D1519231

BAPTISM AND CONFIRMATION

THE HERDER HISTORY OF DOGMA

BAPTISM
AND CONFIRMATION

BURKHARD NEUNHEUSER, O.S.B.

Translated by
John Jay Hughes

HERDER AND HERDER

1964

HERDER AND HERDER NEW YORK

232 Madison Avenue, New York 16, N. Y.

Original edition: "Taufe und Firmung",
(Handbuch der Dogmengeschichte, vol. IV, part 2).
Herder, Freiburg im Breisgau.

Editors of the Handbuch der Dogmengeschichte:
Professor Michael Schmaus
Professor Aloys Grillmeier S. J.

Nihil Obstat: Joannes M. T. Barton, S.T.D., L.S.S., Censor deputatus

Imprimatur: † Georgius L. Craven, Epus. Sebastopolis, Vic. Gen.

Westmonasterii, die 20ª Jan. 1964

The Nihil Obstat and Imprimatur are a declaration that a book
or pamphlet is considered to be free from doctrinal or moral error.
It is not implied that those who have granted the Nihil Obstat and Imprimatur
agree with the contents, opinions or statements expressed.

Library of Congress Catalog Card Number: 64-11974

First published in West Germany © 1964 Herder KG

Printed in West Germany by Herder

CONTENTS

CONTENTS

VI

ABBREVIATIONS

Places of publication:

Antw.	= Antwerp		Lv.	= Louvain
Bln.	= Berlin		Mch.	= Munich
Bs.	= Basel		Mst.	= Münster/Westf.
CbE.	= Cambridge/Eng.		N. Y.	= New York
Dd.	= Düsseldorf		Ox.	= Oxford
Du.	= Dublin		Pa.	= Paris
Ed.	= Edinburgh		Pb.	= Paderborn
FbB.	= Freiburg/Br.		Rgb.	= Regensburg
FbS.	= Fribourg/Switz.		Rm.	= Rome
Gö.	= Göttingen		Stg.	= Stuttgart
Gß.	= Gießen		St. L.	= St. Louis
Gü.	= Gütersloh		Szb.	= Salzburg
HaS.	= Halle/Saale		Tn.	= Turin
Hdb.	= Heidelberg		Tü.	= Tübingen
Ld.	= London		Wn.	= Vienna
Lp.	= Leipzig		Zü.	= Zürich

Periodicals and Collected Works

AAS	=	*Acta Apostolicae Sedis* (Rm.)
AbhGöttGW	=	*Abhandlungen der Gesellschaft d. Wissensch. zu Göttingen* (Gö.)
AntChr	=	*Antike und Christentum, founded by F. J. Dölger* (Mst.)
ArchLW	=	*Archiv für Liturgiewissenschaft* (Rgb.)
BenedMsch	=	*Benediktinische Monatschrift* (Beuron)
Biblica	=	*Biblica: Commentarii, ed. a Pont. Instituto Biblico* (Rm.)
BKV²	=	*Bibliothek der Kirchenväter, ²ed. by O. Bardenhewer et al.* (Kempten)
Catholica	=	*Catholica: Jahrbuch für Kontroverstheologie* (Pb. – Mst.)
CSEL	=	*Corpus Scriptorum Ecclesiasticorum Latinorum* (Wn.)
DACL	=	*Dictionnaire d'Archéologie Chrétienne et de Liturgie* (Pa.)
DBibl	=	*Dictionnaire de la Bible* (Pa.)
Denz.	=	*Denzinger, H.: Enchiridion Symbolorum, ed. 18 ff.*
DieuV	=	*Dieu Vivant: Perspectives religieuses et philosophiques* (Pa.)
DThC	=	*Dictionnaire de Théologie Catholique* (Pa.) (FbB.)
EchOr	=	*Echos d'Orient* (Pa. – Constantinople)
EphLitg	=	*Ephemerides Liturgicae* (Rm.)
GCS	=	*Griechische Christliche Schriftsteller: ed. Preuß, Ak. d. W.* (Lp. – Bln.)
Greg	=	*Gregorianum* (Rm.)
JbLW	=	*Jahrbuch für Literaturwissenschaft, founded by O. Casel* (Mst.)
Kath	=	*Der Katholik* (Mainz)
LitgMöncht	=	*Liturgie und Mönchtum: Laacher Hefte* (FbB.)

LThK	=	*Lexikon für Theologie und Kirche*, ed. by *M. Buchberger* (FbB.)
Mansi	=	*Mansi, J. D.: Sacr. Conciliorum nova collectio* (Flor. – Venet.)
MélScRel	=	*Mélanges de Science Religieuse* (Lille)
Mus	=	*Le Muséon: Revue d'Études Orientales* (Lv.)
OrChr	=	*Orientalia Christiana* (Rm. 1923–34)
OrChrPer	=	*Orientalia Christiana Periodica* (Rm.)
PastorB	=	*Pastor Bonus* (Trier)
PG	=	*Patrologiae Cursus, series graeca*, ed. *J. P. Migne* (Pa.)
PhilJB	=	*Philosophisches Jahrbuch der Görres-Gesellschaft* (Fulda)
PL	=	*Patrologiae Cursus, series latina*, ed. *J. P. Migne* (Pa.)
RechScRel	=	*Recherches de Science Religieuse* (Pa.)
REPTh	=	*Realenzyklopädie für Protestantische Theologie u. Kirche* (Lp. ³1896 ff.)
RevBibl	=	*Revue Biblique* (Pa. – Jerusalem)
RevHistE	=	*Revue d'Histoire Ecclésiastique* (Lv.)
RevHistPhRel	=	*Revue d'Histoire et de Philosophie Religieuses* (Strasb. – Pa.)
RevScPhTh	=	*Revue des Sciences Philosophiques et Théologiques* (Kain – Pa.)
RevThPh	=	*Revue de Théologie et de Philosophie* (Lausanne)
RGG	=	*Religion in Geschichte und Gegenwart* (Tü. ²1927 ff.)
RömQ	=	*Römische Quartalschrift für christl. Altertumskunde* (Rm. – FbB.)
SBHeidelbAk	=	*Sitzungsberichte der Heidelberger Akad. d. Wiss.* (Hdb.)
Schol	=	*Scholastik* (FbB.)
ST	=	*Studi e Testi: pubblicazioni della Biblioteca Vaticana* (Rm.)

StdCth	=	*Studia Catholica* (Roermond – Nijmegen)
ThGl	=	*Theologie und Glaube* (Pb.)
ThQ	=	*Theologische Quartalschrift* (Tü. – Rottenburg/ N.)
ThRev	=	*Theologische Revue* (Mst.)
ThWbNT	=	*Theolog. Wörterbuch zum Neuen Testament,* founded by G. Kittel (Stg.)
TLitg	=	*Tijdschrift voor Liturgie* (Affligem)
TU	=	*Texte und Untersuchungen zur Gesch. d. altchristl. Literatur* (Lp. – Bln.)
ZATW	=	*Zeitschrift für die Alttestamentliche Wissenschaft* (Gß. – Bln.)
ZKTh	=	*Zeitschrift für Katholische Theologie* (Innsbruck)

Baptism and Confirmation

GENERAL LITERATURE: J. Corblet, *Histoire dogmatique, liturgique et archéologique du sacrement de baptême* (2 vols.; Pa. 1881). J. Bellamy – G. Bareille *et al.*, "Baptême" in *DThC* 2 (³1923) 167–355. P. de Puniet, "Baptême et Bénédiction de l'eau" in *DACL* 2 (1925) 251–346 resp. 685–713. A. d'Alès, *Baptême et Confirmation* (Pa. 1928). B. Neunheuser, "De benedictione aquae baptismatis. Inquisitiones sec. doctrinam et liturgiam antiquitatis christianae usque ad primam ritus redactionem definitivam" in *EphLitg* 44 (1930) 194–207, 258–81, 369–412, 455–92. Thomas Aquinas, *Die Sakramente. Taufe und Firmung* (*Dtsch. Thomas-Ausg. der Summa theol.*, 29; Szb. – Lp. 1935), with commentary by D. Winzen. *The Summa Theologica of St. Thomas Aquinas*, Third Part, English Dominican Edition (Ld. 1917 et seq.). W. Deinhardt, "Taufe" in *LThK* 9 (1937) 1007–18. Cf. also the dogmatic manuals of B. Bartmann, F. Diekamp, M. Schmaus *et al.* J. Crehan, "Ten years Work on Baptism and Confirmation 1945–1955" in *Theol. Studies* 17, 1956, 494–515. Kurt Aland, *Did the Early Church Baptize Infants?* (Ld. 1963). K. Barth, *The Teaching of the Church Regarding Baptism* (Ld. 1948). David Cairns, *Infant Baptism in the First Four Centuries* (Ld. 1960). J. H. Crehan, *Early Christian Baptism and the Creed* (Ld. 1950). J. G. Davies, *Infant Baptism, History and Modern Practice* (Ld. 1939). G. Every, *The Baptismal Sacrifice* (Ld. 1959). A. Gilmore, *Christian Baptism* (Ld. 1959). N. M. Haring, "One Baptism", *Medieval Studies* 1948 (Vol. X, pp. 217–219). Joachim Jeremias, *Infant Baptism in the First Four Centuries* (Ld. 1960). B. Leeming, *Principles of Sacramental Theology* (Ld. 1956). C. McAuliffe, *Sacramental Theology* (St. L. 1938). P. Palmer, *Sacraments and Worship* (Ld. 1957, Westminster, Maryland 1955). J. Pohle (tr. A. Preuss), *The Sacraments*, 4 vols., (St. L. 1938). E. C. Whitaker, *Documents of the Baptismal Liturgy* (Ld. 1960). R. E. O. White, *The Biblical Doctrine of Initiation* (Ld. 1960).

1

Chapter One

THE SCRIPTURAL DOCTRINE OF BAPTISM

LITERATURE: W. Koch, *Die Taufe im Neuen Testament* (*Bibl. Zeitfragen* III, 10; Mst. 1910; ³1921). A. d'Alès – J. Coppens, "Baptême" in *DBibl* Suppl. (1928) 852–924. K. Prümm, *Der christliche Glaube und die altheidnische Welt,* vol. 2 (Lp. 1935) chap. 15–16 (Nachlaß der Sünden). J. Kostnetter, *Die Taufe Jesu, Exeget. u. religionsgesch. Studien* (*Theol. Stud. d. Österr. Leo-Ges.* 35; Wn. 1936). J. Dey, Παλιγγενεσία. *Ein Beitrag zur Klärung der religionsgesch. Bedeutung von Tit.* 3, 5 (*Ntl. Abh.* 17, 5; Mst. 1937). O. Kuß, "Die vorpaulinische Tauflehre im Neuen Testament" in *ThGl* 41 (1951) 187–309. H. Schwarzmann, *Zur Tauftheologie des hl. Paulus in Röm.* 6 (Hdb. 1950). R. Schnackenburg, *Das Heilsgeschehen bei der Taufe nach dem Apostel Paulus* (*Münch. Theol. Stud.* I, 1; Mch. 1950). V. Warnach, *Das Mysterium der Taufe im Neuen Testament: Lebendiges Zeugnis, Werkh. d. Akad. Bonifatius-Einigung* 14 (1952) 8–30. The same author, *Das Abbild seines Todes (Röm.* 6, 5*) und der Taufritus: op.cit.* 50 (1955) 1–21. W. Brandt, *Die jüdischen Baptismen oder das religiöse Waschen und Baden im Judentum mit Einschluß des Judenchristentums* (*Beih. z. ZATW* 18; Gß. 1910). A. v. Stromberg, *Studien zur Theorie und Praxis der Taufe in der christl. Kirche der ersten zwei Jahrhunderte* (*N. Stud. z. Gesch. d. Theol. u. d. Kirche* 18; Bln. 1913). J. Leipold, *Die urchristliche Taufe im Lichte der Religionsgeschichte* (Lp. 1928); cf. for this work O. Casel in *JbLW* 9 (1929) 203–5. A. Oepke, Βάπτω in *ThWbNT* 1 (1933) 527 ff. K. Barth, "Die kirchl. Lehre von der Taufe" (*Theol. Stud.* 14; Zr. ²1943; also: "Theol. Existenz heute", NF 4; 1947). M. Barth, *Die Taufe — ein Sakrament? Ein exeget. Beitrag zum Gespräch über die kirchl. Taufe* (Zü. 1951). Joh. Schneider, *Die Taufe im Neuen Testament* (Stg. 1952). Cf. also the relevant works on the theology of the NT, *e.g.* B. F. Prat, *Théologie de S. Paul* (2 vols.; Pa. [33]1942; [28]1941), Engl. tr. *The Theology of St. Paul* (Ld. 1959). A. Wikenhauser, *Pauline Mysticism. Christ in the Mystical Teaching of St. Paul,* Engl. tr. (Ed. 1960). E. Stauffer, *Theologie des Neuen Testamentes* (Stg. [3]1947), Engl. tr. *New Testament Theology* (Ld. 1955). D. M. Stanley, "The New Testament Doctrine of Baptism; an Essay in Biblical Theology" (*Theol. Stud.* 18, 1957, 169–215). W. F. Flemington, *The New Testament Doctrine of Baptism* (Ld. 1948). O. Dullmann, *Baptism in the New Testament* (Studies in Biblical Theology I.), (Lo. 1950). G. W. H. Lampe, *The Seal of the Spirit; Baptism and Confirmation in the New Testament and the Fathers* (Ld. 1951). E. Dinkler, "Taufe im Urchristentum" (RGG 6, 1962 627–637). H. H. Rowley, "Jewish Proselyte Baptism and the Baptism of John" in *Hebrew Union College Annual* (Cincinnati, Ohio) 15, 1940, pp. 313–14. *The Biblical Doctrine of Baptism:* A study document issued by the special commission on baptism of the Church of Scotland (Ed. 1958).

AT THE beginning of the apostolic preaching about Jesus the Christ we find baptism prominently mentioned: "The beginning of the gospel of Jesus Christ. As it is written in Isaiah the Prophet: Behold, I send my angel . . . John the Baptist (literally: "the Baptizer") . . . preached a baptism of repentance for the forgiveness of sins. And they all came . . . and had themselves baptized by him in Jordan, confessing their sins" (Mark 1:1–5). The Apostles begin their own preaching similarly, when they testify to "that which has come to pass in Judah, beginning from Galilee, after the baptism which John preached, concerning Jesus of Nazareth" (Acts 10:37; cf. 1:22; 13:24). Jesus himself undergoes this baptism.[1] But as the "Baptizer" on that occasion makes very clear, this is merely "a baptism with water", whereas his mightier successor will baptize "with the Holy Spirit" (Mark 1:8; cf. Acts 1:5 and 11:16 where this distinction is put into the mouth of Christ).

---

[1] "He was baptized (immersed) in the Jordan by John" (Mark 1:9).

Both oral and written proclamation of the gospel begin, then, with an act of baptism – and not without reason. Later, however, it is John alone who, in his report of the nocturnal conversation between Jesus and Nicodemus, speaks of being "born of water and the spirit" as the prerequisite for entry into the kingdom of God (John 3:5). Without doubt it is that higher form of baptism "with the Holy Spirit" mentioned in Mark 1:8 which is referred to here. We hear no more of any such baptism, however, until the Risen Christ gives the command which we find set in solemn and impressive form by the evangelist Matthew, at the end of his Gospel: "Go therefore and make disciples of all nations, baptizing them in the name of the Father and of the Son and of the Holy Spirit" (Matt. 28:19). In accordance with this command, Peter answers the question of the contrite Jews as to what they should do in order to obtain salvation by telling them: "Repent, and be baptized every one of you in the name of Jesus Christ for the forgiveness of your sins; and you shall receive the gift of the Holy Spirit" (Acts 2:37f.).

This is, then, in broad outline, what the New Testament – apart from the Epistles – says with regard to baptism. Today we quite naturally understand these four scriptural passages as stages in a single line of development. It was the criticism of liberal theology which stimulated this approach. It encouraged research into the relationship of these passages to one another and the discussion of the question whether primitive Christian baptism could actually be traced back to Jesus.[2]

[2] See J. Coppens in *DBibl* Suppl. 1 (1928) 877–86: Independent critical hypotheses as to the origins and the development of the ceremonies and doctrine of Christian baptism (Hypothèses critiques indépendantes sur les origines et le développement des cérémonies et de la doctrine baptismale

The starting point for our discussion is the scriptural evidence for baptism taken in its entirety. The character of this evidence as a part of revelation does not prevent us from recognizing that the individual authors, having as they do different styles and different reasons for writing, express the same truth in various forms, with a changing terminology, from continually shifting points of view, and not always with the same clarity. Thus Paul in Rom. 6:3 ("Do you not know that . . ." *i.e.* "you know very well") assumes in his hearers a rather profound insight into the meaning of baptism. And inasmuch as Christ's words to Nicodemus about being born again (John 3:5) – likewise a penetrating interpretation of the meaning of baptism – were doubtless uttered by Jesus himself at a relatively early date,[3] this line of thought must have been familiar to those who proclaimed the apostolic message. And even if at first sight their presentation of this teaching about baptism seems to be characterized by a certain archaic simplicity, we are nevertheless able, by observing the manner in which they write and the words which they use to describe the act of baptism, to gain new insight into the significance and meaning which they wished to ascribe to this very rite.

The technical term which is used in the New Testament, first for the outward act of baptism, but then for everything implied and accomplished thereby, is βαπτίζειν, resp. βαπτίζεσθαι and βάπτισμα. What do these words mean? From the simple word βάπτω, "to dip" or "to dye", we derive the intensive form of the same verb, βαπτίζειν, which means transitively "to plunge" or "to submerge". The intransitive meaning of the

chrétiennes). See also the bibliography given in this work, p. 921 ff. Cf. also the bibliography in *ThWbNT* s. v. βάπτω (1, 527).
[3] Cf. W. Koch, *Taufe im NT* 27–9.

word is „to sink", "to die". In general usage the word has the connotation of "to perish, to be destroyed". So much for the profane usage.

In the New Testament βάπτω appears only in the sense of "to dip" (cf. John 13:26). βαπτίζω always has a religious meaning, mostly the technical one of "baptize", or "to baptize with water".[4] But even if the word tends to be used only as a technical term for a religious action, the basic meaning of its parent stem still clings to it: "to submerge in water", "to dip", "to plunge into a bath".[5] Even the use of the word in Mark 1:9f. ("and he was baptized by John in the Jordan. And when he came up out of the water . . ."; Matt 3:16 is similar) presupposes this basic meaning of "submerging" or "dipping" which βαπτίζω has from its root in the common word βάπτω.

Indeed everything that we know of John's baptismal practice points in the same direction. And it is just such a baptism, a sacred and religious bath, but one which involves a real submersion in water, which we find in a prominent position right at the beginning of the gospel. This is the baptism of John, as it is called in Acts 19:3. With probably a very similar baptism, that is by immersion, "Jesus baptized" (John 3:12) – or rather, to be strictly accurate, his disciples baptized (John 4:2). And the disciples of John remark jealously that "all are coming to him", instead of to John, as previously (3:26). This Johannine baptism is differentiated in Acts 19:3-5 from baptism "in the name of the Lord Jesus" (εἰς τὸ ὄνομα . . .) – that is, from a form of bap-

---

[4] See ThWbNT 1, 527f.

[5] Cf. O. Casel in JbLW 14 (1938) 209f. against K. Prümm, Christlicher Glaube und altheidnische Welt 2, 293; cf. K. Prümm, Religionsgeschichtliches Handbuch für den Raum der altchristlichen Umwelt (FbB. 1943) 340, note 1.

tism which first came to be practised after the Resurrection and Ascension of Jesus, as the use of the title Kyrios makes clear. The difference between the two forms must therefore lie not so much in their symbolical outward actions as in the relationship of these actions to the Lord Jesus and in their consequent inward effect. Indeed the fact that the account of John's baptizing and of Jesus' baptism by John is placed at the beginning of the relatively late written account of the apostolic preaching allows us to conclude that the symbolical actions were essentially the same in the case of both baptisms. In each case we are dealing with genuine immersion.[6]

[6] This in no way implies, however, agreement with the simple identification of the two forms of baptism, such as is made by Barth *(Taufe)*, p. 173: "The Johannine baptism and Christian baptism are in essence one and the same thing. ... It is, therefore, incorrect to consider the Johannine baptism merely as a preparation and Christian baptism as fulfilment...". It is, to be sure, true, when Barth says (p. 393): "The baptism which was first performed by Jesus or by his disciples must have been a baptism with water similar to, if not identical with, that practised by John." But the conclusions which he proceeds to draw with regard to the essence of baptism as it was administered after the death of Christ are untenable. His conclusions are only possible through a daring interpretation of texts which in cases such as Acts 19:2–6 (p. 165–72) amounts to a distortion, and through the assumption that baptism with water is nothing else than "man's 'Yes' and 'Amen' to God's election, deed, and will" (p. 185) in which things alone, apart from any human means or anything of the sort, our salvation is accomplished. On Barth's exegesis of Acts 19:2–6 cf. the sharply critical comments of the Protestant Ch. Masson, *Le baptême, un sacrement?* in *RevThPh* 3, 3 (1953) 22f., who comes to the conclusion: "Ainsi le texte invoqué par M. Barth pour établir que le baptême chrétien n'est en lui-même que le baptême de Jean, atteste bien fortement, qu'il s'agit de deux baptêmes distincts." ("Thus the very text invoked by Barth to demonstrate that Christian baptism is in itself only the baptism of John bears strong witness to the fact that the two baptisms are distinct.") We shall have occasion to return a number of times to Barth's views. For a general appraisal see below (Chap. 1) notes 10f., 27, 37, and p. 230f.

Ritual washings were known to the Old Testament through the Mosaic legislation, as the evangelists themselves testify (*e.g.* Mark 7:2–4; John 2:6; Acts 16:13). They were further developed especially by the Essenes. In addition, we have the evidence for the existence of so-called Proselyte-Baptism[7] in the time prior to the Johannine baptism, and it had probably already become customary in the first century B.C. It was a part of the rite by which a proselyte was received into the Synagogue. In the presence of witnesses the convert descended into water and immersed himself fully. Despite this notable difference from Johannine baptism and the orientation of the entire rite towards exterior Levitical purification, the significance of Proselyte-Baptism (which was coupled with the resolution to lead a new life, and through which the proselyte became, legally, like a "new-born child") seems to be of no small importance for our understanding of Johannine baptismal practice. At any rate it appears that an immersion in water as a means of initiation into the life of a religious community or into a new and higher way of life was by no means unknown. Finally, there is embodied in this bathing the universal human necessity for symbolic expression, which we meet so often in the old cults. When "in several cults that longing which dwells within every man for purification from his sins and liberation from everything which he feels in any way to be a stain or guilt, seeks its satisfaction in a religious

---

[7] For what follows cf. also: W. Brandt, *Jüd. Baptismen.* J. Zellinger, *Bad und Bäder in der altchristlichen Kirche* (Mch. 1928) 93–129; *ThWbNT* 1, 528-33. K. Prümm, *Religionsgeschichtl. Hdb.*, Vzchn. VIII, s. v. Taufe, Wasser, Reinigung; on proselyte baptism see especially H. Strack – P. Billerbeck, *Kommentar zum Neuen Testament aus Talmud und Midrasch,* vol. 1 (Mch. 1922) 102–8.

ceremony, then it is entirely natural that this ceremony will be a washing with water, perhaps even a water bath or a water baptism".[8] This need not in the slightest imply that other and parallel ritual washings are in any sense the origin of Christian baptism. In this connection we must also mention here the descent into the water of the pool of Bethsaida (John 5) and the washing in the pool of Siloam, where the evangelist's translation of "Siloam" with the word "sent" points towards the deeper, symbolical meaning of this washing.

From the foregoing, our picture of Johannine baptism gains background and colouring. Admittedly the figure of the Baptist is itself too prominent to be interpreted entirely in terms of that which had preceded him. He is, in his own right, prophet, messenger of God, forerunner, and proclaimer of the Parousia of the Lord, preacher of repentance and of new life. He makes use for his purposes of something – the immersion-bath – the richness of meaning and practicality of which at Proselyte-Baptism become clear to us against the background of Jewish purification rites. But at the same time he creates a new form for this water bath. A confession of sin is placed prior to it (Mark 1:5), and the purpose of this baptism is no longer Levitical purity, which the water of Jordan could in no way impart, but rather purity from sins. John does not wish to receive those whom he baptizes into a new religious community, but rather to prepare the way for the Parousia of the Messiah and of the kingdom of God. In addition it is he who carries out the immersion of the baptismal candidate – there is no longer any self-immersion on the part of the one baptized. For the first time it is the "Baptist",

---

[8] K. Prümm, *Religionsgeschichtl. Hdb.* 331.

the one who administers baptism, who becomes prominent.

It is this baptism – which already in itself has a strong moral significance, and which serves the coming of the kingdom of God – which Jesus now receives. However, this baptism, which he in no way needed and which he took over as representative of the whole human race in preparation for the kingdom of God, becomes for him the occasion for a mighty and glorious revelation of his divine Sonship, for the proclamation of his Father's witness to him, and for the proof of the fulness of the Spirit which he has been given. For the Baptist this baptism offers an opportunity of pointing specifically to a new baptism with the Holy Spirit still to come: "This is he who immerses in (ἐν) the Holy Spirit" (John 1:33; cf. Matt. 3:11). Also of importance in this connection are the Baptist's words about the "Lamb of God, who takes away the sins of the world" (John 1:29).[9] What was formerly an immersion-bath of repentance and preparation for the coming of God's kingdom has now, through being carried out on Jesus, become the solemn act which reveals his divine glory and sets him forth as the decisive man in the coming of God's kingdom. It is he who will baptize from now on; he it is, the man who is filled with the Spirit, whom we are to hear as the Son of God. He will baptize (immerse), and this no longer with (or in) water, but rather with (in) the Holy Spirit and fire (Matt. 3:11).

It is this immersion bath, which Jesus himself had received under such extraordinary circumstances, as the apostolic preaching and the primitive Church again and again emphasize, and as the ancient Christian liturgy was already celebrating at an early

---

[9] On this point see O. Casel in *ArchLW* 1 (1950) 314.

date in the Feast of the Epiphany, which the Risen Christ commands to be performed: ". . . baptize them in the name of the Father and of the Son and of the Holy Spirit" (Matt. 28:19). The liberal critics are wrong when they claim that this command could be ascribed to the Lord himself only if he had directly prepared the way for such a command in his preaching, that is, only if he had spoken about baptism more frequently. Through the fact that he had himself undergone baptism – a fact which is recorded by all four evangelists not without a special purpose – Jesus had given this sacred immersion bath a weighty sanction. In addition he had himself, through the agency of his disciples, to be sure, had people baptized (John 4:1f.). But his preaching had another immediate purpose: it was to bring the message of repentance, of belief in the kingdom of God and in the Son of Man – and it was intended gradually to prepare the way for his sacrificial death. Only after the entrance of Jesus into his glory had the moment logically come to go back once again to that solemn commencement and finally to give the command to open to all believers (cf. Mark 16:16) the entrance to God's kingdom through the administration of the immersion-bath in the name of the Father and of the Son, and of the Holy Spirit.[10] And this

[10] For a detailed reply to the difficulties raised by modernistic-liberal theology, one might consult the work by E. Koch, *Taufe im NT*, p. 29–40. "The claim that Matt. 28:19 was once different from the version in our traditional text, *i.e.* that the baptismal command and the trinitarian formula originally were lacking, is just as much to be rejected as the assertion that the universality of Christ's missionary commission proves that this saying cannot have come from his lips." So writes M. Meinertz, *Theologie des Neuen Testaments* (Bonn 1950) 122, note 2. See also the reference there to G. Ongaro, "L'autenticità e integrità del comma trinitario in Matt. 28:19" in *Biblica* 19 (1938) 267–79. On this question Barth takes the following position (*Taufe*, p. 525–54): "The alternatives are inescapable: a) either baptism

11

immersion-bath, administered in obedience to this command, is the baptism with the Holy Spirit and with fire which the Baptist had once prophesied.[11]

Even though this was just as much a bath of immersion as was John's baptism, it must, according to the evidence in Acts 19:3–5, have been distinguishable from the latter in its outward form alone, since it was "baptism in the name of Jesus" – no longer baptism by John but by Jesus himself, or by those whom he had sent. From the beginning it is obvious that the actual

is a sacrament, in which case Matt. 28:19 is certainly a product of the later Christian community ... or b) baptism is not a sacrament, in which case ... we must maintain the authenticity of this passage" (p. 528). This conclusion is a natural result of Barth's categories, since for him a "sacrament" is synonymous with the "natural or magical healing power of a bath" (p. 522). If, however "sacrament" is the word which the later tradition coined for the means through which precisely the saving act of God becomes effective, then there is nothing to prevent us from accepting the authenticity of the baptismal commission in Matt. 28:19. In this case one does, to be sure, find: "une interprétation plus congéniale de certaines thèmes du christianisme primitif, sans pour le moins retomber dans des interprétations 'magiques'" ("a more congenial interpretation of certain themes in primitive Christianity, without in the least falling back into 'magical' interpretations"): J. Héring, Kritik zu Barths Buch in *RevHistPhRel* 33 (1953) 260.
[11] The radical denial of the equation of water and spirit baptism is the heart of the thesis proposed by Barth in his book. He is, to be sure, able to maintain this thesis only by means of such a strange exegesis as that which he gives of John 3:5 ("born of water and the spirit"), which he explains by the epexegetical interpretation of the word "and", in the sense of "namely" or "that is", so that his reading of the passage becomes "of water, *i.e.* of spirit"; "in contrast to all baptisms with water, so the passage asserts, new birth comes about only 'from the spirit'; for the genuine water is the spirit" (p. 446). Ch. Masson in *RevThPh* 3, 3 (1953) 29 says that the acceptance of a spirit-baptism independent of water-baptism would mean "se mettre hors d'état de comprendre dans leur sens le plus évident la plupart des textes du Nouveau Testament relatifs au baptême" ("making it impossible for us to understand most of the New Testament texts with regard to baptism in their most obvious sense").

identity of the baptizer in each case is quite irrelevant. John's prophecy, "He will baptize in the Holy Spirit", is in every case fulfilled, regardless of whether the Apostles themselves baptized (which may be the case in Acts 2:41 and 4:4) or not (1 Cor. 1:14f.), or whether the baptism was administered by the deacon, Philip (Acts 8:12), or by another authorized person. What is decisive is in whose name the baptism is performed. This is expressed as early as the report of the baptisms on the first feast of Pentecost (Acts 2:38). The seeming contradiction between the baptismal command in Matt. 28:19 and the mention here of a baptism "in the name of Jesus" does not really raise for us today, as it once did, an essential difficulty.[12]

---

[12] Cf. in connection with this question which was once felt to be so difficult, W. Koch, *Taufe im NT*, 6–10. Our treatment of this subject was written some time previous to the publication by A. Stenzel of his instructive essay on "Cyprian und die Taufe im Namen Jesu" in *Schol* 30 (1955) 372–87. He underlines first the point about which general agreement prevails today. First, "there can be no doubt that every baptism has theologically a trinitarian structure". But with regard to "the liturgical clarity of this basic theological finding" opinions differ (p. 373). Nevertheless Stenzel states, that "Catholic scholars have good ground to be cautious"; for "all of the direct and convincing pieces of evidence point in the direction of a baptism which was also in its liturgical form trinitarian" (p. 374). He adds that one could hardly hazard a statement about any practice of the Church at large with regard to a baptism in the name of Jesus alone. Nevertheless Stenzel considers that the existence of such a baptism in the name of Jesus is not completely excluded, at least for "circles outside the main stream of Church life". At most such baptisms could be proved only from the time of controversy over baptism by heretics (p. 377). We are also in agreement with Stenzel in his assent to the view first put forward by P. Puniet (*DACL* 2, 341 ff.), that in primitive Christian times, "an indicative form of baptism (ego te baptizo) was not in use" (p. 378). We should like, however, to hold more strongly than Stenzel does, that each confession of Jesus made by the primitive Christians contained at least implicitly, and in most cases probably explicitly as well, the beginning of a

Baptism "in the name of Jesus" is baptism administered in obedience to Jesus' command and with his authority, in the manner prescribed by him. The expression is, therefore, intended primarily to convey that it is a question of Jesus' baptism, in contrast to that of John. This is quite clear from the linguistic usage of the time. However, from the solemn manner in which the names are mentioned in the baptismal commission which stands with such emphasis at the close of the gospel, we must conclude that in addition to the meaning which in all probability is primary (that this baptism is to be administered on behalf of Christ and with his authority) something even more important is intended.

It is certainly illegitimate to see in the names mentioned here an actual baptismal "formula". It has been quite correctly pointed out that Jesus did not speak in "liturgical formularies" – a truth which, of course, applies equally to the other "formula", "in the name of Jesus Christ".[13] What is true here, however, is that "in a summary of the foundations of salvation we are told the direction in which baptism exercises its effect: it is that which binds us to the Father..., to the Son..., to the Spirit...".[14] How these names were uttered in the individual case we cannot with certainty say from the evidence of these texts. Despite the evidence of the *Didache,* which freely uses both the trinitarian form and that in the name of Jesus side by side, we must assume that as far as

confession of the Father, who sent Jesus, and of the Spirit, whom the Father sends in Jesus' name. This would then be the kernel of truth in "Ernst's final admission" mentioned on p. 387.

[13] Cf. Jos. Schmid, *Das Evangelium nach Matthäus* (*Regensb. NT,* 1; Rgb. 1948) 273.

[14] M. Meinertz, *Th. d. NT,* 123; cf. the entire passage there, pp. 122f.

the administration of baptism is concerned – and we have definite evidence for this in the second and third centuries from Hippolytus, for instance – the practice with regard to the invocation of these names was very elastic. At the same time, the immersion-bath is supposed to be administered with the mention of these names. It is a "water-bath in the word" as St. Paul will later say in Eph. 5:26, that is, a water-bath which receives its distinctive feature through these sacred names and which in precisely this way becomes the baptism of Jesus. Such a naming of the three persons is an epiclesis in the primitive sense. The name of the Father, and of the Son, and of the Holy Spirit is invoked upon him who is being immersed in the water-bath. For the man of antiquity such an epiclesis means that the godhead which it invokes is present with its efficacious power.[15] But the godhead is also present in order that he, over whom the name of God is invoked, may entrust himself to God – indeed more simply, that he may consecrate himself to God. That may be quite specially suggested by formulas like "εἰς τὸ ὄνομα" (not ἐν τῷ ὀνόματι), "be baptized into the name". Moreover, by understanding the invocation of the names as an epiclesis it is possible to explain the evidence from the primitive period in a way which is inherently consistent. Furthermore, it opens the way to an understanding of the further line of development, which – as we can already see clearly indicated in the *Didache* – led to the establishment of these names as the baptismal formula in the proper sense of the word.

[15] Cf. O. Casel, "Zur Epiklese" in *JbLW* 3 (1923) 100–2, and "Neue Beiträge zur Epiklesenfrage" in *op. cit.* 7 (1924) 169–78. That such a conception has nothing to do with "name-magic" will, surely, hardly require specific emphasis.

The inner meaning and effect, then, of this "water-bath in the word", and, therefore, the manner in which it is basically distinguishable from the baptism of John – all this is contained in the words of our Lord to Nicodemus (John 3:1–10). There we find first the reference to the Johannine immersion-bath in water. In clear parallel to the words of the Baptist, but going beyond them, Jesus speaks of "water and Spirit" (John 3:5), putting the accent strongly on "Spirit" (3:6–8). Even more revealing for the meaning of the whole action is its description as γεννηθῆναι ἄνωθεν (3:3), γεννηθῆναι ἐξ ὕδατος καὶ πνεύματος (3:5), "being born from above" (or "anew"), and "being born of water and Spirit".[16] Baptism – for it is clear from the use of the words "from water and Spirit" in this connection that baptism is meant – is, therefore, birth from above, birth given by the Spirit and from the Spirit, whereby a spirit, a spiritual man, is born. It is only as such that he can see (3:3) and enter (3:5) the kingdom of God.[17]

Let us now look at the entire picture as it is given to us from the apostolic preaching in the inspired words of Holy Scripture, before we turn our attention to further theological interpretation. At a time when baptismal practice had long since become a matter of course and its interpretation was rather developed, the four evangelists sketch in a few strokes and in the framework of an effective composition a striking picture of baptism from the first beginning of the apostolic preaching. Jesus had commissioned

[16] Translated in the *Vulgate* by *renasci,* resp. *renasci denuo.*
[17] Even according to M. Barth (*Taufe,* 449f.) John 3:5 refers to water-baptism, "but refers polemically to belief in water-baptism". The verse "is consequently a vigorous limitation of superstitious belief in the effectiveness of any kind of water-baptism at all for salvation".

16

this baptism. Since the first feast of Pentecost the apostles have been administering it. It is the immersion-bath in water which was familiar from John, and which now transcends this Johannine baptism and becomes baptism in the name of Jesus, since it is administered "in the name of the Father and of the Son and of the Holy Spirit" that is, with invocation (epiclesis) of these names. And this baptism of Jesus is more than a mere water-bath; it is baptism "in the Holy Spirit and fire" and constitutes a new birth, a birth from the Spirit. It is the birth of a man of the spirit – a spiritual man. It is the prerequisite for the attainment of salvation.

We now come upon this act of baptism in the other New Testament writings in many passages which lead us deeper into its meaning. At the beginning of Acts (1:5) a saying of the Lord states once again the superiority of the new baptism to the mere water-bath of Johannine baptism: "you will be baptized with the Holy Spirit". This administration of the new baptismal bath is in Acts clearly distinguished from the rite of the laying on of hands for the conveying of the Holy Spirit. In the Pauline epistles, on the other hand, it is impossible to find any text which contrasts with compelling clarity the "bath of regeneration and renewal in the Holy Spirit" (Titus 3:5) with the laying on of hands for the visible imparting of the Spirit. Even in 1 Cor. 12, where Paul speaks extensively of the gifts of the Spirit, which according to Acts appear in connection with the laying on of hands, he ascribes them to the working of the Spirit given in baptism (1 Cor. 12, 13). The intention of his teaching makes that understandable. For he wishes to show that those endowed with these gifts must therefore serve the *one* body of which they are the severally different members. But it is through baptism and

17

through the *one* Spirit which works in baptism that we become members of the *one* Body of Christ. Acts 2:38 connects the imparting of the gifts of the Spirit with the reception of baptism. But in so doing it fails to tell us with complete certainty what the nature of the inner connection between these two realities is.[18] Nevertheless, other passages (like Acts 8:15–17; 19:5f.; and similarly, even if different, 10:47f.) show quite clearly that Acts does distinguish between baptism with water in the name of the Lord Jesus Christ for the forgiveness of sins and the laying on of hands for the imparting of the Spirit, of which the Spirit's charismatic gifts are the visible result. But already in the water-bath of baptism the Holy Spirit is in a basic manner imparted. This is clear from Acts 1:5, as well as from 19:2–5. But the decisive passage is Acts 2:38, where the assurance is given that with the act of baptism "you will receive the gift of the Holy Spirit".[19] The later Pauline practice confirms this. Even M. Barth admits these connections: "Both the baptism with water and the laying on of hands are conditioned by the promise that the Holy Spirit will be poured out." But he interprets both these rites as merely "forms of prayer for the Holy Spirit".[20] He is forced to this interpretation, since his viewpoint prevents him from recognizing in these actions the means which the Lord chooses to use

---

[18] Cf. the commentaries on this passage, *e.g.* A. Wikenhauser, *Die Apostelgeschichte (Regensb. NT*; Rgb. [2]1951) 42f., M. Barth, *Taufe,* 141–5.

[19] Cf. H. Elfers: *ThGl* 34 (1942) 335: "The καί (in Acts 2:38) is to be taken in a consecutive sense. Both classical and New Testament Greek are very fond of this usage, especially after imperatives. It should therefore be translated: 'And so you will receive the gifts of the Holy Spirit'." Elfers disputes here the interpretation of B. Welte in *Die postbaptismale Salbung* (FbB. 1939).

[20] M. Barth, *Taufe,* 153.

in order to fulfil his promise of the Spirit. Barth's basic error is that he equates such an efficacy in baptism with magic. Provided, however, that we avoid such a confusion, there is nothing to prevent us from seeing in the water-baptism of Acts 2:38 – which must be read in connection with Acts 8 and 10 as well as with the Lucan statements about the Holy Spirit (cf. Luke 11:13) – the normal and basic means for the imparting of the Spirit.[21] The laying on of hands effects, then, a further imparting of the Spirit, which becomes manifest primarily in the gift of tongues and in prophecy.

When we disregard the unusual occurrence on the occasion of Cornelius' reception, it is "water", that is, the immersion-bath in water, which is the foundation of the Christian confession (Acts 10:47). Peter says this in his sermon on the feast of Pentecost: "Repent, and be baptized every one of you in the name of Jesus Christ for the forgiveness of your sins; and you shall receive the gift of the Holy Spirit" (Acts 2:38). "So those who received his word were baptized" (2:41). This first "baptismal catechism" preserves chiefly the connection with the Baptist's preaching of repentance as well as with that of the Lord himself (Matt. 4:17; Mark 1:14–15). To be ready for the approaching kingdom of God, it is necessary to repent. And as John had administered baptism as a sign of the kingdom so now the Apostles do the same. But this time the clause, "for the forgiveness of your sins" expresses no longer the distant goal of a purely exterior symbolic action, but rather a goal which is really present. Moreover, the forgiveness of sins is actually elevated by

[21] M. Barth (*Taufe*, 143) to the contrary notwithstanding. He considers such a view as "early catholic", seems to deny that it is the view of Acts, and to trace it back to Simon Magus (p. 146 ff.).

the gift of the Holy Spirit – the gift *par excellence* of the fulfilled Messianic time (cf. Acts 2:39). In a middle position between the prerequisites for the act of repentance and the realization of messianic salvation, stands the immersion-bath in water, at once the symbolic expression of this attitude of repentance and of the grace of salvation which is really given. The connection between the bath of immersion and the above-mentioned prerequisites is expressed frequently in Acts – especially, for instance, in the conversion of the Ethiopian eunuch, from whom is required, as prerequisite for baptism (at least this is the reading of the "western" texts) faith in Jesus Christ as the Son of God (Acts 8:37; cf. also 8:12; 16:30–32; 19:4). We must understand that the relationship between the forgiveness of sins and the water-bath is such that the latter is normally the prerequisite for receiving forgiveness. According to Acts 10:43 this forgiveness of sins through the name of Jesus comes to all those who believe in him. But that in no way excludes the water-bath from the crucial central position which it normally occupies in other passages. Repentance, faith, immersion-bath: these three build an undivided unity, which imparts salvation (cf. the baptismal scene in the prison at Philippi, Acts 16:29–35). What the relation is between these things in detail is not yet stated here.

The liturgy in which the act of baptism was performed was probably very simple, plain, and brief. The immersion-bath forms its core. We learn almost nothing of other forms. According to chapters 2, 8, 16, and 19 of Acts, a baptismal catechism in the form of an alternating dialogue must have preceded the bath of immersion. To this was joined the proclamation of the Word of God (16:32, *i.e.* of the word "about the Lord", according to the reading in many manuscripts), of the good news of Jesus

(8:35) with questions and answers concerning belief in this good news. The evidence in Matt. 28:19 indicates that the immersion-bath itself, given εἰς τὸ ὄνομα or ἐπί, ἐν τῷ ὀνόματι Ἰησοῦ Χριστοῦ, according to (the good news of) the name of Jesus Christ, is administered εἰς τὸ ὄνομα τοῦ πατρὸς καὶ τοῦ υἱοῦ καὶ ἁγίου πνεύματος.[22] Immediately following comes normally the laying on of hands, preceded by a prayer for the imparting of the Holy Spirit (Acts 19:6; cf. 8:15–17). We can recognize the simplicity and brevity of the entire action by considering in detail the circumstances attending the baptisms of the Ethiopian eunuch and the jailer at Philippi. Nevertheless, baptism remains that action by which the newcomers were "added" (Acts 2, 41) to the flock of the first-born, that they might from thenceforth participate in the fellowship of the apostles' teaching, of the breaking of bread and of prayer (2:42).

The apostles' letters, and especially those of Paul, 1 Peter and 1 John, give us a rich fund of information as to the nature of the act of baptism which is reported so simply in Acts. It is the λουτρὸν τοῦ ὕδατος ἐν ῥήματι, the "water-bath in the word" (Eph. 5:26), through which (instrumental dative!) Christ, who "loved the Church and gave himself up for her", "cleanses her for sanctification, that the Church might be presented before him in splendour ..." (Eph. 5:25–27). This passage brings out the close relationship between three elements: first, Christ's *agape* and self-oblation unto death on behalf of the Church and for the

---

[22] That the two usages "in the name of Jesus", and "in the name of the Father, etc." do not imply any contradiction has already been briefly demonstrated above on p. 9. Cf. also W. Koch, *Taufe im NT,* 6–10, as well as M. Meinertz, *Th. d. NT,* 122f. For the views of the Fathers and Scholastics on this question, see below pp. 50, 51f., 76, 83 and 91.

purpose of her sanctification; second, this water-bath, through which the Church *in concreto* is to be purified; and third, the Church's holy and immaculate presentation as the final goal. Baptism, which is already doing its purifying work, stands in between the original saving work of Christ and its final consummation at the end of time. It is also remarkable that this passage makes the Church the *subject* of baptism. This refers to the fact that baptism lays the foundation of Christian fellowship and builds up this fellowship – a truth which we see expressed in Eph. 4:4–5 as well, and more especially in 1 Cor. 12:13: "In one Spirit we were all baptized into one body." The one (*i.e.* and only) baptism (Eph. 4:5) as concrete foundation, the one faith in the one Lord and in the one Father-God – these correspond to the one hope of our calling. Accordingly we are incorporated into the one unity of the one body and the one Spirit.

The formula "baptism in (or with) the Spirit" allows us, as we meet it in similar passages in Acts and in the Synoptic gospels, to see how completely new this immersion-bath is in comparison with the mere Johannine baptism. Therefore it is irrelevant who baptizes (cf. 1 Cor. 1:13–17). The Apostle does not need to concern himself with this matter, since baptism is not administered "in his name". Alongside this formula, however, appears another: "to be baptized into Christ" (Gal. 3:27; Rom. 6:3). This formula the Apostle equates with the previous one (baptism in – or with – the Spirit) in accordance with the central position occupied in his thought by the parallelism "Christ – Pneuma". In Gal. 3:27 ("You who were baptized into Christ have put on Christ") "baptism into Christ" is the equivalent of "putting on Christ". This transformation through Christ is so powerful that it causes the dicisive distinctions of nation, of social position, and of sex to recede: "You are all one in Christ Jesus" (3:28). What we have here is a total reality, established through baptism. The Apostle mentions baptism here in order to strengthen his argument, coupling the clauses with the conjunction "for" (γάρ). And he says (3:26) that the Galatians are sons of God through belief in (on) Christ Jesus. Here too, then, we find baptism standing in close relationship to faith. Without going beyond what is directly said in the text we can say, therefore, that faith assumes concrete form in baptism. Baptism and faith in their totality cause, then, the effects we have just mentioned – putting on Christ, and so forth.

The metaphor of putting on clothes is very rich in meaning and a figure of which the Apostle is fond. Thus he warns in Rom. 13:14 that after turning from walking in the works of sin, we must "put on the Lord Jesus Christ". The same figure is used in Col. 3:10 and in Eph. 4:23 in a more limited sense, inasmuch as he is speaking there of putting off and laying aside the old man, and "putting on the new man".[23] Even if there is no direct reference in the latter passage to a cult act, still the entire context permits us without hesitation to associate the very important theological content of these metaphors with Gal. 3:27. Baptism, considered as the putting on of Christ, then becomes the putting off of the old man with his works and the putting on of a new man. On the basis of conformation with Christ the whole man is refashioned and renewed in accordance with the original image which the Creator had designed. Thus this new man will be finally a man conformed to Christ: "Christ is all, and in all" (Col. 3:11).

---

[23] Cf. E. Peterson, "Theologie des Kleides" in *BenedMsch* 16 (1934) 347–56.

In Eph. 5:26 Paul says that Christ "cleansed" his Church through baptism. We find a similar metaphor in Hebrews 10:22: "Our hearts (have been) sprinkled clean (to free us) from an evil conscience and our bodies washed with pure water." We can understand that only as referring to baptism, which stands behind the words of 1 Cor. 6:11 as well: "You were washed, you were sanctified, you were justified in the name of the Lord Jesus Christ and in the Spirit of our God." The external act of bathing in water, done in the "name" of the Lord, that is, in accordance with his command and in the strength of his Spirit, implies in the last analysis sanctification and justification. We are forced to such an interpretation above all by Rom. 6 and by parallel passages such as Titus 3:5 – passages which constitute the climax of St. Paul's theology of baptism.

It is true that the Apostle brings up the subject of baptism in Rom. 6 more or less incidentally, in a larger ethical and theological framework. But nevertheless baptism is in these verses (6:1–14) to such a degree the central theme, that this passage can quite properly be called the *locus classicus* of Pauline baptismal theology. In recent times it is especially the experts in the field of comparative religions, on the Catholic side notably Odo Casel, who have through their exhaustive investigations thrown fresh light upon the meaning of this passage.[24] Even though

---

[24] An objective report of the pertinent works of O. Casel and S. Stricker and their opponents is to be found in Th. Filthaut, *Die Kontroverse über die Mysterienlehre* (Warendorf 1947) 81–5: "Das Kultmysterium im Zeugnis der Heiligen Schrift: die Exegese von Röm. 6:2–11". From amongst the most recent studies mention should be made of R. Schnackenburg's work listed at the outset, *Heilsgeschehen,* as well as of *Taufe und Christusgeschehen* by V. Warnach. See also the corresponding sections in M. Barth, *Taufe,* 187–318.

there is no prevailing agreement in all points by any means, we can still base our brief presentation upon these investigations.

The immediate goal of the Apostle's argument here is the statement that the Christian's moral life requires a break with sin. To substantiate this statement he refers to the basic fact of baptism, declaring it to be the underlying pattern which determines the form of Christian life. In this connection St. Paul assumes that his Roman readers are thoroughly familiar with the fact that Christian baptism is a baptism "into Christ's death" (6:3).[25] The apostolic *kerygma* must therefore have presented this – outside St. Paul's missionary territory, as well as within it – as a self-evident truth of the faith. In fact, such a teaching is nothing more than the logical conclusion which one must come to with regard to baptism when one takes the view of Christ's saving death which we find already presented in his own preaching in the Synoptics (cf., for example, Matt. 20:28 and Luke 22:20). Such a conclusion is supported by the dominical command in Matt. 28:19, as well as by evidence in Acts and by the developed Pauline theology of baptism mentioned above. But this teaching is not merely a "theological inference"; it is the teaching of St. Paul and the testimony of Scripture – in short, the revealed truth of God.

This "baptism into Christ's death" is, then, to follow the argument of the Apostle further, the equivalent of Christ's death, burial, and resurrection. Important in this connection are the compound words with σύν which occur frequently in this sixth chapter of Romans: συνετάθημεν (buried with), σύμφυτοι (grown along with), συνεσταυρώθη (crucified with), ἀπεθάνομεν σὺν Χριστῷ (died with Christ), συνζήσομεν (to live with). It is generally

---

[25] Cf. R. Schnackenburg, *Heilsgeschehen*, 29. O. Kuß, *Vorpaulin. Tauflehre.*

25

recognized that these compounds with σύν relate to the moment of the conformation with Christ which is so crucial in the Pauline system of thought.[26]

The argument of Rom. 6:4–14 in detail is, briefly, as follows: We have been buried with Christ by "baptism into death" (v. 4). Consequently, and continuing the parallel now with the risen Christ as well, we walk in newness of life. Verse 5, which begins with "for", gives the reason: just as we have been united with the ὁμοίωμα, with the likeness of his death (in order that in this likeness, *i.e.* in the immersion-bath in water, we may ourselves become partakers of his death), so we shall also have a share in the resurrection. The following verses (6–9) emphasize this basic fact with a number of fresh modes of expression. The old man has been crucified with Christ; thus the sinful body has also been destroyed and the slavery to sin abolished. By virtue of our conformation with Christ a common life with him grows up, and we receive an increasing share of his freedom from death and from the dominion of death. In 6:10f. the Apostle draws the conclusion, first, with regard to Christ, who is now once for all dead to sin and who lives for God; and then, second, with regard to the baptized: they are "dead to sin and alive to God in Christ Jesus". Verses 12–14 apply what has been said to the ethical goal of these statements: it is therefore not permissible that sin reign over us; rather is it incumbent upon us to show ourselves "as men who have been called from death to life", as men serving

---

[26] Cf. in this connection F. Prat, *Théologie de S. Paul,* 2 (1941) 20–2, especially the summary on p. 21, note 1. (Engl. tr. *The Theology of St. Paul,* Ld. 1959). E. Lohmeyer in *Festgabe für Adolf Deissmann* (Tü. 1927) 218–57. R. Schnackenburg, *Heilsgeschehen,* 149–59, 163–75. V. Warnach, *Agape. Die Liebe als Grundmotiv der neutestamentlichen Theologie* (Dd. 1951) 383–94, 574ff.

God in the battle for righteousness, no longer under the law, but under grace.[27]

Of primary and crucial importance for the interpretation of this passage is our understanding of the word ὁμοίωμα.[28] We

[27] For comment on this passage in detail cf. R. Schnackenburg, *Heilsgeschehen* 290–322. Schnackenburg summarizes as follows (p. 106): "St. Paul states his argument most deeply and most individually in Rom. 6:3ff., where he describes entrance into the Christian community as the process through which we subsequently undergo the same experience which Christ once underwent – subsequently, and yet also *with* Christ. Here the events of Christ's life, which lie historically in the past, take on direct significance for the Christian's attainment of salvation in the present. Christ in his total reality, both as spiritually present now and as a figure out of the historical past, is the one great way of salvation. . . ." These remarks are all the more worthy of attention, since Schnackenburg criticizes O. Casel sharply in detail (cf. pp. 139–44). In a final interpretation he comes obviously to agree with his adversary. It is therefore not incorrect for M. Barth, the antipode of both men, to say (*Taufe*, p. 212): "From the equivalent results arrived at by both the comparative religions and conservative schools of thought in the Catholic as well as in the Protestant Church one can conclude that there is probably in matters of sacramental theology no final and unbridgeable opposition between the Rome, Wittenberg, and Geneva of the Reformation period and the Heidelberg, Oxford, Maria-Laach and Munich of the present. The roots of this consensus (which understands baptism as the mystery in which the death of Christ is made present and its validity and significance for us realized) may well lie in Tertullian's work *De baptismo* . . . ." For M. Barth all these attempts fall, of course, under the heading "magic" (pp. 212–18), since everything which is ascribed to baptism is "torn away from Christ". "Must not such a means, if it is really effective for salvation by virtue of divine institution and through correct performance 'ex opere operato', stand in competition with the one mediator, Jesus Christ, and with his perfect service of God, the unique death on the cross . . . ?" (p. 220). This question can only be answered in the negative, since such a baptism is, of course, by its very nature intended to bind us to Christ, and is quite simply the implement for his own most personal work.

[28] See also R. Schnackenburg, *Heilsgeschehen*, 39–48. V. Warnach, *Taufe u. Christusgeschehen*, 302–11. M. Barth, *Taufe*, 235–44; in addition, H. Schwarzmann, *Taufth. d. Paulus*, 7: "The real concern of the work is to analyse the sentence structure and interpret the meaning of verse 5. . . ."

should like to interpret the word as V. Warnach does in a concrete sense, with the meaning "image" or "likeness" (related to the dynamic word ὁμοίωσις), and not in the abstract sense of "identity" (like, perhaps, the word ὁμοιότης). Such an interpretation does not entail sliding anachronistically in the Platonizing direction of later Church Fathers, but is rather a simple, matter-of-fact rendering of the sense of this word, which is supported by its meaning in other passages in Paul's writings, and which takes account of the context here.[29] Baptism ("the baptism of death") is, therefore, ὁμοίωμα, a likeness of the death of Christ; this is the fundamental reality in baptism. In and through this likeness of Christ's death, the baptismal candidate enters into the most intimate association with the Lord crucified, and in consequence, with the risen Lord as well. He does this by being crucified with Christ, dying with him, being buried with him, and by being raised with him to life again, freed from the dominion of sin, in order that he may henceforth live with Christ and in Christ for God. From this condition of being united with this likeness of Christ's death proceed the consequences already mentioned: being dead to sin and alive to God in Christ.[30]

[29] Warnach, *Taufe u. Christusgeschehen,* 306 f., note 66 reports the opinions of the most important exegetes as to the interpretation of this passage.

[30] It cannot be our task to go more deeply here into the (at present still disputed) theological evaluation of this passage. The best insight into this controversy is offered by R. Schnackenburg, *Heilsgeschehen,* above all pp. 132–207, and – in conflict with him – by V. Warnach, *Taufe u. Christusgeschehen,* which also contains extensive bibliographical references. E. Stommel, *Das "Abbild seines Todes" (Röm. 6: 5) und der Taufritus,* 16 ff. comes to a somewhat different conclusion from Warnach. According to him Rom. 6:5 cannot say that in baptism we "have been united with" the ὁμοίωμα of Christ's death as Warnach translates. The meaning is on the contrary literal: "We have become those-who-have-been-united-with." It is true, he adds, that ὁμοίωμα must be understood in a concrete sense, but pre-

THE SCRIPTURAL DOCTRINE OF BAPTISM

However, this immediate result of baptism must not be understood in a mechanical and external sense. The intention of the entire chapter is, of course, precisely to admonish the baptized to manifest in their future lives these unique and permanent fundamental facts, and not to fall back again into the dominion of sin (which is, therefore, entirely possible), but rather to prove themselves in this new life of theirs as men who have been raised from the dead. This is perfectly clear both from the beginning and end of the Apostle's argument, 6:2 and 6:12f. And the noteworthy future verbs in 6:4, 5, and 8 point in the same direction: we shall walk, we shall be (united), we shall live with. The reality which is given to us in baptism is something which, at least in a certain respect, is completely fulfilled only in the future. This is entirely consistent with the teaching of the Apostle in other passages. In 1 Cor. 10:2, where he comes to speak of the baptism of Moses received by "our fathers" as they passed through the Red Sea, he issues an express warning against lulling one's self into false security. All the same, it is clear from the whole context here that baptism imparts a new life which furnishes the foundation for a Christian life of moral and mental

cisely for this reason it cannot refer to the baptismal action in the sense of the performance of the rite. For this event is unique and transitory. With the mere performance of baptism it is, therfore, impossible for us to be "those-who-have-been-united-with"; such a condition is possible only if the reception of baptism has translated us into a new state of being. ὁμοίωμα is the state of being alive for God and dead to sin, which is effected by the living Spirit at the time baptism is received, and which corresponds to the condition of the dead and buried Saviour. Cf. also E. Stommel, *"Begraben mit Christus" und der Taufritus.* It seems to us, however, hardly probable that one can, consistently with the Apostle's conception of baptism, leave the baptismal rite fully out of consideration – as this view requires.

freedom, and the consummation and crowning of which will be future holiness (cf. Col. 3:4) and eternal life. The Apostle then proceeds in the following chapters, and especially in chapter 8, to show the grandeur of the life which this "baptism of death" imparts.

The Epistle to the Colossians contains the same train of thought. The baptized are made members of Christ in such a manner that they are dead for the service of the elements of the universe, and in order that they may lead a new life with its corresponding moral consequences. The crucial sentence is 2:12: "You were buried with him (Christ) in baptism, in which you were also raised with him through faith in the working of God, who raised him from the dead." What happens in baptism is made a completely integral part of the saving work of Christ. In Christ the Colossians have come to the fulness of life (2:10), in him they have also been circumcised, "not with a circumcision which was made with hands, but rather by putting off (taking off) the body of the flesh (2:11); hitherto they have been dead, but they have been made alive with Christ (2:13), and freed from all sins. Their bond of indebtedness has been cancelled (2:13f.), and they are free from the burdens and confinements of alien mystery cults (2:16–23). Therefore those who have been raised with Christ are to lead a life hid with Christ in God (3:3), "seeking that which is above" (3:2), in the hope that when the Lord comes again this hidden life with him will be made manifest (3:4). The remainder of chapter 3 sets forth the standards of this life which results from the union with Christ in death and in life that has been established in baptism.

In these two passages, Rom. 6 and Col. 2–3, we have the most comprehensive portion of Paul's theology of baptism. To this Titus 3:5–7 is, despite its relative brevity, a characteristic supplement.[31] "He saved us, not because of deeds done by us in righteousness, but in virtue of his own mercy, by the washing of regeneration and renewal in the Holy Spirit, which he poured out upon us richly through Jesus Christ our Saviour, so that, justified through his grace, we might become heirs in hope of eternal life."[32] The Greek text of the decisive passage here runs as follows: διὰ λουτροῦ παλιγγενεσίας καὶ ἀνακαινώσεως πνεύματος ἁγίου. It is the notion of παλιγγενεσία, regeneration, which is important here – something which appears for the first time, and uniquely, in the Pauline writings. One might perceive here the influence of 1 Pet. 1:3 and 23, were it not for the fact that we find in the latter passage different terminology (ἀναγεννᾶν) for a metaphor which is certainly the same in content. But however we decide this really quite formal question, it is certain that this notion is at heart merely the completion and crystallization of a train of thought which the Apostle has long had in his mind. Indeed we need look no further than the following word ἀνακαίνωσις, "renewal", to find the connection easily. In the dying of the old man, in the putting off of this man, in the resurrection of the new man, and in the putting on of this new man – in short, in the renewal which all these things constitute, we have something so new coming to being that we can even speak of a new birth, or re-birth, or of regeneration. The reason why this metaphor is self-evident, is because the Apostle applies it likewise to the resurrection of Christ, which he sees as the basic type

---

[31] M. Barth (Taufe, 455; cf. 454–71) disputes the view that Titus 3:5 refers clearly and expressly to baptism. Despite a number of good thoughts his demonstration is not convincing. He comes himself to the resigned conclusion: "To all appearances and on the basis of present-day scholarship it is not possible to give a proper and exact explanation of Titus 3:5" (p. 471).   [32] Cf. for this passage J. Dey, Παλιγγενεσία.

of the baptismal resurrection. And behind Christ's resurrection he perceives the prophetical words of Psalm 2: "Thou art my Son, today I have begotten thee" (cf. Acts 13:33). The author of this baptismal regeneration is the "soter", who, after his epiphany on earth, effects this re-birth by means of the baptismal bath. The foundation of regeneration is not one's own works of righteousness, but the mercy of God the Saviour. Regeneration, or the renewal which is given along with it, is characterized by the addition, in the genitive, of the words "in the Holy Spirit" (Titus 3:5): in this renewal the sacred *pneuma* operates in a special way. Just how this *pneuma* is poured out by Jesus Christ we do not learn in any detail. However, on the basis of the context it is not possible to exclude at least the possibility that this takes place within the framework of the whole act of baptism. The final sentence gives to the whole passage once again an eschatological orientation: in such a justification there is granted an hereditary claim in accordance with the hope of eternal life.

Paul's doctrine of baptism is, therefore, presented in integral form in Romans and in 1 Corinthians, his principal letters, as well as in Colossians, and Ephesians, in the late Epistle to Titus, and in Galatians and Hebrews, even though the various passages show different shades of meaning. In order to arrive at a full understanding of this doctrine of baptism it is absolutely necessary to set it in the framework of the Apostle's total doctrine of salvation. It is, therefore, imperative to refer at this point to this teaching.[33] We recall for instance the mystical teaching with regard to Christ in Gal. 2:19f., our adoption as sons and the giving

---

[33] See *Hdb. d. Dogmengeschichte (The Herder History of Dogma)*, vol. 3, parts 2 and 4; also vol. 2, parts 2 and 3.

of the Spirit referred to in Gal. 4:17 as well as in Rom. 8:14–17, the opposition between flesh and spirit in Gal. 5, and the comparison of light and darkness in Eph. 5:8–14. It is true that such thoughts and others like them are not applied by the Apostle expressly to baptism. But it is only in connection with baptism that they achieve their full and proper significance; and they are, on the other hand, of the greatest value for a full understanding of the Apostle's doctrine of baptism.

Finally, in the framework of the other New Testament writings, this doctrine of baptism receives further deepening and interpretation in 1 Peter and in 1 John. The first Epistle of Peter mentions baptism expressly only once, to be sure (3:20): ". . . in the ark only a few, that is, eight souls, were saved through water. Baptism, which corresponds to this, now saves you, not as [being so much] a removal of dirt from the body but as an appeal to God for a good conscience through the [power of the] resurrection of Jesus Christ." Just as the ark in olden times saved from the flood and from the death to which the unbelievers were doomed, so now does baptism do the same. The water-bath is, in this connection, more than external, bodily washing. It is a request (and a request granted, ἐπερώτημα) to God for a good conscience by means of Christ's resurrection – which takes effect in baptism.[34] Here as well we find reference, therefore, to the mysterious parallel with Christ. The conformation of the bap-

---

[34] Within the framework of his system of thought M. Barth is very concerned to show that the words, "baptism now saves you", mean merely that baptism is a prayer with the utterance of which there begins that good way of life which is the confirmation and exercise of faith and obedience (*Taufe,* p. 519). Such words are intended to warn Christians against "having faith in baptism instead of placing their trust in the Holy Spirit . . . Christians are to know that the Holy Spirit alone . . . sanctifies, and that

tismal candidate to Christ can be even more clearly recognized from the context. Chapter 3, verse 18, says of Christ, that he "was put to death in the flesh but made alive in the spirit". And following the mention of baptism, we read in 4:1 f. that since Christ suffered in the flesh the believer should also take on himself the same disposition. Here is another passage where what happens in baptism becomes the standard which is to give to the candidate's entire life the stamp of moral effort according to the pattern of Christ, to whose death and resurrection he has been conformed in baptism.

The resurrection life, which is thus given in baptism, is mentioned also in other contexts in the first Epistle of Peter. To be sure, these passages do not report any cult or ritual action directly. But one can claim that such references achieve their full significance only in connection with the act of baptism. "By the great mercy of (God the Father) we have been born anew (ἀναγεννήσας) to a living hope through the resurrection of Jesus Christ from the dead, and to an inheritance which is imperishable . . . kept in heaven for you" (1:3–5). The Father has effected this new birth to hope by means of the resurrection of Christ. We must therefore supplement this by reference to 3:21, where it is expressly stated that Christ's resurrection imparts salvation through baptism, which is, in accordance with the original

their salvation is guaranteed by the resurrection of Christ, and not by cult acts . . ." (p. 520). Cf. the contrary opinion expressed by the (Protestant) Jean Héring in *RevHistPhRel* 33 (1953) 259: "M. B. s'efforce d'enlever ce formidable obstacle qui s'oppose à sa thèse . . . Nous ne serons sans doute pas les seuls à n'être qu'à moitié convaincus par cette exégèse" ("M. B. strives to remove this formidable obstacle which stands in the way of his thesis . . . We shall doubtless not be the only one to remain but half convinced by this exegesis").

34

pattern of Christ's resurrection, the raising of a new man from the death of sin. 1:23 is to be taken in the same sense: "born anew (ἀναγεγεννημένοι), not of perishable seed but of imperishable, through the word of the loving and abiding God". People who have in this way been born anew are, in fact, like "newborn babes" (ἀρτιγέννητα 2, 2). They are like living stones built into a spiritual house, called to the dignity of a holy, royal priesthood (2:5, 9) and of a holy people, summoned from darkness into the wonderful light of God (2:9).

Baptism, a water-bath in which the imperishable seed of God's Word (cf. Eph. 5:26) is at work giving life, means, therefore, for Paul the same thing as new birth. This new birth is effected by means of the assimilation to Christ's passion and resurrection which takes place in baptism. It makes him who is newly born a member of a new people with a sacred and exalted dignity. It is true that the expression used here for new birth (ἀναγεννᾶν) is different from that in Titus (παλιγγενεσία). And John's expression is different again: he uses the simple verb (γεννηθῆναι, γεγεννημένος etc.) without prefix. This linguistic freedom in referring to the same thing excludes, of course, the possibility that the passages are textually dependent upon one another. But it brings out the interpretation of baptism as regeneration, new birth, or quite simply, as "birth", even more strongly than would be the case if we found from the very beginning a completely uniform usage in this matter.

To this evidence must be added from the Johannine writings the first Epistle and John's own words in his Gospel, that is, essentially, the Prologue. Here as well we do not find any direct mention of baptism itself. But it is, of course, the same author who records the nocturnal conversation of the Lord with Nicodemus:

35

"Unless one is born from above, . . . unless one is born of water and the Spirit . . ." (John 3:3 and 5). We may, then, indeed we must, explain the passages in John 1 and 1 John which speak of such a birth in such a way that they at the very least include baptism. The Logos gave to those who received him the power "to become children of God – to those who believe on his name, who were born, not of blood . . . but of God" (John 1:12f.). The same expression "born of God" is one of the fundamental notions of the first Epistle (3:9; 5:1, 4, and 18). Christians are "the children of God", not merely in name, but in very truth (3:1). And they remain God's children even if this condition is to become manifest only in the future, at the last appearance of Christ (3:2). "He who is born of God commits no sin; for his (God's) seed abides in him; indeed he cannot sin, because (to the extent that) he is born of God" (3:9). There is nothing to prevent our equating this "birth from God" with the "birth from water and the Spirit" which was mentioned in the conversation with Nicodemus. It is true that 1 John 5:1 says: "Every one who believes that Jesus is the Christ is born of God." But that in no way excludes a ritual performance of baptism. It merely says that faith belongs necessarily to baptism, which is stated in Acts 8:35–38 and in other passages as well: baptism is in a certain measure just the concrete expression of faith. At the time that John wrote, baptism was, of course, long since a practice taken for granted in the Church. And about things taken for granted the Apostle did not need to speak. But the emphasis of faith is a valuable supplement to the theology of baptism, and one which is quite in line with the other New Testament writings as well.

Just how important the baptismal action was for John is shown by 1 John 5:6–8 as well: "This is he who came by water and the blood. . . . There are three who bear witness: the Spirit and the water and the blood, and these three are one." We can interpret the water best as meaning the water of Jesus' baptism in Jordan, when the Spirit appeared above him as witness. But this witness which was given on the occasion of his baptism in water is supplemented by the witness of the blood which flowed on the cross. In John 19:34 the Evangelist had borne witness to the stream of water and blood which flowed from the pierced side of Jesus. A number of Fathers see in this remarkable event, which had so much significance for the Apostle, a reference to the Eucharist and to baptism.[35] It is true that the validity of this symbolical interpretation is disputed. Nevertheless, the Johannine doctrine of baptism does deserve to be considered sometime against such a background as well.

In this connection we must mention passages like John 4:14, where living water is promised, as well perhaps as the miracle of healing at the pool of Bethesda (John 5:1–15), but very specially the healing of the man born blind, who is to wash

---

[35] For the exegesis of this and of the following passages see M.–J. Lagrange, *L'évangile selon S. Jean* (Pa. ³1927) 499, which presents a moderate view of the historic reality and its value as a symbol: "C'est la réalité qui importe avant tout, comme base du symbole, quoique le symbole, s'il y en a un, confère une singulière valeur. Il n'est d'ailleurs pas aisé de définir ce symbole, et les pères ont proposé de nombreuses explications" ("What matters most of all is the reality, as being the foundation for the symbol, although the symbol, if there is one, confers special value. It is, moreover, not easy to define the symbol, and the Fathers have proposed numerous explanations"). A brief survey of these interpretations follows. On the whole question in the framework of the problems presented by the Fourth Gospel, see *op. cit.* pp. xc–xcii: *Le symbolisme du quatrième évangile.* Cf. also O. Casel in *ArchLW* 1 (1950) 4f., 312–15 (and review of the same by O. Cullmann, *Urchristentum u. Gottesdienst* (*Abh. z. Theol. d. A. u. N. T.*, 3: Bs. 1944) (Engl. tr. *Early Christian Worship,* Studies in Biblical Theology 10, Ld., 1953).

himself in the pool of Siloam (John 9:1–38). Even if it is quite impossible to do complete justice to these passages by interpreting them symbolically, still such symbolical interpretation does retain its place – and not merely in the exegesis of later times, but right in the composition of the gospel itself and in the express statements of the Evangelist: baptism proceeds from the crucified Lord and is enlightenment and healing, a spring of living water for eternal life.

As we look back, we perceive that the New Testament doctrine of baptism, amidst all the variety of metaphors in detail, presents as a whole an impressively unified structure. Taken over at first from the "Baptist" in the form of an external rite of immersion, but then supplemented and perfected in its own right through the epiclesis of the names in accordance with the Lord's commission, baptism remains always in immediate and definite proximity to the act of repentance and to the confession of faith. It is, accordingly, always a question of adult baptism: the question of infant baptism is not raised.[36] Baptism is an image of, and at the same time conforms us to, the death and resurrection of Christ, and is so far-reaching in its potency that

[36] It would probably be difficult to find in the New Testament even the *practice* of infant baptism. We might well feel obliged to agree here with the conclusions which are to be found in numerous Protestant studies of this question, as for example, Joh. Schneider, *Taufe im NT* (which also contains a list of the most important writings on this question). This, however, implies nothing contrary to the legitimacy of infant baptism and its compatibility with Holy Scripture. This problem is solved from Tradition, where we find the legitimate development of what is stated in Scripture. Of course, anyone who denies the legitimacy of such development will hardly be able to assent to infant baptism. At any rate, Tradition shows that nothing can be produced from the New Testament which would prove infant baptism to be contrary to Scripture. Cf. below pp. 32, 39, 100f.

it effects a new creation, a new birth, or regeneration. To be sure, what is given in baptism achieves its fulfilment only at the end of time. Nevertheless, it displays its effectiveness in the present through forgiveness of sins, through purification, by doing away with the old man and by bringing to birth in the Spirit a new man who is the child of God, as well as through the putting on of Christ. In this way baptism imparts fundamentally the gift of the Holy Spirit, and is, in fact, the promised baptism in the Holy Spirit. This all means, furthermore, the reception and incorporation into the Body of Christ, into the fellowship of his Church with all the duties and rights that this involves. Because baptism is reception and incorporation, it is unique, and therefore *one*. The minister has direct importance, as standing in the foreground. He need not be an Apostle; a deacon can also administer baptism, in the last analysis, anyone at all. The relationship of baptism to the name of God or of the Lord, with the mighty acts of Christ's saving work, with his death and resurrection as well as with his holy *pneuma* are all clearly brought out.

These ideas form, in their diversity, an admirably organic unity.[37] Although we have in our presentation up to this point,

---

[37] M. Barth comes to the same conclusion (*Taufe*, p. 522): "The New Testament statements about baptism with water are surprisingly uniform and consistent." However, this consistent doctrine of baptism consists according to Barth in the view that the performance of baptism which Christ had commanded (Matt. 28:19) is an act of obedience. "Baptism is *not* a mystery . . ." p. 553. Barth's book contains an abundance of interesting and sometimes even valuable thoughts. It is true that he interprets all the texts in one very definite direction and on the basis of one very definite presupposition. This comes to light in the dilemma which we have already mentioned a number of times, according to which the recognition of even a very slight efficacy in baptism does injury to the cross of Christ and even means magic. Thus he says in closing: "Whoever expects all

and indeed in the summary immediately above, allowed Holy Scripture to speak for itself, we do see already in the Scriptures the basic patterns of the subsequent teaching of the Church. The presentation which has been given here has caused us to recognize clearly that the New Testament teaching about baptism, which possesses such inner consistency, may be traced right back to Christ and to his work; and furthermore that Christ himself "instituted" this baptism (in the strictest sense of that word) when, in his baptismal commission in Matt. 28 he joined the immersion-bath in water, which was already familiar from his Forerunner, with the epiclesis of the trinitarian God, uniting the two in "baptism" in the proper sense of the term. There is no evidence that the Lord, in giving this commission, or his disciples, in carrying it into practice, had drawn upon other non-Christian or non-Jewish usages – indeed this is entirely improbable. R. Reitzenstein's attempt to trace Christian baptism back to Mandaean baptism may be considered a complete failure.[38]

Even if we have demonstrated the independent character of Christian baptism, we are still not dispensed from the task of seeking an explanation for the parallels with Hellenistic initiation rites which do, in fact, exist. A sober answer must be content with one point, which in this difficult question is actually no longer really disputed: namely, that without there being any causal in-

---

salvation from the cross . . ., can say that baptism is a good work of the praying community, by which the cross of Christ and the vivifying Spirit are praised" (p. 553). The equating (at least in a certain sense: see p. 173) of the baptism of John and Christian baptism shows likewise for its part that Barth, with his interpretation of baptism, remains standing at the threshold of the New Testament.

[38] R. Reitzenstein, *Die Vorgeschichte der christlichen Taufe* (Lp. 1929); see the review of this work by O. Casel in *JbLW* 9 (1929) 206–19.

fluence, there are nevertheless forms on both sides which can be traced back simply to the basic mental and bodily structure of man as it relates to religious celebrations in general and initiation rites in particular. In the case of Christian baptism the incarnate God-Logos has created quite independently a rite having a concrete connection with the Johannine baptism, and yet one which remains his own genuine work; a rite which is in large part, above all in its essential characteristics, unique, and which at the same time displays in a number of ways something analogous to other initiation rites. But as regards non-Christian initiation rites, the worshipping community has in each case created from its more or less elevated power of religious expression cult actions, in which these analogies are likewise to be observed.[39]

The awareness of such analogies can be of great value for a deeper understanding of the cult actions concerned. We shall come back to this point later on (p. 92–100), when we shall have to show how the contemporary witnesses themselves become aware of these analogies, and how their recognition of these parallels influences both terminology and theology.

---

[39] See on this point O. Casel, *Das christliche Kult-Mysterium* (Rgb. ³1948) 95-115 (Engl. tr. *The Mystery of Christian Worship,* Ld. 1962); also, by the same author, *JbLW* 14 (1938) 197–224 (the controversy with K. Prümm). A brief summary of this controversy is to be found in Th. Filthaut, *Kontroverse* 86–98. M. Barth has also treated this entire matter in detail (*Taufe,* 187–221). It is, within the framework of his entire view, natural that he rejects any relationship between Christian and non-Christian initiation rites. But he grants the existence of such a relationship (in a pejorative sense, it is true) once one begins, in line with Tradition since the time of Tertullian, to describe baptism as a "sacrament" (cf. *e.g.* p. 212).

Chapter Two

THE SCRIPTURAL DOCTRINE OF CONFIRMATION

BIBLIOGRAPHY: L. Jannsens, *La confirmation. Exposé dogmatique, historique et liturgique* (Lille 1888). F. J. Dölger, *Das Sacrament der Firmung, historisch-dogmatisch dargestellt* (Wn. 1906). C. Ruch, "Confirmation dans la S. Écriture" in *DThC* 3, 1 (1908) 975–1026. P. de Puniet, "Confirmation" in *DACL* 3, 2 (1914) 2515–44. M. O'Dwyer, *Confirmation. A Study in the Development of Sacramental Theology* (Du. 1915). J. B. Umberg, *Die Schriftlehre vom Sacrament der Firmung* (FbB. 1920). J. Coppens, *L'imposition des mains et les rites connexes dans le Nouveau Testament et dans l'Église ancienne* (*Univ. Cath. Lovan. Dissert.* II, 15; Wetteren-Pa. 1925); by the same author, "Confirmation" in *DBibl Suppl.* 2 (1934) 120–53. B. Welte, *Die postbaptismale Salbung. Ihr symbolischer Gehalt u. ihre sakramentale Zugehörigkeit nach den Zeugnissen der alten Kirche* (*Freibg. Th. Stud.* 51; FbB. 1953). N. Adler, *Taufe und Handauflegung. Exeget. theol. Untersuchg. v. Apg.* 8, 14–17 (*Ntl. Abh.* 19, 3; Mst. 1951).

HOWEVER one interprets the relationship between baptism and confirmation in detail, three New Testament texts make it certain that a laying on of hands for the imparting of the Spirit – performed after the water-bath and as a complement to this bath – existed already in the earliest apostolic times. These texts are: Acts 8:4–20 and 19:1–7, and Hebrews 6:1–6.

The two texts from Acts are the most important. Following his sermon about the kingdom of God and the name of Jesus Christ (8:12), the deacon, Philip, has administered the baptismal bath in the name of the Lord Jesus (8:16). The Apostles hear "that Samaria has received the word of God" (8:14), whereupon they send Peter and John there. These two apostles "prayed for them that they might receive the Holy Spirit; for it had not yet fallen on any of them, but they had only been baptized in the name of the Lord Jesus. Then they laid their hands on them and they received the Holy Spirit" (8:15–17). Acts 8:18–19 confirms this connection once more, as it is reflected in the scene with Simon the magician: "the Spirit was given through the laying on of the apostles' hands".

We hear of something similar in Acts 19:1–7. The disciples of John – introduced simply as "disciples" – are asked whether after their acceptance of the faith (that is, obviously, after reception of baptism) they had received the Holy Spirit. They answer that they had not even known that there was a Holy Spirit; they have been baptized with "John's baptism" only. The Apostle refers to the preparatory character of this baptism, whereupon the disciples allow themselves to be baptized in the name of the Lord Jesus.[1] "And when Paul had laid hands upon them, the Holy Spirit came on them; and they spoke with tongues and prophesied."

The passage in Hebrews (6:1–6), although not quite so clear

---

[1] M. Barth tries to weaken this passage, which is so crucial for his entire interpretation, by the daring expedient of changing the punctuation: he makes Acts 19:5 a continuation of St. Paul's own speech, so that the passage gives the appearance of saying that the disciples were not baptized again, but that they had merely received the laying on of hands (cf. *Taufe*, p. 165–72). This fails, however, alone through the impossibility of describing the baptism of John as a "baptism in the name of the Lord Jesus".

in meaning, distinguishes likewise a doctrine of "baptismal actions" from the doctrine of "the laying on of hands". The two passages in Acts must be referred to if one is to arrive at a fuller understanding of this excessively brief passage.

The texts distinguish clearly between the administration of the immersion-bath (denoted by the word βαπτίζεσθαι) and a subsequent laying on of hands. The difference is the more tangible in that different "ministers" are named for the two actions. Acts 8 shows this at the first glance: it is not the deacon, but only the apostles who are able to impart the *pneuma* through the laying on of hands. But in Acts 19 as well an identical situation is presupposed. For we hear there first of the baptism of the disciples in quite general terms, without the minister being identified. (According to 1 Cor. 1:17 it could not have been St. Paul, since he left baptism to others as a matter of principle.) But then it is expressly stated that it is St. Paul who lays hands upon them. Both these passages in Acts ascribe to this laying on of hands an imparting of the Holy Spirit, which has not been effected by the "mere" performance of the immersion-bath. On the other hand, a passage like Acts 2:38 shows that even the water-bath cannot be conceived of apart from the Spirit; and the same is shown, though in a different manner, by Acts 10:47. And finally Acts 8 shows that the laying on of hands is joined with a prayer for the descent of the Spirit.

The criticisms of liberal theology, which deny to Acts as a whole, and especially to chapters 8 and 19, all historical value for the first apostolic period, have been conclusively refuted by the studies of C. Ruch and J. Coppers.[2] The attempt to claim (as

[2] C. Ruch: *DThC* 3,1 (1908) 975–1001; J. Coppens, *L'imposition* 220–48.

German liberal theologians[3] and A. Loisy[4] in particular have done) that the two passages in question are clumsy compilations of older sources, filled with internal contradictions, has failed. And it is just as mistaken to try to shake confidence in the value of the evidence offered by Acts as to the laying on of hands by pointing to the allegedly contradictory and inconsistent meaning which the word πνεῦμα possesses in Acts. It is claimed, on the one hand, that the word represents a Hellenistic conception, "signifiant l'esprit-élément, influx psychologique, principe intrinsèque, immanent de vie religieuse et morale"("signifying the elemental spirit, a psychological influx, an intrinsic and immanent principle of religious and moral life"). And on the other hand the term is said to be based upon a Judaic-Christian conception and "introduisant dans les Actes l'Esprit personnel avec tout le cortège de ses interventions charismatiques, pro-phétiques et thaumaturgiques" (to "introduce into Acts the personal Spirit with his whole accompaniment of charismatical, prophetical and miraculous interventions").[5] Despite the varying connotation of the word *pneuma* in Acts, Coppens maintains that there is definitely no contradiction, and in particular none between the conception of the Spirit as a person and its conception as a gift. In Acts we find the most varying shades of meaning for *pneuma*, depending on the particular occasion of the narrative in each case. In the first part, which presents principally

[3] A brief summary of the more recent Protestant view is to be found in *RGG* 1 ([2]1927) 439f.; for examples of the older trend of opinion see, perhaps, H. Waitz, "Simon Magus" in *REPTh* 18 (1906) 351–61. H. H. Wendt, *Die Apostelgeschichte* (Gö. [9]1913).
[4] A. Loisy, *Les Actes des Apôtres* (Pa. 1920).
[5] J. Coppens describes these views in this summary fashion in his work, *L'imposition*, 246.

a picture of the religious life of the first Christians, the sanctifying effects of the *pneuma* are to the fore; whereas in the reports of the activity of the apostle St. Paul, it is the influence of this *pneuma* in the activity of the Christian messengers which is more prominent.[6] It will, accordingly, not do to create a gap between the *pneuma* which descends upon the apostles at Pentecost and which is promised by Peter to the baptismal candidates in his Pentecost sermon, and the *pneuma* which is imparted through the laying on of hands, as reported in Acts 8 and 19. We are dealing essentially with the same *pneuma,* even if we have in each case, perhaps, to distinguish a different primary significance.[7]

We can state, therefore, in conclusion that the evidence of Acts is valid. The bath of baptism and the laying on of hands are, then, separate happenings which can be well distinguished from one another. However, they complement each other mutually, as follows. The baptismal bath in the name of Jesus (which is the first imparting of the Spirit), and the (complementary) imparting of the Spirit through the laying on of hands make up together the full and complete process by which believers become Christians, and by which they are initiated into the Christian life. They are the two components of Christian initiation, in which the full sense of Peter's demand to the repentent Jews is brought to realization: "be baptized every one of you . . . and you shall receive the gift of the Holy Spirit" (2:38).

This total initiation corresponds exactly to the conception which the original Christian community had of the Spirit as the

---

[6] *op. cit.* 247 f.; cf. also J. B. Umberg, *Schriftlehre v. S. d. Firm.,* 77–96.
[7] For the entire problem here see also B. Neunheuser, "Die Lehre vom Geist Christi nach der Enzyklika 'Mystici Corporis' in Liturgie u. Mönchtum" in *Laacher Hefte* 4 (1949) 60–2.

messianic gift *par excellence*.[8] The Prophets had predicted this pouring out of the Spirit under the metaphor of saving streams of water. "Jesus' appeal to the Scriptures (in John 7:37f.) must be referred not to a single passage in the psalms, but rather to the entire Old Testament prediction that the Messiah was to impart water bringing with it the fullness of blessing."[9] We find the pouring out of God's Spirit clearly prophesied in Ezech. 39:29, in Zach. 12:10, and especially in the well-known passage quoted by St. Peter, Joel 3:1–2. We may quite legitimately follow the interpretation of both Patristic and modern theology in seeing the first fulfilment of these prophecies in the descent of the Holy Spirit upon Jesus at his baptism in Jordan.[10] "And the holy *pneuma* descended upon him in bodily form, as a dove" (Luke 3:22 and parallels). This descent of the Spirit takes place after the water-bath which the Lord has undergone. It is the pattern for that descent of the Spirit which the disciples receive after the glorification of Jesus (cf. also Acts 1:8). This descent occurred in an extraordinary manner on the feast of Pentecost. On the occasion of Cornelius' conversion the accompanying and equally unusual descent of the Spirit upon the Gentiles is taken by St. Peter to be a sign that those so favoured must receive the water-bath, in order that they may belong completely to the Christian community (Acts 10:47f.). Admittedly these are special cases. But already on the feast of Pentecost St. Peter makes a connection between the bath of baptism and the imparting of the Spirit. And we see that by the time of the

---

[8] For what follows see: J. B. Umberg, *Schriftlehre v. S. d. Firm.*, 78–96.
[9] *op. cit.* 81f.
[10] J. Coppens in *DBibl* Suppl. 2, 148. L. Koch, "Die Geistessalbung Christi bei der Taufe im Jordan" in *BenedMsch* 20 (1938) 18–20.

events in Samaria recorded in Acts 8, at the latest, a distinction was made between two rites, the water-bath and the laying on of hands, which now, taken together and mutually complementing one another, confer full membership in the fellowship of the disciples and impart the promised *pneuma*.

Just how the apostles actually came to adopt such a practice we can hardly say with certainty merely on the basis of the texts which have been handed down to us. J. Coppens refers to the fact that there was at this time a laying on of hands in Judaic usage.[11] In addition there was the example of the Lord, reaching out his hands as he ascended to heaven, to which we must in all likelihood add a direct dominical command, similar to that given to Ananias (Acts 9:17). But it is highly unlikely that the apostles would have introduced on their own authority a rite of such dynamic power. At any rate, the laying on of hands was in the eyes of the apostles an efficacious symbol for the imparting of the Spirit.[12]

It is, however, true that the terminology of the Apostle Paul is unique. He himself is, so to speak, *the* apostle of the holy *pneuma*. According to Acts 19:6 he was familiar with the laying on of hands in the sense adopted here, and he administered it. Nevertheless, he never mentions it in his letters. St. Paul seems rather to ascribe to what he himself terms baptism all the effects of Christian initiation, and in particular, therefore, the possession of the *pneuma*. The various individual gifts are merely different facets of the single new life, whose ultimate source is, for him, the *pneuma*. But there is nothing to prevent us from assuming –

[11] J. Coppens, *L'imposition*, 368–73; by the same author: *DBibl* Suppl. 151.
[12] J. Coppens, *L'imposition*, 373.

and indeed passages like Acts 8 and 19 and Hebrews 6 really require such an assumption – that the Pauline βαπτισμός includes several actions. This is exactly parallel, for instance, to Acts 19, 1–6, the terminology of which requires such an assumption. And in the following centuries the several initiatory rites continued to be referred to simply under the one term, baptism.[13] It is true that "we cannot find in (St. Paul's) writings evidence for a distinction between individual stages in the rite of Christian initiation. But just as the individual external rites do not stand out from one another in St. Paul's thought, so it is likewise impossible to differentiate in his writings between several successive stages in the internal effects of Christian initiation. In his view of the matter becoming a Christian and receiving the Spirit occur together. 'Anyone who does not have the Spirit of Christ does not belong to him' (Rom. 8:9)."[14]

Due to the more or less incidental way in which St. Paul's letters came to be written, there was for him simply no need to go into all the details of the total action. Even in the subsequent period, when people had for some time clearly defined in theory the distinction between baptism and confirmation, the two rites remained firmly united in one. Therefore the conclusion which liberal theology draws from St. Paul's terminology, in opposition to the Catholic doctrine of confirmation, is not compelling. Even St. Paul presents the life of the baptized as something which can be augmented: such augmentation he ascribes to a sending of the Spirit. "Because you are sons (obviously because

---

[13] There is a good presentation of these facts to be found in B. Welte, *Postbapt. Salbg.*, 14; cf. J. Coppens, *L'imposition*, 258; F. J. Dölger, *Sphragis. Eine altchristl. Taufbezeichnung* . . . (Pb. 1911) 185, 192f.

[14] B. Welte, *Postbapt. Salbg.*, 16; cf. J. Coppens, *L'imposition*, 265f.

of the adoption as sons which has been effected in baptism) God has sent the *pneuma* of his Son into our hearts . . ." (Gal. 4:6).[15] Further evidence for this point could be found in the letters written by St. Paul during his imprisonment, if it were legitimate to interpret the metaphor of the seal of the Spirit,[16] which we find in these letters, as referring to baptism alone. But this interpretation seems to us hardly likely, since one must in all probability take this "seal of the Spirit" as referring rather to baptism in the fullest sense, that is, to the immersion *and* to the laying on of hands.[17]

It is, further, important, as B. Welte has rightly pointed out, to investigate the connotation of the term "anointing" as it is used in the New Testament.[18] It is stated that Jesus himself has been anointed: "God anointed him with the Holy Spirit and with power" (Acts 10:38; cf. 4:27; Luke 4:18; Heb. 1:9). The word, which is taken from the Old Testament, should certainly be understood figuratively. And the statements about Christians being anointed, which are analogous to this anointing of the "Christos" (cf. 2 Cor. 1:21; 1 John 2:20, 27), can hardly be interpreted other than figuratively. At the same time, proceeding

[15] Further passages in J. Coppens, *L'imposition,* 258–65 and J. B. Umberg, *Schriftlehre v. S. d. Firm.,* 101–4.
[16] Eph. 1:13: "In him you also, who have heard the word of truth, . . . and have believed in him, were sealed with the promised Holy Spirit;" cf. 2 Cor. 1:21f. and Eph. 4:30. See, on this point, J. Coppens, *L'imposition,* 267–73 and J. B. Umberg, *Schriftlehre v. S. d. Firm.,* 104f. We would agree with these authors in their view that in these passages St. Paul can have had in mind the laying on of hands, and that he at any rate does not say anything to exclude a laying on of hands. We should not, however, so readily follow them in the more far-reaching conclusion which they draw.
[17] Thus F. J. Dölger, *Sphragis,* 78f.
[18] B. Welte, *Postbapt. Salbg.,* 4–13.

from the background of Old Testament conceptions and usages, it was not difficult to speak, in connection with the "anointing" received by Christians, of their priestly and royal dignity (cf. 1 Pet. 2:9; Apoc. 1:6; 5:10; 20:6; 22:5). But when Welte seeks to conclude from this that "one cannot dispute the possibility of an actual anointing in connection with the act of initiation in primitive Christianity", he goes beyond the New Testament texts. These allow the purely theoretical possibility that there was such an anointing, but contain no evidence that it did in fact exist. In contrast to Welte, Elfers has quite rightly remarked: "Only in the third century can we begin to see more clearly how the liturgical rite of anointing has evolved out of these . . . elements."[19]

Though the connotation of the term "anointing" will prove to be of value especially for the later theological development, it offers us nothing of immediate importance for our understanding of confirmation in the New Testament. In particular, we must content ourselves with the fact that although St. Paul speaks about a sealing and an anointing with the Spirit, there seems to be nothing in his writings pointing to the existence of a rite separate from the act of baptism in its totality. It is only the later theology which will evaluate the beginnings which are made here, utilizing them for the individual stages of the one total act in the Pauline sense as they subsequently become clear. This will be all the more possible inasmuch as Acts attests with certainty to the existence as early as the New Testament period

---

[19] H. Elfers, "Gehört die Salbung mit Chrisma im ältesten abendländischen Initiationsritus zur Taufe oder zur Firmung?" in *ThGl* 34 (1942) 336; cf. the position taken by O. Casel on the views expressed by Welte and Elfers in *ArchLW* 1 (1950) 327f. (no. 269f.).

of a complementary laying on of hands for the imparting of the Spirit. But at first both tradition and St. Paul speak of a single rite of initiation, which includes both the water-bath and the laying on of hands.[20] The rite is called quite simply "baptism", from its fundamental and impressive act. The laying on of hands is not specially mentioned. In addition, neither tradition nor St. Paul felt as yet any need to distinguish between the different and mutually complementary manner in which the Spirit was imparted in baptism and in confirmation.

[20] The view that "baptism" in St. Paul's writings denotes a rite of initiation which includes the water-bath and the imparting of the Spirit through the laying on of hands is held by F. J. Dölger, H. Elfers, P. de Puniet (*DACL* 3/2 1914, 2516), F. Prat (*Theol. de S. Paul* 2[23], 315), O. Casel (*JbLW* 7, 1927, 265, nr. 224), A. Oepke (*ThWbNT* 1, 541) and indeed even to a certain degree by B. Welte (*Postbapt. Salbg.*, 14) and by J. Coppens (*L'imposition*, 283f.).

Chapter Three

SECOND CENTURY EVIDENCE

AND INITIAL DEVELOPMENT

BIBLIOGRAPHY: F. J. Dölger, "Die Firmung in den Denkmälern des christlichen Altertums" in *RömQ* 19 (1905) 1-41; same author, Sphragis. *Eine altchristliche Taufbezeichnung in ihren Beziehungen zur profanen und religiösen Kultur des Altertums* (Pb. 1911). A. v. Harnack, *Die Terminologie der Wiedergeburt und verwandter Erlebnisse in der ältesten Kirche* in *TU* 42, 2 (1918). H. Elfers, *Die Kirchenordnung Hippolyts von Rom. Neue Untersuchungen unter besond. Berücks. d. Buches v. R. Lorentz: De Egyptische Kerkordening en Hippolytus van Rome* (Pb. 1938). W. M. Bedard O. F. M., "The Symbolism of the Baptismal Font in Early Christian Thought" (The Cath. Univ. of America. *Studies in Sacred Theology,* 11, 45, 1951).

IT IS difficult, primarily because of the scantiness of the sources, to trace the first beginning of the process by which the revealed truth of faith evolved into a fully developed dogma. Moreover, the sources available to us offer for the most part nothing but purely occasional statements, so that we can but seldom hope for a complete picture. We shall try, first, to get a picture of the actual performance of baptism as a cult act, that is, of the liturgy of baptism. Following this we shall discuss the first theological

53

reflections about baptism. The earliest monograph about baptism which has been preserved, Tertullian's work *De baptismo,* will be our most important source.

We have from as early as the end of the apostolic period – the dating is today once again disputed – a witness for the liturgy of baptism: the seventh chapter of the *Didache.*[1]

"Regarding baptism. Baptize as follows: after first explaining all these points, baptize in the name of the Father and of the Son and of the Holy Spirit, in running water. But if you have no running water, baptize in other water; and if you cannot in cold, then in warm. But if you have neither, pour water on the head three times in the name of the Father and of the Son and of the Holy Spirit. Before baptism, let the baptizer and the candidate for baptism fast, as well as any others that are able. Require the candidate to fast one or two days previously."

This brief ritual of baptism speaks of the preparation which precedes baptism. This is the catechizing about the way of life and death, treated in chapters one to six of the *Didache.* To this is joined the fasting of those who take part in the baptism. In these two elements we have the beginnings of the liturgical action, which will develop in ever richer form and continue to occupy a place prior to the act of baptism itself. These elements are nothing else than the development of the apostolic preaching and summons to repentance.[2] "Baptisma", baptism, is the quite natural technical name of the central action, and is still used, without modification, in the original full sense of the word, that is, as equivalent with an immersion-bath. Hence the direc-

---

[1] In *ACW* VI, p. 19 ff.
[2] Acts 2:38 and Peter's entire speech, 2:14–36; 8:5; 19:4.

tion: "Baptize in running, that is, in flowing water."[3] Of course, the condition that the water be flowing is not crucial. Other water can be used as well, even warm water. Indeed if there is not sufficient water to permit immersion,[4] it suffices to pour the water over the head of the candidate three times. We have here the first piece of evidence – and it remains right into the third century the only evidence – for baptism by infusion. Accordingly it is taken completely for granted that baptism is primarily "the immersion-bath". But the application of this custom is left elastic and free. Baptism is performed "in the name of the Father and of the Son and of the Holy Spirit". But this same baptism is later (9, 5) described simply as baptism "in the name of the Lord", which shows once again how little these two formularies are mutually exclusive.

It is only in the following period that the sacred action sketched all too briefly in this primitive Christian ritual book becomes clearer. The evidence is contained in chapter 61 of Justin Martyr's first *Apology,* in the various indications given by Tertullian, and finally in the more precise information supplied for the first time by Hippolytus in his *Apostolic Tradition.* The preparation for baptism consists, according to Justin, of the confession of faith, the promise of an upright life, prayer, fasting, and petition for the forgiveness of sins. Tertullian gives the liturgical and ritual setting even more clearly: "He who is about to approach the baptismal bath must (beforehand) pray with repeated prayers,

---

[3] Cf. here Th. Klauser, "Taufet in lebendigem Wasser! Zum religions- und kulturgeschichtl. Verständnis von Didache 7, 1–3" in *Pisciuli. Relig. u. Kultur d. Altertums. Festgabe F. J. Dölger* (Mst. 1939) 157–64.

[4] *Didache* 7, 3 (*ACW* VI, p. 19); cf. F. J. Dölger, "Die Taufe Konstantins und ihre Probleme" in *RömQ* (1913) 19. Suppl.-H. 440–2.

fasts, bendings of the knee, and vigils all night through, and with confession of all his bygone sins . . ."[5]. He mentions the Easter Eve celebration (the Pascha) and Pentecost, that is, the fifty-day Easter season, as the solemn times for baptism. But "every Lord's day, every hour, every time" is really "suitable for baptism".[6] The form of the immersion-bath may be seen with equal clarity in the descriptions of both Justin and Tertullian: "They are brought by us where there is water . . . , they then receive the washing with water."[7] Tertullian speaks of "immersion" ("in aquam demissus") and of "coming out of the bath".[8] He mentions further details: he is familiar with a blessing of the water *(De baptismo 4)*, and reports that the candidate is immersed three times.[9] After the immersion-bath, "we are completely anointed in the blessed unction according to the old custom" (c. 7); "then comes the laying on of hands, and the Holy Spirit is invoked and called down by this benediction" (c. 8). This is all, of course, a simple and plain act, in contrast to the pagan mystery rites with their "suggestus" and "apparatus": "In the greatest simplicity, without pomp, without any kind of new paraphernalia, and finally, without any expense, the person is immersed in water and washed with a few words . . ." (c. 2).

The *Apostolic Tradition* of Hippolytus describes for us the exact procedure followed in the baptismal act. According to the

---

[5] Tertullianus, *De baptismo* 20.

[6] *Op. cit.* 19; for the notion of Pentecost cf. O. Casel in *JbLW* 14 (1934) 17 f.

[7] Iustinus, *Apologia* I. 61, 3.

[8] Tertull., *De bapt.* 2 and 7.

[9] Tertull., *Adv. Praxean* 26: "Nam nec semel, sed ter, ad singula nomina in personas singulas tinguimur" ("For we are immersed not once, but thrice, with the individual names for the individual persons"). Cf. Tertull., *De Corona* 3.

assured results of modern scholarly research we are justified in seeing in the liturgical and disciplinary regulation which he gives "in essence the forms of religious life in the Roman community... which Hippolytus belonged to before his apostasy as presbyter, around the end of the second and beginning of the third century".[10]

In the part concerning baptism we hear first of all of regulations concerning the preparation for baptism.[11] Statutes 28 to 34 contain rules about reception into the catechumenate. Then Statute 35 gives directions for the actual act of baptism: "At the time of cock-crow they shall first pray over the water. And it shall be, if possible, such as flows into the tank of baptism or is caused to flow down upon it. And it shall be thus unless there is a scarcity of water; but if there is a scarcity they shall pour water into the tank. And they shall put off their garments and be baptized naked. And they shall baptize the little children first; and if

[10] H. Elfers, *Kirchenordnung Hippolyts*, 330f. The doubts which have recently been expressed by H. Engberding about ascribing this work to Hippolytus are refuted with good reasons by B. Botte (cf. *ArchLW*, 1952, 130) and by J. A. Jungmann, *The Mass of the Roman Rite: its Origins and Development*, vol. 2 (N. Y. 1951–55).

[11] We have used for the translation of the text given here the English reconstruction by Dom R. Hugh Connolly, *The so-called Egyptian Church Order and Derived Documents* (*Texts and Studies* 8; CbE. 1916). For comparison we have referred to: E. Haulers, *Lateinische Fragmente* (1900) no. 73, 74 (1–3) p. 110–12; also *Der äthiopische Text der Kirchenordnung Hippolyts*: edited and translated by H. Duensing in *AbhGöttGW* Philol.-hist. Kl., III, 32 (1946) 41–61; cf. also: *Der koptische Text der Kirchenordnung Hippolyts*: edited and translated by W. Till – J. Leipoldt in *TU* 58 (1954) 17–23. The critical reconstruction of G. Dix, *The Treatise on the Apostolic Tradition of St. Hippolytus of Rome* (Ld. 1937) is also valuable. It has the following arrangement: Part II 16–20: Preparatory regulations (p. 23); 21: Administration of baptism (p. 33); 22: Confirmation (p. 38f.); 23 The Easter Mass (p. 40.). No. 21 = Stat. 35.

they can speak for themselves, let them speak. But if they cannot, their parents shall answer for them, or one of their relatives. And afterwards they shall baptize the grown-up men. And afterwards all the women shall loose their hair; and they shall be forbidden to wear their ornaments and their gold; and none shall go down having anything alien with them into the water. . . ." (Then follow regulations regarding the bishop's prayer of thanksgiving over the oil of exorcism, and regarding the renunciation of the devil and the anointing with oil.) "Thus he (the deacon) shall deliver him to the bishop, naked, or else the presbyter who stands at the water of baptism shall do this. Let the deacon go down with him to the water.[12] Then let the priest descend into the water, let him lay his hand on the candidate's head and question him with the words: Do you believe in God the Father almighty? The candidate answers: Yes, I believe. The priest keeps his hand on the candidate's head and immerses him once (*i.e.* he baptizes him). Then he says: Do you believe in Christ Jesus, the Son of God, who was born of the Holy Spirit by the Virgin Mary . . . who will come again to judge the quick and the dead? And when the candidate says, I believe, he is to be immersed (baptized) again. And again let the priest say: Do you believe in the Holy Spirit and the holy Church and the resurrection of the flesh? Then the candidate should say: I believe. And so let him be immersed the third time. Then when he has come up let him be anointed with consecrated oil by the presbyter, who shall say: I anoint thee with sacred oil in the name of Jesus

---

[12] The text which has been handed down has here an entire baptismal creed immediately after the first baptismal question. This is probably an interpolation, since the contents point to the end of the fourth century. See H. Elfers, *Kirchenordnung Hippolyts,* 23f.

Christ. Then the individual candidates should dry themselves, get dressed, and then go into the church. But let the bishop lay his hand on them and say with invocation (epiclesis): Lord God, thou hast made them worthy to merit forgiveness of sins through the bath of regeneration in the Holy Ghost: send thy grace upon them, that they may serve thee according to thy will; thine is the glory, to the Father and the Son, with the Holy Spirit in the holy Church now and forever. Amen. Then let him pour consecrated oil from his hand on their heads and say: I anoint thee with sacred oil in the Lord, the almighty Father, and in Christ Jesus and in the Holy Spirit. And making (sealing, 'consignans') their foreheads, he gives the kiss of peace and should say: the Lord be with you. And he who is sealed shall say: And with thy spirit. So shall the bishop do to all. And then he is to pray together with the whole congregation, but he is not to pray with the faithful before they have done all this. And when they have prayed they are to bring the kiss of peace with the mouth." (The celebration of the Eucharist follows.)

We do not need here to go into the features peculiar to Hippolytus.[13] We are concerned with the common and essential outlines of the solemn act of baptism, which, evolving out of the foundations given in scripture, are testified to by the *Didache,* Justin Martyr, Tertullian, and Hippolytus for the period from the end of the first century until the beginning of the third, at least for the Churches of Rome and North Africa. Preceding baptism and separate from it we find a (catechetical) preparation of the candidates, who – with the exception of Hippolytus' reference to children – are in general assumed to be adults. Then

---

[13] See H. Elfers, *op. cit. passim.*

follows a more immediate preparation, consisting of fasting, prayers and vows. From the time of Tertullian we know also of a sanctifying or blessing of the water. The baptism itself is normally a genuine immersion-bath in running water, for which, therefore, the candidate must undress. From Tertullian's time – and probably already in that of Justin Martyr – this immersion-bath is performed by immersing the candidate three times in water, with the epiclesis of the three divine names, one being named at each immersion.[14] Joined to this we find the following elements, which are testified to from Tertullian's time: anointing, sealing, laying on of hands (or, after Hippolytus, a further anointing and sealing). Only at this stage is the entire action completed, as we can see from the evidence of Justin and Hippolytus, according to whom the novice is from henceforth admitted to the common worship of the brethren or of the faithful, to the kiss of peace and to the celebration of the Eucharist.[15]

Over against the "simplicity of the divine works which is visible in the act" (of baptism) stands the "grandeur which is promised thereto in the effect", namely, the truly "incredible attainment of eternity".[16]

In contrast to this impressive picture of the act of baptism, the evidence for theological reflection about the salvation imparted by the sacrament is relatively meagre. The earliest piece of evidence is the so-called Epistle of Barnabas, dating from the first decade of the second century.

[14] See F. J. Dölger, "Die Eingliederung des Taufsymbols in den Taufvollzug nach den Schriften Tertullians" in *AntChr* 4 (1934) 138–46.
[15] Iustinus, *Apologia* I., 65, 1 f.; Hippolytus, *Apost. Trad.* 74 (Dix, *op. cit.* 38).
[16] "Simplicitas divinorum operum quae in actu videtur et magnificentia quae in effectu repromittitur" – "incredibilis . . . consecutio aeternitatis"; Tertull., *De bapt.* 2.

Chapter 11 takes up the Old Testament prophecy "about water and the cross".[17] In contrast to what is true with regard to the Israelites, baptism, for Christians, φέρον [εἰς] ἄφεσιν ἁμαρτιῶν "brings the forgiveness of sins". Water (that is, baptismal water) and the cross are, according to the author of the epistle, placed with emphasis side by side in the prophetic passage from Psalm 1; "with hope set upon the cross one descends into the baptismal water", "laden with sins and filth; but then one comes out bearing fruit, namely, the fear (of God) in the heart and the hope of Jesus in the spirit". He says in connection with Ezechiel 47:12 that he who hears and believes "will live for evermore". Despite the unclear language it does become clear what is imparted by the immersion-bath of baptism, how the cross of Jesus stands in the most intimate relationship to it, and how it becomes possible that from the sacrament there proceeds in fear and in hope a fruitful life which extends into eternity.

Justin Martyr speaks more clearly:

Baptism is "consecration to God" (ἀνεθήκαμεν ἑαυτοῦς τῷ θεῷ), a new creation through Christ (καινοποιηθέντες διὰ τοῦ Χριστοῦ) and regeneration. Without this regeneration there is, according to John 3:3, 5, no entrance into the kingdom of heaven. In contrast to our first birth – which takes place without our willing it – and in contrast to the sinful manner of life followed by the candidate hitherto, he is now no longer the "child of necessity and of ignorance, but the child of choice and of knowledge, who attains the forgiveness of sins formerly committed, after he has decided to be born again and has repented of his sins".[18] The

---

[17] Barnabas *Epistle* 11, 1; the following quotations: 11, 8, 11.
[18] Iustinus, *Apol.* I, 61.

source of these effects is the immersion-bath, conceived of in a completely realistic manner. It is described as "taking a bath in water" and as "being bathed (washed)". What is decisive in this act of bathing by immersion is the epiclesis of the three divine names, with accompanying mention of the attributes of the three persons. The candidates "are then led by us to the water, and are born again in the same manner in which we ourselves became regenerate; in the name of the Father of the universe and of the Lord God, and of our Saviour Jesus Christ, and of the Holy Spirit they take the bath in water".[19] This bath is also called "illumination" (φωτισμός), "because the spirit of him who is learning (the deposit of faith) is illuminated".[20] Neither here nor in chapter 65 do we meet the term "baptisma". Instead Justin's habitual technical terms for baptism are "rebirth", "water-bath" (with the most varied uses of the word λούω), and "illumination". The fundamental gifts of baptism are liberation from all sins "formerly committed" (there is no mention of original sin despite the reference to the first birth); illumination of the spirit (that is, understanding, which probably perfects the faith which is termed in chapters 6 and 65 the prerequisite of baptism); and new creation. Through baptism the baptized is consecrated to God, delivered over to the brethren for the fellowship of the kiss of peace, of prayer and of the eucharistic celebration (chapter 65), and has entrance into the kingdom of heaven. Furthermore, he must from henceforth strive, "to know the truth, to walk in good works, and to be found observing the commandments . . .".[21]

The *Shepherd of Hermas* moves in a similar train of thought: "Your life has been saved by water (in baptism) and will

---

[19] *Loc. cit.*   [20] *Loc. cit.*   [21] *Op. cit.* I, 65.

remain saved. It is founded upon the word of the almighty and venerable name . . .".[22] "There is but *one* repentance: that according to which we descend into the water and (there) receive the forgiveness of our bygone sins, . . . with the obligation, from henceforth to sin no more, but to persist in chastity."[23] "They had to ascend by means of water in order to be made living. Otherwise, if they had not shed the death of their former life, they could not enter the kingdom of God. Those, also, who were deceased so received the seal of the Son of God and entered the kingdom of God. For a man is dead before he receives the name of the Son of God, but, when he receives the seal, he puts off death and receives life. The seal, therefore, is water. The dead go down into the water and come out of it living. Therefore this seal was proclaimed to them and they put it to use to enter the kingdom of God."[24]

Even if we may wonder at the view that the righteous of the old covenant have actually been baptized by the apostles who descended to them, still the conception of baptism we meet in all the passages cited is that it is man's decisive repentance, the water-bath founded on the word of the name, and the seal which imparts liberation from death and transition into the life of God's kingdom, and hence salvation. The performance of baptism is, in the complete vividness of its symbolic action, something tangible. Accompanied by the epiclesis of the divine name the candidate descends into the water, there to wash off his earlier mortality; his ascent from the water is ascent from death to life.

[22] *Pastor Hermae,* Visio 3, 3, 5.
[23] *Op. cit.* Mandatum 4, 3, 1f.
[24] *Op. cit.* Similitudo 9, 16, 2–4.

The testimony of Clement of Alexandria must be placed a little later, around the last decade of the second century. For him the Lord's baptism is a type of what happens to us. He continues his argument: "Being baptized, we are illuminated; illuminated, we become sons; being made sons, we are made perfect; being made perfect, we are made immortal . . . . This work is variously called grace [χάρισμα] and illumination and perfection and washing: washing, by which we cleanse away our sins; grace by which the penalties accruing to transgressions are remitted; and illumination, by which that holy light of salvation is beheld, that is, by which we see God clearly. But we call perfection, that in which there is nothing lacking. For what does he yet lack who has acknowledged God? Indeed it would probably be unthinkable that we could give the name of divine grace to something imperfect . . . . Moreover, the liberation from evils is itself the beginning of salvation."[25]

The order in which the expressions are mentioned is especially important in this fundamental presentation: baptized, illuminated, made sons, made perfect, made immortal. The series of names, with the interpretation which follows, is also significant: grace (χάρισμα), illumination (φώτισμα), perfection (τέλειον), washing (λουτρόν). At the beginning of this same chapter six (25, 1) the name "regeneration" (ἀναγεννηθείς) is added as well. We miss the term σφραγίς, seal, which Clement uses several times in other passages.[26] Nevertheless, F. J. Dölger has demonstrated that the word-group τελεῖν, τελεῖσθαι, τελείωσις (= finally initiate into the mysteries) is to be equated with

---

[25] Clemens Alex., *Paedagogus* I, 6, 26, 1–3.
[26] *e.g.* Clemens Alex., *Quis dives salvetur* 42, 4.

64

σφραγίζειν, σφραγίζεσθαι (to seal) and σφραγίς (a seal).[27] The inner richness of baptism becomes clear through the use of so many names to describe it. It is like the borderline between death and life. He who has reached this line has escaped death. In touching this line he is made "complete" and "perfect". Once across this boundary he stands "in Christ", in life. "For that which has come to being in him is life", as Clement says by way of proof, adopting the older reading of John 1:3–4. "It is, therefore, deliverance to follow Christ."[28] He maintains that there are two elements which constitute this perfection of life: "bare faith and being regenerate".[29] Naturally the term "perfecting" does not imply that the candidate has already received a gift which is absolutely "perfect". But the baptized is, nevertheless, "in the light, and the darkness no longer holds him".[30] "Just as soon as someone has been born again he is as one illuminated . . . , he is freed at once from darkness, and has from this very moment on received the light."[31] The – final – perfection is to be found in the resurrection. If this is arrival at the goal, then baptism is "the (mental) anticipation of this arrival".[32] Clement attaches great importance to the fact that already in baptism a perfection is given, "as far as that is possible in this world".[33] But this is a gift of grace. Of course, previous instruction must supply the necessary preparation. However, "that instruction leads to faith (only up to it); but faith is effected at the moment of baptism through the instrumentality of the Holy Spirit".[34] Human co-operation is required,

---

[27] F. J. Dölger, *Sphragis,* 159.
[28] Clemens Alex., *Paedag.* I. 6, 27, 1.
[29] *Op. cit.* 27, 2.   [30] *Op. cit.* 28, 3.   [31] *Op. cit.* 27, 3.
[32] *Op. cit.* 28, 4.   [33] *Op. cit.* 29, 1.   [34] *Op. cit.* 30, 2.

although it is not the decisive element. It is not this co-operation which makes "disciples" out of "the ignorant". They receive this name ("disciple") rather in baptism, "because knowledge arises simultaneously with illumination, and irradiates the spirit".[35] The passage immediately before this one speaks of the efficacy of baptism. The bonds of ignorance "are loosed right swiftly by human faith and divine grace when our offences are forgiven by a single liberating means of salvation, baptism of the Logos. We are purified from all sins, and at once we are no longer bad. It is one unique grace of illumination that our whole manner of being is no longer the same as before baptism." In connection with Gal. 3:26–8 Clement asserts (ch. 6, no. 31, 1–2): "There are not, then, in the same Logos some illuminated (gnostics), and some animal (or natural) men; but all who have abandoned the desires of the flesh are equal and spiritual before the Lord. And elsewhere he writes again (1 Cor. 12:13): 'For by one Spirit we were all baptized into one body' . . . ."

The picture of baptism sketched by Clement in this passage can be supplemented by various other passages in his works as well. Mention should be made here of the close relationship between the bath of baptism and the Logos, which is brought out in two such passages. In the same chapter 6 of the *Paidagogos* he speaks of the "fellowship of the word with baptism".[36] We must think here of the close relationship between the baptismal bath and the Logos in the name of God. But in another passage it is the close relationship between the preceding catechizing and the actual act of baptism which is brought out: "By the barbarian philosophers catechizing and illumination are

[35] *Op. cit.* 30, 1.   [36] *Op. cit.* 50, 4.

called being born again."[37] Finally, reference should be made to a passage where he speaks also of a sanctification of the water.[38]

With all his various names for baptism Clement moves completely within the conceptual world of the second century. But he brings forth these thoughts in great fullness by referring to the intellectual gifts imparted in baptism; and his terminology refers with special emphasis to the illuminating and vivifying effect of this washing. Baptism is the baptism of the Logos; but the *pneuma* is active in it as well. It is, completely in the Pauline sense, the foundation – in the most comprehensive manner – of the Christian life.

Clement's successor as leader of the catechetical school of Alexandria, Origen, brings the doctrine of baptism within the framework of the fruitful conception τύπος, σύμβολον, μυστήριον– though his presentation is not, to be sure, systematic.[39] Three dangers cause Origen to emphasize especially the moral side of baptism. These are: the magical conception of the mysteries, the Gnostic tendency to turn grace into a natural and cosmological process, and the abuse, which Origen sometimes complains is abroad in the Church, of performing merely the traditional rite of baptism, without bothering about understanding its significance.[40] Here, as indeed everywhere, Origen is the advocate for the priority of the interior, spiritual order over the external and visible order which must be its servant.

[37] Clemens Alex., *Stromata* V, 2, 15, 3.
[38] Clemens Alex., *Excerpta ex Theodoto* 82, 2: "The water, both that which is exorcized as well as that used for the baptismal bath, does not merely keep away evil but takes on sanctification."
[39] The most thorough presentation is given by H. U. v. Balthasar, "Le Mysterion d'Origène" in *RechScRel* 26 (1936) 513–62; 27 (1937) 38–64.
[40] Origenes, *In Rom. comm.* V, 8 (*PG* 14, 1040B).

For Origen and for his age the content of the mystery is revealed in the types of holy Scripture,[41] which are signs of the "invisible, spiritual baptism".[42] The historical incarnation of the types guarantees the mystical reality of the sacramental effect.[43] The mystery recapitulates these historical types mystically in the soul.[44] Faith, sacrament, and ministry accomplish in us the process of redemption in history. In the economy of salvation the "economy of the bath of regeneration"[45] has its place in between John the Baptist and rebirth in the new heaven and the new earth.

Origen does not describe the rite of baptism. It is explained by means of typology, since the rite features biblical types of baptism. The rite is secret and is solemnly performed by priests with the assistance of Levites.[46]

Baptism is an exodus, an "exire, relinquere, proficere"[47] ("a going out, a leaving, a setting forth"); it is a "transire" ("crossing over") to the other shore, to God.[48] It is an exodus of Israel, which the catechumen accomplishes through his renunciation.[49] In the passage through the Salt Sea Origen sees "the bitter element in baptism", the flight from Satan, which leads

---

[41] Cf. P. Lundberg, *La typologie baptismale dans l' Ancienne Église* (Lund 1941).
[42] Origenes, *In Jo. comm.* fragment 76; *In Lc. hom.* XXIV.
[43] "haec in prioribus gesta sunt . . . omnia complentur in te secundum mysticam rationem" ("these things were done in former things . . . everything is embraced in thee according to a mystery"); *In Jos. hom.* IV, 1.
[44] The later doctrine of character is already prepared in Origen's doctrine of types, though in historical categories: "puto quod sacramentum Ioannis usque hodie expleatur in mundo" ("I think that the sacrament of John is accomplished in the world until the present day"): *In Lc. hom.* IV.
[45] *In Jer. hom.* XVI, 5.   [46] *In Jos. hom.* IV, 1.
[47] *In Ex. hom.* III, 3.   [48] *In Jos. hom.* V, 1.
[49] It is probable that parts of the formula of renunciation are given in *In Ex. hom.* VIII, 4 and *In Num. hom.* XII, 4.

to the death of the old generation, namely, the old man, in the desert.[50] In this manner the catechumen forsakes his previous life. Baptism is also, therefore, the beginning and the principle of the spiritual struggle.[51]

By means of the promise of discipleship to God baptism becomes a covenant with God[52] and a betrothal. Rebekah, Rachel, and Zipporah are all chosen as brides beside a well. "The Patriarchs come to the wells and find their marriage beside the waters." Just so the Church is betrothed to Christ in the water-bath.[53] Of course, the catechumens belong already to the Church by virtue of their obedience.[54] But whoever comes to the sacramental spring of baptism has crossed over Jordan.[55] "He who is re-born is translated into paradise, that is, into the Church."[56] Baptism is necessary and great above all measure, since one receives it in order to enter the kingdom of God.[57] It elevates "an insignificant earthly human being into a temple of God and makes what was flesh and blood a member of Christ".[58] We become children of God and brothers of Christ.[59]

Baptism is renunciation of sin, conversion, and repentance. This principle is so fundamental that all subsequent repentance presupposes this first decision and takes it up again.[60] Sin is

[50] *In Jo. comm.* VI, 44.
[51] *In Judic. hom.* IX, 2 and *In Ex. hom.* VIII, 4.
[52] *Exhort. ad martyrium* 17.   [53] *In Gen. hom.* X, 5.
[54] *In Rom. comm.* VIII, 5 (*PG* 14, 1166 C).
[55] *In Jos. hom.* IV, 1. Origen likes to interpret the passage through the Red Sea as the entrance into the catechumenate and the passage through Jordan as baptism.
[56] *In Gen. comm.* fragment (*PG* 12, 100 B).
[57] *In Jo. comm.* fragment 36.   [58] *In Jos. hom.* V, 6.
[59] *In Jo. comm.* XX, 37.   [60] *Op. cit.* VI, 33.

blotted out after we have broken with it. This is symbolized by the Flood, the drowning of the Egyptians, and the destruction of Jericho after the crossing of Jordan, but above all by the death of Jesus.[61] In the case of Jesus, symbol and mystery are one. Baptism is dying to sin and sin's burial. The catechumen's ascetical death and his renunciation of sin are sacramentally perfected in baptism. Therefore Origen demands of the adult candidate for baptism a corresponding spiritual preparation: "Come, catechumens, do penance, that you may attain baptism for the remission of sins . . . ; for when someone comes (still) sinning to the water-bath, he does not receive forgiveness of sins."[62] This passage is of further significance because it presupposes that a washing with water can be valid in itself without forgiving sins.[63] Such a state of affairs is – as is also, in similar fashion, the disputed recognition of baptism at the hands of heretics – the foundation for the view of medieval Latin theologians concerning the "character sacramentalis".

The power of baptism to forgive sins applies not only to adults; it applies even to the smallest children: "The little ones are baptized for the forgiveness of sins. Which sins? Or at what time have they sinned? Or how can there be the slightest reason for the baptism of little children, unless it is to be found

---

[61] *In Gen. hom.* II, 6; *In Ex. hom.* V, 5; *In Jos. hom.* VI, 4; *In Rom. comm.* V 8 (*PG* 14, 1038 C).
[62] *In Lc. hom.* XXI.
[63] *In Ex. hom.* VI, 5 is similar: "Nec sic lavemini ut quidam qui loti sunt, sed non in salutem; accipit aquam, non accipit Spiritum Sanctum; qui lavatur in salutem, et aquam accipit et Spiritum Sanctum" ("and do not get washed like those who have been washed but not unto salvation; he receives the water, but not the Holy Spirit; he who is washed unto salvation receives both the water and the Holy Spirit").

in the passage: 'No one is free from taint, not even he whose life upon earth lasts but a day'? Even little children are baptized. Because the taint which we have from the moment of birth is removed in the sacrament of baptism."[64] As reason for sin Origen says: "quod in corpore peccati et corpore mortis atque humilitatis effecta sit" ("because [the child] is conceived in a sinful body, in a mortal and lowly body").[65] Infant baptism, which blots out this taint, is for him an "ecclesiastical practice" going back to the apostles.[66]

The actual symbol is that of new birth. Jesus accepted this sacrament, "so that you too, robbing your previous birth of its power, might in regeneration pass over to a second birth".[67] By rebirth Christ replaces our first birth from Adam.[68]

Origen sees a perfect symbol of baptism in the sacred Triduum. "Hear the prophet: 'After two days God will revive us, and on the third day we shall arise' (Osee 6:2). The first day is for us the Saviour's passion; the second, that on which he descended into the underworld; but the third is the day of the resurrection. Therefore God went before them on the third day as well, by day in a cloudy pillar, by night in a pillar of fire. If the Apostle is

---

[64] *In Lc. hom.* XIV.

[65] *In Rom. comm.* V, 9 (*PG* 14, 1047 C). – However, this does not make Origen a witness for the doctrine of original sin. It is true that he speaks more clearly than the other Oriental theologians of the ancient Church of an innate blemish. But he does not deduce this from the sin of Adam, but adopts instead a doctrine of pre-existence and explains this blemish sometimes as the result of a pre-historic fall of souls, and at other times as the result of the soul's union with the body. Cf. J. Freundorfer, *Erbsünde und Erbtod beim Apostel Paulus. Eine religionsgesch. u. exeget. Untersuchung über Römerbrief* 5, 12–21 (*Ntl. Abhdlgn.* 13, 1–2; Mst. 1927) 110–14.

[66] *In Rom. comm.* V, 9. (*PG* 14, 1047 B); *In Lev. hom.* VIII, 3.

[67] *In Lc. hom.* XXVIII.   [68] *In Jo. comm.* fragments 121 and 36.

71

right in teaching us to see in these words the sacrament of baptism it is a necessary consequence that 'those who are baptized in Christ, are baptized into his death'; they must be buried with him and on the third day rise with him from the dead.... Therefore when you have received the sacrament of the third day, the Lord begins to lead you and to show you the way of salvation."[69] This important text shows to what an extent Origen's theology of baptism is inspired by that of St. Paul. We also see here how he describes baptismal grace by means of types drawn from the drama of redemption, and how the sacrament of baptism places us within this redemptory process, and, in fact, reproduces this whole history of redemption in us. Baptism is rising with Christ to new life. "The resurrection is already prepared."[70] The raising of Lazarus belongs, in Origen's view, to the material to be covered in the baptismal catechizing.

A further aspect of baptism is the freedom it brings from Satan's tyranny and from guilt: "Jerusalem, the house of freedom, and the heavenly Jerusalem, the mother of freedom"[71], are opened to him who is baptized.

Finally the reception of the Spirit is a consequence of baptism. Fire fell upon Elijah's sacrifice after he had poured water upon it.[72] Under Moses all were baptized in the sea and in the cloud, and Jesus also received the Holy Spirit at baptism.[73] "The Spirit, which at the beginning of creation hovered over the water, makes this bath also a bath of regeneration with renewal of the Holy Spirit."[74] With a series of types, which from his

---

[69] *In Ex. hom.* V, 2. [70] *In Jer. hom.* I, 16. [71] *In Ex. hom.* VIII, 1.
[72] *In Jo. comm.* VI, 23. [73] *Loc. cit.* VI, 44. [74] *Loc. cit.* VI, 33.

time on became traditional,[75] Origen sums up the effect of baptism: "Those who have been baptized by bathing in Jordan lay aside the ignomy of Egypt (*scil.* like Joshua); they become capable of being received into heaven (like Elijah); they are cleansed of their dreadful leprosy (like Naaman); they experience increase of the gifts of grace and are prepared to receive the Holy Spirit (like Jesus). That is baptism's advantage for salvation; for over any other river (than Jordan) the dove of the Spirit does not hover."[76] Origen calls the laying on of hands in Samaria (Acts 8:18) a baptism,[77] and says: "We are baptized in visible water and in visible chrism, according to the type which has been handed down to the churches."[78] This brings out both the close connection and at the same time the clear differentiation between the water-bath and the anointing with chrism. Both actions are included here under the single name "baptism", exactly as the tradition hitherto had already done, in completely natural manner.

The *pneuma* which is received in this water-baptism is the pledge of the "resurrectio perfecta".[79] Actual baptism takes place only at the end of time. The resurrection from the dead "is actually that regeneration which is really a new birth, when a new heaven and a new earth will be created for those who are renewing themselves . . . . The introduction to that re-birth is what Paul calls the bath of regeneration . . . . By regeneration in water everyone is, of course, . . . free from sin, but . . . he is pure only as in the mirror and in a mystery. Only when that other regeneration comes . . . will all . . . be completely free

---

[75] Cf. J. Daniélou, *Bible et Liturgie* (Pa. 1951) 136–55.
[76] *In Jo. comm.* VI, 48.   [77] *De principiis* I, 3, 3.
[78] *In Rom. comm.* V, 8 (*PG* 14, 1038 C).   [79] *In Ez. hom.* II, 6.

from sin. . . . He achieves this re-birth (only, of course,) through the bath of regeneration."[80] In accordance with his soteriological interest Origen sees baptism as having three dimensions: first the revealing type, which was a mere symbol (antea in aenigmate fuit baptismum in nube et in mari – in time past there was in a mystery a baptism in the cloud and in the sea): second, the Spirit-filled symbol in the time after Christ, which is efficacious for salvation (nunc autem in specie regeneratio est in aqua et Spiritu Sancto – but now there is visible regeneration in water and in the Holy Spirit),[81] and this symbol is "at once the realization of the Old Testament sign and a sign of the reality to come";[82] and third, the eschatological baptism of the resurrection and transfiguration (in Spiritu et igne – in the Spirit and in fire) for which we bear in us already the preparation and "signum".[83] The Church's baptism both imparts and binds. It is at once a sign and the truth; not yet the fulfilment, however, but a symbol which both points ahead and is efficacious.

All types point to Christ. He is Jordan, "the actual, the saving water".[84] His death in exaltation is the symbol that recapitulates all previous types of baptism. Therefore Jesus does not begin his death without the initial type of the Johannine baptism. And he brings his course to completion when he is exalted in his sacrificial death and resurrection – the symbol

---

[80] *In Mt. comm.* XV, 22.   [81] *In Num. hom.* VII, 2.
[82] J. Daniélou, *Origène* (Pa. 1948) 71. (Engl. tr. Ld. & N. Y., 1955).
[83] *In Jer. hom.* I, 16; *In Lc. hom.* XXIV; cf. the scholastic notions: sacramentum – sacramentum et res – res sacramenti. Origen means the same thing, but sees it in soteriological terms: the baptismal type (or sign) "in aqua" – the baptismal symbol "in aqua et Spiritu" – the baptismal truth "in Spiritu et igne".   [84] *In Lc. hom.* XXI.

of consummation.[85] Because the signs point to him he does not himself baptize in water – his disciples do that. But "he reserves for himself the administration of baptism in the Holy Spirit and in fire".[86] The power of baptism comes from Jesus, because the *pneuma* dwells in him.[87] Christ is at work in baptism, and is its content and effect as well.[88] Baptism in the name of Jesus means always baptism in the name of the Trinity. But it emphasizes that one is baptized into Christ's death.[89]

In the question as to the relationship between baptism in water and baptism in the Spirit[90] Origen gives the key to the answer in the following important text: "We must know that it is with baptism as with the wonderful miracles of healing performed by the Saviour. These were *symbols* of healings through the word of God from every sickness and weakness. Nor was their value for salvation any the less in that they took place bodily, because they impelled those who received them to faith. In the same way, the bath of regeneration through water is the symbol for the purification of the soul, which is washed free from dirt and evil. And this bath is in itself (that is, as a bodily happening) no less the beginning and the source of divine gifts of grace for him who in the epicleses in which the Trinity is adored puts himself under the divine power which effects salvation."[91] This passage contains essential elements of Origen's

---

[85] *In Jo. comm.* VI, 43.   [86] *Loc. cit.* VI, 23.   [87] *Loc. cit.* VI, 42.

[88] Cf. *In Gen. hom.* XIII, 4; *In Ex.* hom. V, 5; *In Ez. hom.* VIII, 10; *In Jos. hom.* IV, 23 (τὸ γὰρ τῆς ἀναγεννήσεως [βάπτισμα] ... παρὰ τῷ 'Ιησοῦ διὰ τῶν μαθητῶν ἐγίνετο). That is already almost the same as the formula: "Christus est qui baptizat" – "it is Christ who baptizes"); VI, 43, 44; *op. cit.* fragment 76.

[89] *In Rom. comm.* V, 8 (*PG* 14, 1039 D – 1040 A).

[90] *In Lc. hom.* XXIV.   [91] *In Jo. comm.* VI, 23.

doctrine of baptism. First, there is a parallel between Christ's humanity and the sacrament; second, the physical event has an effect in the spiritual order; but third, always in connection with the word. The "divinity of effect" is ascribed to the epiclesis over the water. "The water is healed by a mystical episclesis", to which is added the moral catechizing which initiates the candidate into the mystery. This makes the water share in the power of the Holy Trinity, and joins it to the power of knowledge and goodness."[92] It is actually the soul which the *pneuma* baptizes. "But because the body is also called to salvation . . . it too must in justice be healed"[93] through the embodying of the mystery in a symbol. The symbol is necessary as the instrument by which grace is imparted; and it is useful both as a sign as well to effect the thing signified.[94] The relationship between the symbol and the mystery is one of participation, in fluctuating degrees, in accordance with the Platonic hierarchy of being. Thus we have baptism through the visible sign of water – he who is thus baptized still needs purification by fire after the resurrection.[95] Then there is baptism through spiritual fire which consumes everything earthly in such a painful manner that he who is baptized in this way needs subsequently no further purification.[96] Further, there is baptism through the mystery of suffering, in which sign and truth coincide perfectly.[97] And finally we have baptism "in the firey river. This is received

---

[92] *Op. cit.* fragment 36.   [93] *Loc. cit.*
[94] *In Ex. hom.* XI, 7: "purificatus es corpore, mundatus es ab omni inquinamento carnis ac spiritus" ("you are purified in body, you are cleansed from every pollution of flesh and spirit").
[95] *In Lc. hom.* XIV.   [96] *In Jer. hom.* XX, 8 – 9; cf. *In Judic.* VII, 2.
[97] *In Jo. comm.* VI, 56. In martyrdom equality with the "baptism" of Christ is achieved: *In Mt. comm.* fragment 403.

by him who wants to enter paradise, once this life is ended, but who still requires purification". This baptism with fire is given only to him who bears the sign of previous baptism.[98] The various ways in which baptism can be applied should neither minimize the rite nor cast doubt upon the necessity of water baptism. On the contrary: "without baptism there is no forgiveness of sins".[99] Rather should this very variability of application serve to demonstrate the uniqueness and sole importance of the one and only mystery of baptism, namely of the eschatological death and resurrection. The symbol is the *kenosis* of this unique divine mystery to the level of our bodily existence. "Visible baptism" has meaning only in so far as it conveys "the spiritual baptism".[100] The rite serves merely to convey the mystery which must become a reality in the soul.

The baptismal theology of Clement of Alexandria and of Origen, which is already richly developed, can supply us with the background against which we can see clearly the significance of the names customarily used in the thought of this period to describe baptism.

Βάπτισμα and λουτρόν, that is, immersion-bath and washing but also παλιγγενεσία or ἀναγέννησις, that is, regeneration, new birth, stand in the foreground. The nature of this bath leads both to the whole train of thought associated with the word, washing, as well as to that of the transition from death to life. Already at an early date the water, "living water", was seen as

---

[98] *In Lc. hom.* XXIV; *In Jer. hom.* II, 3. The outer sign of water-baptism cannot be received twice. Origen simply states that: *Exh. ad mart.* 30. The unity of baptism is compared with that of circumcision: *In Jos. hom.* V, 5.

[99] *Exh. ad mart.* 30.   [100] *In Rom. comm.* V, 8 (*PG* 14, 1038 C).

possessing a mysterious efficacy.[101] Thus Ignatius of Antioch, for example, speaks in direct connection with the Lord's baptism of a purification of the water through Christ's sufferings – as indeed Christ's baptism is very often deemed to be the basis for a hallowing of water in general.[102]

The theme of transition from death to life is likewise brought out with clarity, without, however, any express reference to Romans 6. Nevertheless, the close relationship between the cross and baptism is mentioned in the Epistle of Barnabas. And towards the close of the second century Tertullian says specifically that New Testament baptism could not be administered during Christ's lifetime, "inasmuch as the glory of the Lord had not yet been fully attained, nor the efficacy of the font established through the passion and resurrection; because neither can our death see dissolution except by the Lord's passion, nor our life be restored again without his resurrection".[103]

We meet the notion of regeneration again and again in the tradition in direct connection with the act of baptism. The term is even used to denote this act, on the basis of John 3:1 and Titus 3:5. There is a rich world of ideas here, which according to A. v. Harnack's presentation is connected with the experience of regeneration.[104] We can allow the richness of

---

[101] Cf. B. Neunheuser, "De bened. aquae" in *EphLitg* 44 (1930) 258–66, 466 ff.
[102] Ignatius Ant., *Ad Eph.* 18, 2; for a short list of the pertinent Patristic witnesses see B. Neunheuser, *De bened. aquae.* Tertullian should be mentioned here as the most important witness: *Adv. Iudaeos* 8 (*PL* 2, 615 *B*). Also: Hippolytus Rom., *Benedictio Iacobi* 18 (ed. G. N. Bonwetsch, "Drei georgisch erhaltene Schriften von Hippolytus" in *TU* 26, 1 [1904] 304 f.); Clemens Alex., *Eclog. proph.* 7, 2.
[103] Tertull., *De bapt.* 11.
[104] There is a good compilation of the individual ideas belonging to this whole theme of regeneration by A. v. Harnack in *TU* 42 (1920) 97:

these ideas to serve as the background for a comprehensive interpretation of baptism as a form of re-birth. Underneath the abundance of these notions, which are for the most part to be found already in the New Testament itself, lies an entirely uniform conception, the material for which has, as Harnack correctly remarks, grown right out of Christian soil.

"The preliminary stage lies alone and exclusively in the Septuagint, at first – and this is the main point – in Judaic-Hellenistic understanding, and then in increasing measure in Hellenistic understanding. . . . The motivating force came . . . from the metaphors which were at once adopted. None of them was used exclusively, and what was adopted became, as an expression for an historical and interior experience, something new. That is the seal of originality . . . . One synonym replaces another as a proof that none is essential, precise, and exhaustive: the faithful are 'like children' and are 'children'; they are children of God, of Christ, of the Church, but they are also 'friends and house-mates' of God or of Christ, and further his 'brothers'. They are 'renewed', or rather 'created anew', or again 'new-born' they are 'born of God', or rather 'of the Spirit'; they are 'spiritual', 'Spirit-bearers', 'God-bearers', 'Christ-bearers', but again they are men 'born by God', or 'by the Spirit'. The decisive

---

1)῾Ως τὰ παιδία, Νήπιος. — 2)᾽Ανακαινίζεσθαι, ᾽Ανανεοῦσθαι, ᾽Αναπλάσεσθαι, Μεταμορφοῦσθαι. — 3)᾽Εκλογή, Υἱοθεσία, ᾽Ελευθερία. — 4)Φίλοι (Γνώριμοι Οἰκεῖοι) τοῦ Θεοῦ (Χριστοῦ), ᾽Αδελφοὶ Χριστοῦ. — 5) Κτίζεσθαι, καινὴ κτίσις, Παλιγγενεσία, ᾽Αναγεννᾶσθαι, Γεννᾶσθαι ἐκ τοῦ Θεοῦ, Υἱοὶ (τέκνα) Θεοῦ, Σπέρμα τοῦ Θεοῦ. — 6)Δῶρον τοῦ πνεύματος, τὸ χρῖσμα ἀπὸ τοῦ Θεοῦ, Πνευματικοί, Πνευματοφόροι, Χριστοφόροι Θεοφόροι, ᾽Εν Χριστῷ εἶνει. — 7)᾽Επιστήμη, Γνῶσις, ᾽Αλήθεια, Φῶς, Φωτίζεσθαι, Ζωὴ αἰώνιος, ᾽Αθανασία, Ζωοποιεῖσθαι, Θεοποιεῖσθαι, Χριστοποιεῖσθει, Χριστοί, Αἱ νύμφαι τοῦ Χριστοῦ. — 8) ῾Ο καινὸς ἄνθρωπος, ῾Ο ἔσω ἄ., ῾Ο τέλειος ἄ., ῾Ο τοῦ Θεοῦ ἄ., ῾Ο πνευματικός ἄ., ῾Ο ἄνθρωπος ὁ πόρρω τῆς ἀνθρωπότητος.

treasure which they possess is the 'forgiveness of sins', or rather 'knowledge', or 'the truth', or 'the light', or the 'anointing', or rather 'the *gnosis* or eternal life'; they are 'made living', 'made immortal', 'made divine', 'made Christs'; but on the other hand they are only now 'men' – 'new', or 'perfect', or 'spiritual' men, 'God-men', etc."[105]

With masterly skill A. v. Harnack has fitted this picture together as an original Christian picture. But he errs when he attempts from the variability of this terminology to draw the conclusion that there is here "in the background no mystery with firm and settled terminology for the liturgical concepts and images". Both in the New Testament as well as in the following decades of the second century this entire realm of concepts is quite clearly bound up with the water-bath and its accompanying invocation of the divine names. At least this is true with regard to a few of the decisive basic concepts, and especially that of regeneration, to which, according to Harnacks' own words, one can very freely subordinate all other notions. The baptismal bath is the narrow boundary which one must cross in order to enter this comprehensive realm of regeneration. The bath of baptism is the saving power which makes this transition possible.

In similar manner the term "illumination"[106] connects an abundance of ideas from the New Testament with baptism. Clement of Alexandria interprets illumination as follows, basing his argument on Eph. 5:8:

"We, the baptized, wipe away from us like a fog the sins which darken the divine Spirit and stand in his way. And then we have

---

[105] *Op. cit.* 140f.
[106] A. v. Harnack (*op. cit.* 118f., 141) takes "illumination" as a technical expression for baptism.

the eye of the spirit free, fully unhindered, and gleaming bright. With this eye alone do we see the Godhead, when the Holy Spirit streams into us from heaven. In this way there arises a mixture of eternal glory, which is able to look upon the eternal light . . . ." But the wiping away of sins occurs precisely in baptism: "Just as soon as someone is born again, he is as if illuminated, as indeed the word itself implies. He is freed at once from darkness and has from this very moment received the light."[107]

From this point the entire richness of the Johannine light-theology is accessible. Once the darkness has been driven out, then light is given in the form of knowledge of the truth, and knowledge of Christ and of his Father.

There is such extensive evidence for the further term *sphragis* that we may, with F. J. Dölger, take it as certain "that already in the middle of the second century the word σφραγίς as a term for baptism has a tradition behind it".[108] The theological relationships opened up by the conception of baptism as a seal are manifold. However this designation for baptism may have arisen,[109] baptism is considered as *sphragis* more or less inasmuch as it is a sealing of the faith which has been received.[110] It points

---

[107] Clemens Ale., *Paedag.* I, 6, 28, 1–2; 27, 3; cf. also F. J. Dölger, *Die Sonne der Gerechtigkeit und der Schwarze. Eine religionsgeschichtl. Studie zum Taufgelöbnis* (Mst. 1918).

[108] F. J. Dölger, *Sphragis* 80.

[109] For discussion of this point see *loc. cit.* 148–71.

[110] *Loc. cit.* 99 ff. *Pastor Hermae,* Sim. 9, 16, 5 speaks, for instance, of the "seal of the proclamation of doctrine": "as sealing of the faith which has been accepted" (Lavacrum illud obsignatio est fidei quae fides a paenitentiae fide incipitur et commendatur – that cleansing water is a seal of faith, and this faith has its beginning and is commended by genuine repentance): Tertull., *De paenitentia* 6. It achieves in Tertullian's works precisely the meaning of "renunciation and baptismal confession". It is, of course, the whole action which is meant, but this act of sealing, which

to a "spiritual circumcision",[111] by virtue of which the baptized
is designated or marked, and because of which he bears himself
the stigmata, the distinguishing marks of Jesus.[112] The concept
of baptism as re-birth may suggest the thought that the soul
which has in baptism been formed according to the image of
Christ, who is considered as the mould or seal (χαρακτήρ, σφραγίς),
"has been sealed with the Logos, with the Spirit of Christ".[113]
The term *sphragis* also points to the fact that baptism is a pre-
ventive measure of defense "against sin and the temptations of the
devil".[114] According to Ignatius of Antioch "this should remain
as military equipment".[115] Especially important is also the significance of the word in the sense of a "sigillum infragile", a sign
which may not be broken. Here we run into the "problem of the
primitive Christian baptismal obligation", the tremendous seriousness of which "we meet everywhere in primitive Christian
literature".[116] Finally, baptism is "the seal of eternal life and
re-birth in God". It is "as the necessary means for entrance into

is so essential in the whole action, is emphasized. It must be remembered
that "in the ancient Church the three-fold baptismal confession was
inserted in question and answer form between the three immersions, so
that each immersion did actually appear as a confirmation and sealing of
the baptismal contract" (Dölger, *op. cit.* 103).

[111] F. J. Dölger, *op. cit.* 108, with a reference to Barnabas, *Epistle* 4, 8:
"Therefore the new covenant was sealed through faith in Christ. But the
full acceptance of faith came about through baptism. Now what is more
natural than to see in the word ἐγκατασφραγισθῇ a reference to the seal of
baptism understood in contrast with the seal of circumcision?"

[112] *Op. cit.* 105–9; Clemens Alex., *Exc. ex Theodoto* 86, 2: "After reception
of the seal of truth the believing soul bears the stigmata of Christ."
Dölger comments here: "The stigmata are Christ's name and his image
= the Spirit of Christ."

[113] *Op. cit.* 113.   [114] *Op. cit.* 119.   [115] *Ep. ad Polycarpum* 6, 2.
[116] F. J. Dölger, *Sphragis,* 126–40.

the kingdom of heaven" and as "the pledge of incorruption, of the glorified resurrection".[117]

Right here in this far-reaching circle of associations bound up with the word *sphragis,* we have a reminder of the comprehensive nature of "baptism" in the full sense of the term. And it is clear that the mutually complementary stages by which the Spirit is imparted have not yet been distinguished conceptually. Baptism is at this period, as we have already shown, a comprehensive rite of initiation, in which baptism in the stricter sense of the word, that is, the immersion-bath of water in the word, and the laying on of hands in confirmation which immediately follow it, stand side by side quite as a matter of course. It is, therefore, legitimate for us to take up here likewise the whole line of symbolism suggested by the so-called anointing, even though we cannot distinguish strictly between baptism and confirmation. B. Welte, whose view on this point is supported by his critic, H. Elfers, says with regard to the second century in general: "The whole circle of connotations suggested by the anointing of Christ, the elements of which are to be found already in the New Testament, has remained alive in the Christian consciousness, and has, though not in any essential points, developed further. The individual elements which together make up this circle of connotations can be seen as a more solid and more conscious unity. In addition, and as a new element, there comes to the fore the related thought of the *chrisma-christianus.*"[118] It is probably true that we have already in this period an actual rite of anoint-

---

[117] *Op. cit.* 141–8 in dependence on a text from Irenaeus of Lyons, *Epideixis, et al.*

[118] B. Welte, *Postbapt. Salbg.,* 21f.; see also H. Elfers in *ThGl* 34 (1942) 337.

ing.[119] But also quite independent of, or at any rate without any necessary connection with, any such rite, there is ascribed to the entire act of baptism that anointing which makes a man a Christian.

These various theological statements, which still exist in isolation from one another, will fall into place in a single complete picture, if we place them now, by way of conclusion, within the framework of Tertullian's treatise, *De baptismo.* This is the earliest monograph about baptism which has been preserved for us, and is for that reason alone noteworthy. The work comes from the pen of that striking African whose work in so many realms is decisive for the development of Latin theology, and can serve to illustrate in detail the developed theology of baptism at the end of the second century.

The enthusiastic attitude of primitive Christianity characterizes his short work: "Felix sacramentum aquae nostrae" ("O happy sacrament of our water!"). The fundamental importance of baptism for the entire life is expressed in the following words: "We are little fishes, born in water according to our *ichthys,* Jesus Christ, and we live only by remaining in the water."[120] In his presentation, which is also directed against the false teaching of the Gaians, Tertullian wants to offer a deeper understanding of the traditional faith (chap. 1). He treats all the points which have already turned into a "controversy over baptism" (chaps. 12 and 15). His most frequently used terms for baptism

[119] According to the testimony of Theophilus of Antioch, *Ad Autolycum* 1, 12 (*PG* 6, 1041): "We are called Christians because we are anointed with the oil of God."
[120] Tertull, *De bapt.* 1. The translation of this and the following text is based upon the German translation of Reifferscheid-Wissova (*CSEL* 20, 201–18).

are, in general, the following: "baptismus, baptisma (chap. 15), lavacrum, sanctissimum lavacrum novi natalis" ("most sacred bath of regeneration": chap. 20), quite simply "aqua" (*e.g.* chap. 12), literally water or water-bath ("in aquam demissus et inter pauca verba tinctus": chap. 2), "tinguere" (to wash off, to immerse: *e.g.* chap. 14), and the like.

The treatise is divided into three sections. The first embraces chapters one to nine. This treats the theme "de universis quae baptismi religionem struunt" (chap. 10), and concerns, therefore, all the foundations of the act of baptism. In strong contrast with the "solemnia" and the "arcana", that is, with the solemn secret cults of the heathen, Christian baptism is plain and simple. In chapter 2 Tertullian makes a telling presentation of the antithesis to this exterior simplicity, namely the "consecutio aeternitatis", the attainment of eternal life, which baptism imparts. But he is also at pains to bring out the dignity and importance of the water. He does this by reference to the story of creation (chap. 3), and to the fact that water was originally hallowed by the Spirit – to which is joined the santification by the epiclesis of the name of God.[121] Water's importance is underlined by reference to parallel water rites in the "sacra" of Isis, Mithras, and in the myths of water gods in general. Chapter 6 proceeds, then, to say quite clearly that the Holy Spirit is not actually obtained in baptism, despite the Spirit's efficacy in sanctifying the water. "Rather are we, who have been cleansed in the water, prepared for the Holy Spirit by an angel. But the angel of baptism ('angelus baptismi arbiter') prepares the way for the descent of the Holy Spirit by the washing away of sins, attained by faith, and sealed in the

---

[121] Cf. B. Neunheuser, *De bened. aquae,* 200–4.

85

Father and in the Son and in the Holy Spirit." After the water-bath follows the anointing, corresponding to the priestly anointing of the Old Testament and to the anointing of Christ. "This is 'a physical event . . . as indeed the act of baptism is also physical' . . . but the effect is spiritual, in that we are freed from sins" (chap. 7). Then follows "the laying on of hands, which by a blessing (a word of blessing) invokes and invites the Holy Spirit" (chap. 8). Chapter 9 mentions once again in rich abundance the Old and New Testament types for water, which have played a part in the "sacred service (religionem) of water" (*i.e.* of the water-bath). This sacred service includes water-bath, anointing, and laying on of hands, to which the following effects are ascribed: forgiveness of sins, priestly anointing, and descent of the Holy Spirit. But these effects take place in such a manner that they form together a unity. This unity is summed up as "baptismus", "aqua", and so forth. In its entirety this unity gives "eternal life" (chap. 2 and 1), liberation from previous blindness, and possesssion of peace with God, together with the obligation to lead a sinless life (chap. 8).

The second section (chaps. 10–16) treats a number of smaller questions with regard to aspects of baptism's essence not yet touched upon. In contrast to the baptism of John this baptism is "divine", not only in respect of its origin and the command in obedience to which it is administered, but also because of its power. It is able to impart something "heavenly", "the Holy Spirit and forgiveness of sins". But for this faith is the prerequisite, "for true and firm faith is washed with fire for judgment" (chap. 10). Christ is the minister of baptism in and through his servants. Without baptism no one is entitled to salvation (chap. 12). But Tertullian admits that we know nothing definite about any baptism of the apostles, apart from the case of St. Paul. He would like, therefore, to see the faith of the apostles as having alone constituted a "compendium baptismi", "a truncated baptism" or a "substitute for baptism", in virtue of which they have achieved salvation. By that he does not mean to say, however, that baptism is "not necessary for those for whom faith is already sufficient" (chap. 13). The proponents of such views he calls "criminal men" (chap. 13). For after the Lord's passion and resurrection "salvation is no longer given through mere faith (per fidem nudam). Since faith has been broadened through the confession of Christ's birth, his passion, and resurrection, the sacrament has been broadened as well through the sealing of baptism, the garment of faith, as it were. Faith was hitherto naked, but can no longer exist without its law. For a law commanding baptism has been given which also prescribes its form."[122] The baptismal command of Matt. 28:19 gives the content of this form, and the direction added to this command in John 3:5 "has joined faith to the necessity of baptism. Therefore

[122] Tertull., *De bapt.* 13: "at ubi fides aucta est credendi in nativitatem, passionem resurrectionemque eius, addita est ampliatio sacramenti (instead of "sacramento", as suggested by Harnack), obsignatio baptismi, vestimentum quoddammodo fidei, quae retro nuda erat nec potest iam sine sua lege. Lex enim tinguendi imposita est et forma praescripta. Ite, inquit, docete nationes tinguentes eas in nomen Patris. . . . Huic legi collata definitio illa, nisi quis renatus fuerit . . ., obstrinxit fidem ad baptismi necessitatem. Itaque omnes exinde credentes tinguebantur" ("But when faith has advanced to the point of belief in his nativity, passion, and resurrection, there is added the fullness of the sacrament, the signing of baptism, the garment of faith, as it were, which was naked without it, but which garment has no efficiency without its law. For a law to baptize has been imposed and a prescribed form. Go, he said, and teach all nations, baptize them in the name of the Father. . . . The definition attached to this law . . . unless a man is born again . . ., imposes on the faith the necessity of baptism").

from that time on all believers have been baptized" (chap. 13). Chapter 15 demonstrates emphatically the unity of baptism, and the fact that it is unique and cannot be repeated. "For there is *one* God and *one* baptism and *one* Church in heaven." According to Tertullian, heretics do not possess valid baptism. Along with this doctrine there is the further thought that baptism washes away sins but once, "because one cannot, of course, receive it again" (chap. 15). There is certainly a further means of help, a "secundum lavacrum", the baptism of blood (lavacrum sanguinis). This "represents (repraesentat) baptism, in case it has not yet been received, and gives back what has been lost (perditum)" (chap. 16).

The third section (chap. 17–20) treats "of the manner of administering and receiving baptism". The minister legally entitled to baptize is, in the first place, the bishop. But then priests and deacons can also be the ministers, though only on behalf of the bishop. In fact, even laymen may baptize, though only in cases of strict necessity. Tertullian claims that women are not entitled to baptize (chap. 17). Baptism is not to be "rashly" (temere) administered. And its delay (cunctatio) is in general "utilior", especially in the case of children.

"They should become Christians only when they are able to know Christ. Why should the age of innocence hasten to the forgiveness of sins?" (chap. 18). Accordingly, Tertullian rejects infant baptism. The thought of original sin does not occur to him. It is true that his words against infant baptism show that this was in all probability a widespread practice. Tertullian's advice about judicious delay in the reception of baptism is inspired by the thought of the seriousness of the baptismal obligation: "If the burden of baptism is understood, its reception will be feared more than its delay. Integral faith (fides integra) is certain of salvation" (chap. 18). It is, accordingly, quite clear that Tertullian ascribes to integral faith alone an adequate assurance of salvation.

Baptism gives the right of admission to the common (eucharistic) worship. When the baptized "come up out of the sacred water-bath of new birth", they are permitted "for the first time to open their hands in prayer beside their mother (the Church) and in company with their brethren" (chap. 20). This entrance into the Christian realm proper is the fulfilment of the Old Testament type of the passage of the chosen people through the sea and their feeding in the desert. Therefore the baptized have a "necessitas gaudii et gratulatio salutis" (chap. 20).

To sum up, then: Tertullian presents us with a coherent picture, which is confirmed and supplemented by the fragmentary accounts of the other witnesses we have mentioned. We have before us a single, integral action. Certain statements are made about this action in its integrity, among which we can, however, clearly recognize those elements which in Acts were separated in the water-bath and the laying on of hands, and which later theology will separate even more clearly into baptism and confirmation. Indeed, when Tertullian denies that the Holy Spirit is received in baptism (chap. 6), he stands either in opposition to all other tradition, or else he is merely stating in exaggerated form a position which we find put forward elsewhere, namely, that the water-bath and the laying on of hands are mutually complementary stages in the imparting of the Spirit. At any rate, he is able quite naturally to distinguish baptism in the strict sense, which prepares for the Holy Spirit, from the laying on of hands, by which the Holy Spirit is invoked and imparted (chap. 8). And

89

this is evidence of great importance for the history of dogmatic development![123] At the same time, the unity of the entire action is preserved – even in the case of Tertullian. It effects forgiveness of sins, priestly anointing, descent of the Holy Spirit – in short, eternal life. The forgiveness of sins stands in the foreground. Baptism is the fulfilment of the repentant disposition demanded of the candidate. The fact that baptism cannot be repeated and the necessity of continually renewed repentance are decisive factors in the gradual development of a separate penance after baptism.[124] Moreover, baptism already conveys the gift of the Holy Spirit. This cannot be seen so clearly in the case of Tertullian. But he brings out more distinctly the significance of the laying on of hands for the concluding bestowal of the Spirit.[125]

The performance of baptism in the form of a water-bath with accompanying invocation of the divine names is preserved. It is

[123] Corresponding to this is another passage in Tertullian, *De resurrectione carnis* 8, where the individual acts are arranged as follows: ". . . caro abluitur, ut anima emaculetur; caro unguitur, caro signatur, ut et anima muniatur, caro manus impositione adumbratur, ut et anima de deo saginetur" (". . . the flesh is washed, that the soul may be purified; the flesh is anointed and signed, that the soul may be made secure; the flesh is overshadowed with the imposition of hands, that the soul may also be made fat from God").

[124] Cf. here A. Benoit, *Le baptême chrétien au second siècle. La théologie des Pères* (Pa. 1953) 223f.

[125] Anglican theologians, like G. Dix and L. S. Thornton, claim that baptism expunges sin but does not mediate any gift of the Spirit. It is to the credit of G. W. H. Lampe that he has demonstrated in his work, *The Seal of the Spirit* (Ld. 1951), that the gift of the Spirit is indeed attached to baptism. According to him the primitive Church believed that the Spirit was poured out in baptism; but this doctrine was obscured in the third and fourth centuries. J. Daniélou (*RechScRel* 38 [1951] 286–89) agrees in his criticism of Lampe's work with these statements on the whole, but emphasizes quite rightly that Lampe does not bring out sufficiently the significance of the laying on of hands in these early times.

coming slowly to be recognized that the power of these divine names bestows upon the water itself a sanctification which gives it a mysterious efficacy, in stark contrast to the unpretentious external actions (chap. 2 and 7). Alongside this theme stands another: that the efficacy of this water-bath is derived from the Lord's passion and resurrection (19). Just how this takes place is not discussed in any greater detail. And in general this Pauline thesis remains quite definitely in the background in the baptismal theology of the second century.[126]

Faith, works of penance, and the "divine" power of baptism are seen as a unity, though at the same time the *sacramentum* bestows more than can be given by faith alone. The Lord works through the human minister, who changes. But Tertullian is not able to proceed from this point to a recognition of baptism by heretics. It is true that this problem is, in the strict sense, not yet touched upon here. We hear for the first time of infant baptism, which Tertullian is inclined to reject. He also wishes to deny women the right to baptize. In these very points we see that the fundamental elements of a theology of baptism are already prepared. It is the obstacles of another kind, like the still insufficient knowledge of original sin, for instance, which continue to delay the full development of these elements. But the situation is in flux. Already there is discussion about what belongs to the "controversy" about baptism (chap. 15). Errors are being discarded and the original deposit of faith is coming to be grasped more clearly.

---

[126] This is stated, correctly, by A. Benoit, *Baptême chr.*, 227. K. H. Schelkle, "Taufe und Tod. Zur Auslegung von Röm. 6, 1–11" in *Vom christlichen Mysterium. Gesammelte Arbeiten zum Gedächtnis von Odo Casel* (Dd. 1951) 19 f. remarks that this – Pauline – view is not the only form of interpretation for that which is contained in baptism.

Chapter Four

THE FIRST THEOLOGICAL CLASSIFICATIONS;

THE CONTROVERSY OVER HERETIC BAPTISM

(THIRD CENTURY)

BIBLIOGRAPHY: For the word μυστήριον: G. Bornkamm, Μυστήριον, μυέω in *ThWbNT* 4, 809–34. K. Prümm, "Mysterion von Paulus bis Origenes. Ein Bericht u. ein Beitrag" in *ZKTh* 61 (1937) 391–425; a good survey of the literature in K. Prümm, *Religionsgeschichtliches Handbuch für den Raum der altchristlichen Umwelt* (FbB. 1943) 345–51. H. U. v. Balthasar, "Le Mysterion d'Origène" in *RechScRel* 26 (1936) 513–62; 27 (1937) 38–64. O. Casel, "Glaube, Gnosis und Mysterium. IV. Theolog. Philologie. Zum Worte Mysterium" in *JbLW* 15 (1941) 269–305.

– For the word *sacramentum*:
J. De Ghellinck-E. de Backer, J. Poukens, G. Lebacqz. *Pour l'histoire du mot "sacramentum"*: I. *Les Anténicéens* (*Spicil. S. Lovan.* 3; Lv. 1924); cf. review of this work by O. Casel in *ThRev* 24 (1925) 41–7. G. Söhngen, *Der Wesensaufbau des Mysteriums* (*Grenzfragen zw. Theol. u. Philos.* 6; Bonn 1938) 63–6. A. Kolping, *Sacramentum Tertullianeum*. I. T.: *Untersuchgn. üb. die Anfänge d. christl. Gebrauchs der Vokabel sacramentum* (Mst. 1948).

– For the controvery over heretic baptism:
J. Ernst, *Die Ketzertaufangelegenheit in der altchristlichen Kirche nach Cyprian* (*Forsch. z. chr. Lit.- u. Dgmgesch.* 2, 4; Mst. 1901). J. Ernst, "Neue Untersuchungen über Cyprian und den Ketzerstreit" in *ThQ* 93 (1911) 230–81, 364–403; *op. cit.* 230 lists the author's other works on this question; for further bibliography see J. P. Junglas, "Ketzertaufe" in *LThK* 5, 940 ff.

IT IS an undisputed fact that the rites of salvation, such as baptism and confirmation, were after a certain date described as μυστήριον and *sacramentum*.[1] As early as Tertullian we meet the expression "Felix sacramentum aquae nostrae" *(De bapt.* 1*)*. It is of the greatest interest for the history of dogma to ascertain when this happened for the first time, and to discover the reasons for this fact, which are by no means self-evident. This concept is found in authors already in the last decades of the second century. Then in the course of the third century and up until the beginning of the fourth century there occurs "a technical consolidation of the word in this sense".[2] The questions raised here have not yet been finally answered. But there is a good bit of valuable material already available. We shall content ourselves with sketching the main lines of development which seem to us to be certain.

The two words μυστήριον and *sacramentum,* which are used to denote the water-bath of baptism, must, according to O. Casel,[3] be interpreted together and in dependence on one another – and this despite their independent value in their separate linguistic spheres.

The Greek word μυστήριον must be seen as containing the root concept. This word has passed down to the Fathers of the second and third centuries directly from the New Testament and from the subsequent literature. Now the primary meaning of the word

---

[1] Cf., for instance, K. Prümm, "Mysterion von Paulus bis Origenes" in *ZKTh* 61 (1937) 398, which investigates on the basis of the material supplied by H. G. Marsh, the questions, "whether what we today call the sacraments have already taken on the name μυστήριον in Clement's writings, and whether we can ascertain already in his case the beginnings of a technical consolidation of the word in this sense, as is unquestionably the case later".

[2] *Loc. cit.*

[3] O. Casel, "Das Wort sacramentum" (reviewed by J. de Ghellinck *et al.* "Pour l'histoire du mot 'Sacramentum'") in *ThRev* 24 (1925) 41–7.

there expresses nothing with regard to a cult representation, as K. Prümm rightly points out. The word's fullness of meaning can best be analyzed in four categories: "the concrete soterilogical category, the concrete cult category, the abstract symbolic, and the abstract dogmatic categories".[4] We are not concerned here with the question whether, and to what degree, we find in the Christian mysteries some kind of objective influence from the Hellenistic mysteries. In the early period there is certainly no such influence in essential points; but in the later period there is universal agreement that it is present in a number of points.[5] We are concerned to ask, rather: how is it that rites which the New Testament does not yet know under the general term μυστήρια later are so denoted?

First, the most important finding: whereas Irenaeus seldom uses the word μυστήριον with any discernable reference to the Christian cult, but quite frequently with reference to Gnostic usages,[6] a third of the ninety-one cases in which this word occurs in the writings of Clement of Alexandria refers to heathen mystery cults. And Christianity in general is analogously described as *mysterion*. In contrast to Prümm, who interprets this primarily in

---

[4] Thus G. Söhngen, *Wesensaufbau d. Myst.* 64, in dependence on O. Casel (*Wort sacram.*) and against K. Prümm: "On the basis of Casel's researches and insights I am of the opinion that even in theological or dogmatic meaning *mysterium* can denote something concrete and historical; and this is actually the original dogmatic meaning in Christian linguistic usage. The concrete-soteriological and the concrete-cult elements are earlier here than the abstract-theological.

[5] Cf. K. Prümm, *Christentum als Neuheitserlebnis* (FbB. 1939) 442–7, and even more H. Rahner, "Das christliche Mysterium und die heidnischen Mysterien" in *Eranos-Jb.* 11 (1944) 347–98, esp. 387–98. Engl. tr. *Greek Myths and Christian Mysteries* (Ld. 1963).

[6] K. Prümm, "*Myst.*" *v. Paulus b. Or.* 415 f.

a didactic sense, we understand the term, as does O. Casel, in the concrete soteriological sense, as having to do with the saving work of Christ. Certainly, "the problem of the word μυστήριον in Clement's writings is a part of the problem of Clement's *gnosis*", and it is true that μυστήριον is not infrequently the equivalent in meaning of σύμβολον.[7] But Clement certainly does not use *gnosis* in the sense of mere abstract contemplation. He means by *gnosis* really grasping things intellectually. Just how fully and concretely he understood this grasping is indicated by the use of this term in Platonic philosophy. Indeed, it is quite possible that this Platonic background was expressed in a cult action.[8]

Hippolytus' use of the word is influenced above all by St. Paul. In general μυστήριον denotes the realities of Christian salvation. But at the same time it can stand for Gnostic things as well; and finally, for the secret cults of antiquity. And once only it refers to the Eucharist.[9]

Origen's usage is incomparably richer. He too uses the word first of all, and on the basis of "the scriptures and the church's tradition of faith"[10] alone, to denote the various stages in the process of Christian salvation. The most important starting-point for an answer to the question why in growing measure a cult rite like that of the water-bath of baptism is described as a *mysterion* is afforded, in our opinion, by the speculative development of Origen's conception of *mysterion*.

The classification of the various stages of "incarnation, Church and scripture" as "three supernatural facts which are bound

---

[7] *Op. cit.* 399–400.
[8] Cf. O. Casel, *Glaube, Gn. u. Myst.* 275–84, 288–91.
[9] K. Prümm, "Mysterium und Verwandtes bei Hippolyt und Athanasius" in *ZKTh* 63 (1939) 221 f.   [10] K. Prümm, *"Myst."* v. *Paulus b. Or.* 412.

together in the closest manner"[11] creates an analogous unity with regard to the mystery. The one Logos gives himself to men in various stages in such a way that there is a provisional culmination in the mystery of baptism.[12] The mystery of baptism means for Origen conformation to those events by which we are saved, whether this be the foreshadowing event of the Old Testament, the saving act of Christ, or the complete realization of these saving acts. The rite is also termed a symbol, in the full sense in which antiquity understood the term symbol, as being filled with the reality it symbolized.[13] The water-bath of baptism is the *mysterion* and symbol of the death and resurrection of Christ, inasmuch as it is in baptism that his death and resurrection first come to us in their fuller reality. It may well be that in a speculative interpretation of this kind, which is now applied not merely to baptism but to many other New Testament rites of salvation as well, the immeasurable fundamental reality of Christ's unique saving work is perhaps not sufficiently emphasized. But this thesis does do approximate justice to the reality and significance of the cult act. At any rate, it found adherents, and came to determine in increasing measure the course of theological thought for the entire period following. It is, then, first in the writings of Athanasius that we see clearly the use of the word *mysterion* for liturgical actions, and among them for baptism.[14] The Latin

---

[11] *Loc. cit.*

[12] Cf. Origenes, *In Jo. comm.* VI, 26 (*PG* 14, 276 A); the text which follows gives a nice interpretation of Christian initiation in connection with Old Testament types. Cf. also *In Jos. hom.* IV, 1f. On this whole question see H. U. v. Balthasar, *Le Mysterion d'Or.,* p. III in *RechScRel* 27 (1937) 54–8.

[13] Cf. O. Casel, *Glaube, Gn. u. Myst.,* 234f., 240–53.

[14] Athanasius Alex., *Oratio II ctr. Arianos* 42 (*PG* 26, 236 C); *Or. III ctr.Ar.* 33 (*PG* 26, 393ff.). Cf. K. Prümm, *Myst. u. Vw. bei Hipp. u. Ath.* 350–7; his systematic survey could easily be harmonized with the analysis of the

Fathers of the second and third centuries who accepted the suggestions of the Greeks found the foreign expression *mysterium* or the coined word *sacramentum* already existing as Latin translations of μυστήριον. The oldest translation of the Bible had used these terms already. Tertullian's use of the word *sacramentum* brings out more clearly its original meaning of oath or consecration. But that in no way exhausts the meaning of *sacramentum – mysterion*. In the case of baptism the point of comparison is, so far as it is not merely a question of simply continuing what has been handed down, "the μύησις, *initiatio,* initiation into the Christian mysteries (in the cult sense) . . . , in which connection we must consider the *sacramentum* which is described as the baptismal obligation not purely in a military, but also in a mystical sense, just as, conversely, the term *militia Christi* has also a mystical ring about it".[15] With this full sense of the word in mind, Tertullian terms the water-bath a *sacramentum,* "the happy mystery-act, the act by which our water-bath is consecrated". And, referring to the related meaning of the word as denoting the soldier's oath to the flag, he says: "We were already summoned to the battle service of the living God at the time that we answered the words of the consecration (or mystery) pledge."[16] In any case, the essential point is that we refer *sacramentum* back to the Greek word, μυστήριον, with its whole fullness of meaning, even if no final and unambiguous explanation is possible due to the fact that the Greek word itself is not yet fully clarified.

significance of the word *mysterion* which we have worked out above, p. 93–4 in connection with Casel and Söhngen.
[15] O. Casel, *Wort sacram.,* 44; on this whole question cf. also A. Kolping, *Sacram. Tertull.*   [16] Tertullianus, *Ad martyres* 3.

Cyprian takes over the word *sacramentum* from Tertullian, using it to designate the water-bath of baptism, as well as confirmation and the eucharist. In this point Cyprian is following simply the custom of his time. And this becomes most readily understandable with the help of the perspectives supplied by O. Casel. The water-bath is thus not only the "lavacrum carnale" but also "baptismi sacramentum",[17] because it is a "mystery rite", a "sacred act of consecration, an "initiation", which conveys a divine reality figuratively, "so that we . . . follow the way of life by virtue of sacraments (acts of consecration) which bring salvation".[18]

Through the use of the identical terms "mysterium, sacramentum" the water-bath of baptism is also placed in closest association with the act of confirmation and with the eucharist. But this must be treated elsewhere.

It would certainly be exaggerated were we to expect that the terms *mysterion* and *sacramentum* alone would give us decisive insights. We must certainly exercise caution in drawing conclusions from the significance of these words. In particular, the term *mysterion,* which had, of course, already been passed down to the Fathers from Christian tradition, does not imply that the Christian rites were derived in any way from heathen mystery practices. Nevertheless, we can already make the following observations: that the traditional water-bath of baptism is called by the third-century Greeks μυστήριον and by the Latins *sacramentum,* means that this rite is con-

---

[17] Firmilianus, *Ep.* (int. Cypr.) 75, 13 *ad Cyprianum.*
[18] Cyprianus, *Ad Quirinum,* praef.; cf. also the other passages cited by J. Poukens (in De Ghellinck *et al.,* "Pour l'hist. du mot 'Sacr.'") 205 (no. 89–99, 101 ff.).

sidered as a consecration or as an act of initiation. Moreover, this act is – though in just what sense we do not yet learn – an image of the act which saves us, and an image which is also filled with the reality of that act. Through this image we are granted a share in this same saving act. In fact, the image is the realization of this act in a higher form.

The knowledge of the reality conveyed in the act of baptism was decisively deepened by the controversy over heretic baptism, as it was called. As the membership of heretical communities began to be recruited no longer solely from renegade Catholics but also newly converted heathen, there arose the question: what was the situation with regard to the validity of the baptism with which these people had been received into the heretical community, and how ought the Church to treat possible converts?[19] There arose a varying practice. Whereas in the African Churches and in many Churches of the East baptism was repeated, heretic baptism being considered in such Churches as invalid, the Churches of Rome and Alexandria recognized heretic baptism and were content with a rite of reconciliation. The earliest witness for the practice in Africa is Tertullian.[20] As

[19] There is, for instance, a good description of the situation in the introductory arguments of the tractate *De rebaptismate*. For a modern presentation see A. Ehrhard, *Die Kirche der Märtyrer* (Mch. 1932) 341f. The sources for the controversy over heretic baptism are contained essentially in the collection of Cyprian's letters: *Ep.* 69–75. See also the pseudo-Cyprianic work, *De rebaptismate*.

[20] Tertull., *De bapt.* 15: " . . . nec baptismus unus, quia non idem; quem cum rite non habeant, sine dubio non habent, nec capit numerari quod non habetur; ita nec possunt accipere, quia non habent" (" . . . nor one baptism, because it is not the same; since they do not have this baptism in the correct manner, they certainly do not have it at all; and what one does not have at all cannot be counted. And so they cannot receive, because they do not have").

this custom began to appear doubtful to representatives of the African Church, two African synods, which met in the years 255 and 256 under the chairmanship of Cyprian, decided to retain the previous practice. When Pope Stephen I spoke out against this decision the conflict came out into the open, and grew rapidly into a sharp and fundamental opposition. The pope's decision ran as follows: "When someone comes to you from heresy, nothing new should be done save that which is in the tradition, namely, that he be given the laying on of hands in penance, cum ipsi haeretici proprie alterutrum ad se venientes non baptisent, sed communicent tantum" ("because the heretics themselves do not actually baptize those who come to them, but merely receive them into their fellowship").[21] Faced with this decision, Cyprian appealed to the tradition of his own Church, as it had existed at least since the synod under Agrippinus (between 218 and 222).[22] Of course, tradition alone is not decisive, "since custom without (inner) truth is just old error".[23] He therefore tries to demonstrate the inherent reasons for his practice as against Pope Stephen.

Cyprian agrees at the outset with his opponents that there is no such thing as "re-baptism" in the proper sense: "But we say that we do not re-baptize those who come over to us, but we (quite simply) baptize them."[24] But that is, of course, the point of the whole controversy, which has now been clearly brought out: is baptism by a heretic genuine or not? Cyprian answers this question in the negative, in accordance with the practice of his Church,[25] but without wanting on this account

---

[21] In Cyprian, *Ep.* 74, 1.   [22] Cyprian, *Ep.* 73, 3.
[23] *Ep.* 74, 9.   [24] *Ep.* 71, 1.   [25] *Ep.* 74, 12.

to deny other Churches a right to their own usage.[26] Although
this speaks well for Cyprian's conciliatoriness, it does show
that he sees in this affair merely a disciplinary matter and that
he has not grasped its full gravity. The attitude of Rome was
very different and fundamentally severe. Stephen refuses
pointblank to receive Cyprian's envoys and threatens to break
communion with him[27].

These are Cyprian's principal arguments: "If the Church
does not exist amongst the heretics, because the Church is one
and cannot be divided, and if they do not have the Holy Spirit,
because he is not and cannot be with the profane and with
aliens, then there cannot be any baptism amongst the heretics
either, since baptism exists in the same unity. For baptism
cannot be divided from the Church and from the Holy Spirit."[28]
Put in a more sharply personal way, what this actually says is:
"How can someone who is himself unclean, and with whom the
Holy Spirit does not dwell cleanse and sanctify the water? . . .
Or how can someone who himself cannot cast off his sins,
because he is outside the Church, give another the forgiveness
of sins in baptism?"[29] Cyprian's arguments prove too much.
This is shown with special clarity in the letter of Bishop Firmilian of Caesarea-Cappadocia to Cyprian. He agrees with
Cyprian's views and deplores Stephen's recognition of the
validity of heretic baptism. Such recognition says that heretics
can by their act of baptism "wash off the defilement of the old
man, forgive old and deeply-rooted deadly sins, create children
of God through divine regeneration, and by the sanctification

---

[26] *Ep.* 72, 3; cf. *Ep.* 73, 26.   [27] Firmilian, *Ep.* 75, 24–5.
[28] Cyprian, *Ep.* 74, 4   [29] *Ep.* 70, 1.

of the divine bath restore people to eternal life".[30] But Stephen cannot have taught that. Even he could admit the existence of these effects only within the Church, or, if occasion arises, through the laying on of hands in reconciliation. But he defends a fundamental validity for baptism, which must be recognized in all circumstances, even if the heretics cannot in their baptism impart the full condition proper to God's children. The author of the pseudo-Cyprianic tractate, *De rebaptismate* (written about 256) says this quite correctly: "We should either preserve and observe the baptism without qualification, or, if it has already been administered by someone or other in the name of Jesus Christ, we should supplement it, recognizing the most sacred invocation of the name of Jesus . . . and recognizing further the venerable tradition of so long a time and of so many men."[31] In fact, Roman theology ascribes the "effectus", the inner reality of baptism, again and again to the majesty of the divine name.[32] It refuses to make this inner "effectus" dependent in any way upon the personal sanctity of the minister or the degree to which he is filled with the Spirit. "They believe that one should not ask who it was who baptized, since the candidate could obtain grace by invocation of the Trinity . . . ."[33] For Cyprian "this mere (nuda) invocation of the names" is not enough, since a "mens prava" cannot effect the sanctification of the righteous.[34]

Rome asserts, then, definitely and clearly: it is not the personal sanctity of the minister which assures the validity of baptism, but the majesty of God which works through the

---

[30] Firmilian, *Ep.* 75, 17.   [31] *De rebaptismate,* 15.
[32] *E.g.* Cyprian, *Ep.* 74, 5; 73, 16.
[33] Firmilian, *Ep.* 75, 9.   [34] *Loc. cit.*

names. Less clear is the position taken with regard to the fact that the act of baptism and the forgiveness of sins can be separated from one another, so that there can be valid baptism without there necessarily being an immediate forgiveness of sins. Cyprian, at any rate, would like to reject the Roman view, precisely because he fears this identification. "If someone could be baptized by the heretics, then he could well obtain the forgiveness of sins from them as well."[35] As far as we can see from the sources, Rome has, in the face of this criticism, not yet separated these two realities from one another, so that the act of baptism is indeed to be recognized as valid, even though it does not achieve full "efficacia". Because the situation remained unclarified it did not come to a final breach. But it remains regrettable that "two conceptions remained facing one another, one emphasizing exclusively the personal and ethical factor, while the other upholds the official and sacramental element. It is to the credit of the Churches of Rome and Alexandria that they safeguarded the objective and sacramental character of baptism against subjective doubts and considerations, which, despite their deeply religious impact, were certainly in the last analysis rationalistic."[36] Even after the death of the principal opponents it was still a long time before the Churches were reconciled in a common practice. At the Council of Arles (314) even the Africans recognized the validity of heretic baptism, save for the case where the confession of the Trinity had not been sufficiently expressed at the time of the heretic baptism (Can. 8). The Council of Nicaea came to a similar neutral

---

[35] Cyprian, *Ep.* 73, 12.
[36] A. Ehrhard, *Kch. d. Märtyrer* 344.

decision in 325. The Eastern Churches did not in the future associate themselves with the decision of Rome.[37]

But beyond the framework of its own subject matter the controversy over heretic baptism supplies us with a rich picture of baptismal theology in this period. Baptism and the Spirit belong together in the most intimate way: "Baptisma esse sine Spiritu non potest" ("baptism cannot exist without the Spirit").[38] Baptism transforms the new man spiritually, it is a "nativitas secunda spiritalis", it is "spiritaliter nasci", it puts on Christ. Therefore it is called also "lavacrum regenerationis". Despite a number of reminiscences of Romans 6 the fellowship with Christ's death and resurrection is not especially brought out. On the other hand, themes which are already bruited in Tertullian's work (De bapt. 4) are taken up again – as in the demand that the water must first "be purified and sanctified by the priest", so that it can in this way wash away the candidate's sins.[39] Whether we are to see here a blessing of the baptismal water in the proper sense must remain undecided. At any rate, this is an indication that the element of water must be purified and sanctified in order to be capable of serving its purpose.[40]

Great importance is attached to the epiclesis of the names (vocatio nominum), to which the Roman theologians above all appeal. Firmilian also testified to this epiclesis, but is not satisfied with a mere invocation without sanctity, faith, and the Holy Spirit in the candidate.[41]

---

[37] Counc. of Arles, can. 8; Counc. of Nicaea I can. 18f. (Denz. no. 53, 55f.)· Cf. J. Ernst, Ketzertaufangelegenheit in der altchr. Kch. 52–63; see also pp. 135ff. below.   [38] Cyprian, Ep. 74, 5.   [39] Ep. 70, 1.
[40] Cf. B. Neunheuser, De bened. aquae 194ff.
[41] Firmilian, Ep. 75, 9; cf. Cyprian, Ep. 74, 5.

It is also worth noting that the Tractate *De rebaptismate* places side by side individual elements which have not yet been fused into a unity: " . . . the heart is cleansed by faith, souls are washed by the Spirit, but bodies are also washed by water. But through (the pouring out of) blood we speed more swiftly by a short route to the goods of salvation."[42] In this closing summary we find a reference to the three kinds of baptism, baptism of desire, of water, and of blood, which in the view of the author of the tractate do not in any way dissolve the unity of baptism. We find no more precise demonstration of how the external water-bath and the interior working of the Spirit are fused into the unity of the baptismal event. Furthermore, there is evidence here for the so-called clinical baptism and for infant baptism. The latter is justified at length by reference to the "staining of the old death" which comes from Adam.[43] Water baptism in the narrower sense – of spiritual birth – is also distinguished clearly from the laying on of hands in which the newly born receives the Spirit in a manner which clearly supplements the gift of the Spirit in baptism.[44] In connection with Acts 8 Cyprian likewise offers evidence for the act of imparting the Spirit apart from the bath of baptism. He says of the Samaritans who were baptized by Philip: "Because they have now received the legitimate baptism of the Church, it was not necessary to baptize them any further. Rather what was lacking was supplied by Peter and John, so that after a prayer had been uttered for them and they had been given the laying on of hands, the Holy Spirit was invoked upon them and poured out over them. And this still happens amongst us, inasmuch as those who have

---

[42] *De rebaptismate,* 18.   [43] Cyprian, *Ep.* 64, 2–6.   [44] *Ep.* 74, 7.

105

been baptized in the Church are brought to the elders of the Church and they obtain the Holy Spirit through prayer and the laying on of our hands . . . ."[45]

The theological insights which have come to us as the echo of the straightforward practice of the Church, of the controversy over heretic baptism and of very complicated terminological associations are, of course, still incomplete and have not yet been clearly enunciated and fully appreciated. But the essential elements have already been prepared and the lines of demarcation staked out. We can sum up somewhat as follows: the great mystery of Christian "initiatio" is made up of the water-bath in the name of the Trinity and the concluding anointing with chrism or the laying on of hands for the imparting of the Spirit. This single mystery, which is in reality, however, a double action, can be administered but once. The recipients are adults or children. Baptism is supposed to lay the foundations of Christian life by means of the forgiveness of sins and the new birth to heavenly life which it imparts. This initiation mystery stands, finally, as the decisive, efficacious mediating link between the death of Christ and the Christian's participation in this death.

[45] *Ep.* 73, 9 and *De rebaptismate* combine the two actions in one "signum fidei integrum" (c. 10). In fact, confirmation already emerges more clearly and independently as a "signum fidei iteratum atque consummatum" ("a repeated and consummated sign of faith" c. 1); or it is described as "baptisma spiritale" in contrast to the "baptisma aquae" (c. 10). Cf. here F. J. Dölger, *Sphragis,* 104.

Chapter Five

BAPTISM AND CONFIRMATION IN THE WEST IN THE FOURTH AND FIFTH CENTURIES

BIBLIOGRAPHY: P. Galtier, "La consignation à Carthage et à Rome" in *RechScRel* 2 (1911) 350–83; same author, "La consignation dans les Églises d'Occident" in *RevHist E* 13 (1912) 257–301, 467–76. P. de Puniet, "Onction et confirmation" in *RevHistE* 13 (1912) 450–66. T. Hahn, *Tyconiusstudien (Stud. z. Gesch. d. Theol.* 6/2; Lp. 1900). P. Lejay, *(Rite)* "Ambrosien" in *DACL* 1, 1371–1401, 1427–34. J. Hugh, *Die Bedeutung des Wortes Sacramentum bei dem Kirchenvater Ambrosius* (Fulda 1928). K. Adam, *Die Eucharistielehre des hl. Augustinus* (Pb. 1908) 122–46. W. Roetzer, *Des hl. Augustinus Schriften als liturgiegeschichtliche Quelle* (Mch. 1930). F. Hofmann, *Der Kirchenbegriff des hl. Augustinus in seinen Grundlagen und in seiner Entwicklung* (Mch. 1933). J. Ratzinger, *Volk und Haus Gottes in Augustins Lehre von der Kirche* (Mch. 1954). Th. Camelot, "Sacramentum Fidei" in *Augustinus Magister* (Congrès Internat. Augustinien 1954, Pa. o. J., vol. 2: 891–6. E.-R. Fairweather, "Saint Augustine's Interpretation of Infant Baptism" in *Augustinus Magister* 897–903.

THE FOURTH century ushers the Church into a period of freedom, in which its sacramental life is able to develop quietly into a continually more splendid liturgy. Candidates for baptism stream into the Church in droves, the consequence of which is that the Church loses something of its inner purity and

107

holiness. This fact kindles the sacramental rigorism of the Donatists, drives the African Church into schism, and even threatens the Church at large.

In the Donatists' view the visible Church is the immaculate, pure community of the saints. Only a spotless priest can validly administer the sacraments. He is, in fact, the "origo, radix" and "caput" of the new life given to the baptismal candidate. Because the Catholic bishops are either themselves sinners, or else are stained with the sins of others with whom they continue to maintain communion, every baptism administered in the Catholic Church is, in the eyes of the Donatists, null and void. This results in the Donatist practice of "re-baptism" in the case of a Catholic Christian who comes over them. But they consider this, as does Cyprian, not as a new baptism at all, but as the first valid baptism.

Faced with this situation, it was not possible for the Catholics to limit the defence of their conception to a mere exposition of unity by insisting that baptism could not be repeated.[1] Consequently, the question as to the deeper reasons for this fact had become the occasion for a further developement of baptismal theology. It was Augustine who, more than any other, undertook this task. But he has in this respect a predecessor worth naming, in the person of the bishop Optatus of Mileve in Africa. Already around the year 370 he expresses with classical

---

[1] The impossibility of repeating baptism is defended especially by the following: Pope Siricius (384–98), who refers in his *Ep. ad Himerium* to a decree of Liberius (352–66) (*Denz.* 88); Innocent I (401–17, *Ep.* 2, 8 (*PL* 20, 475 B); Optatus of Mileve (ca. 370), *Librorum (de schism. Donatist. ctr. Parmenianum)* V, 1 (ed. C. Ziwsa: *CSEL* 26, 118); Pacian of Barcelona (died ca. 390), *De bapt.* 7 (*PL* 13, 1094 C); Hieronymus, *Dialogus ctr. Luciferianos* 23 (*PL* 23, 177).

clarity the truth that the Church's sanctity is based not upon the sanctity of its individual members, not even that of its bishops and priests, but upon the sanctity of the sacraments. Not to be willing to reckon any but saints as belonging to the Church's fellowship he describes as presumption, in the face of the Lord's words about the sinfulness of the righteous.[2] The sacraments take their sanctity not from their human ministers but from themselves. Men are not their masters but their servants.[3] Three factors work together in baptism: the Trinity, the minister, and the recipient. Weighing these factors one against the other, Optatus draws the conclusion: "principalem locum Trinitas possidet, sine qua res ipsa non potest geri: hanc sequitur fides credentis; iam persona operantis vicina est, quae simili auctoritate esse non potest"[4] ("the Trinity possesses the chief place, for without it the thing itself could not be done; next comes the faith of the believer; and now comes the person of the minister, who cannot have the same weight of authority"). Assuming that the recipient has the proper faith, God always gives grace, if the baptism is administered in the correct trinitarian form, whether the minister be a saint or a sinner.[5] The unrepeatable character of such a baptism is taken by Optatus to be based upon Christ's words at the washing of the apostles'

[2] Optatus Milev., *Citr. Parm.* VII, 2 (Ziwsa 168f.).
[3] *Op. cit.* V, 4 (Ziwsa 127₁₄ff.): "operarii mutari possunt, sacramenta mutari non possunt. Cum ergo videatis omnes, qui baptizant, operarios esse, non dominos, et sacramenta per se esse sancta non per homines . . ." ("the workers can be changed, but the sacraments cannot be changed. Therefore you see that all who baptize are workers, not lords, and the sacraments are holy in themselves, and not through men . . .". Cf. also Hieronymus, *Dial. ctr. Lucif.* 6 (*PL* 23, 161 A).
[4] Optatus, *loc. cit.* (Ziwsa 126₁₉₋₂₂).　　[5] *Op. cit.* V, 1 (Ziwsa 120f.).

feet.[6] He divides baptism administered outside the Church into two categories: heretic and schismatic baptism. He recognizes the validity of the latter only, its basis being the faith which is common both to Catholics and to Donatists, which finds expression in the trinitarian formulary of baptism. The heretics, on the other hand, have falsified the creed.[7] Heretic baptism is understood therefore as being essentially a falling away from the teaching of the faith. He thus comes to exclude heresy, but not schism. Donatism's actual error – apart from its separation from the unity and love of the true divine bride, the Church – is its very practice of re-baptism. Optatus rejects the Donatistic errors regarding the sacrament of baptism, but is not able to explain the permanent effect of baptism. Above all, the position he adopts with regard to heretic baptism is contrary to the teaching of the Church.

Tyconius[8] must also be mentioned as one who prepared the way in baptismal teaching for Augustine. Although a Donatist, he was a very decided opponent of re-baptism and of re-ordination, and separated himself from his friends in a number of other respects as well. Tyconius holds, as does Optatus, that the sacrament is in the first place an expression of the life of the Church. Baptism is the first resurrection from sin. Humanity falls into two large groups: into the people of the baptized and that of the unbaptized. Within the fellowship of the baptized he distinguishes three groups, according to their proximity

---

[6] *Op. cit.* V, 3 (Ziwsa 125).
[7] Cf. *op. cit.* I, 10, 12; III, 9; IV, 8; V, 3 (Ziwsa 13ff., 93, 114, 125).
[8] On Tyconius see P. Monceaux, *Histoire littéraire de l'Afrique chrétienne: Le Donatisme* vol. 4–7 (Pa. 1912–23), esp. vol. 5, 165–219. T. Hahn, *Tyconiusstudien*. Augustins Urteil über Tyconius: cf. *Ctr. ep. Parm.* 1, 1, 1 (*PL* 43, 337).

110

to the fellowship of Christ: the saints, the schismatics, and the "false brethren". The last he considers to be a danger on account of their reprehensible manner of life. But this does no damage to the validity and sanctity of the sacraments. In thus distinguishing between the objective and sacramental aspect, and the subjective and ethical aspect, Tyconius seems sometimes to have had in mind the notion of "character".

Before we treat Augustine we must also touch briefly the figure of St. Ambrose, who, of course, prepared and instructed Augustine for the reception of baptism. It is true that the ideas which have been handed down to us from Ambrose were not nearly so decisive for the shaping of Augustine's theology of baptism as was the evidence for the tradition of his African predecessors. Ambrose turns back in many points to the beginnings of Latin baptismal theology, to investigations into the notion of *sacramentum,* for instance. His two works, *De mysteriis* and *De sacramentis*[9] are our chief sources for his understanding of baptism, while furnishing, at the same time, comprehensive evidence for the celebration of baptism customary in the Church in this period.

The cult fullness of the Greek *mysterion* shines forth in his writings (especially in *De myst.* 4) more clearly than in the previous period. Baptism is the mystery or the water-bath of regeneration in the name of the Father and of the Son and of the Holy Spirit. An abundance of smaller acts surrounds the heart of the action; they are also "mysteria, sacramenta" (cf. *De myst.* 1, 3). They are not merely images of what the candidate is

---

[9] The texts are quoted from the edition of J. Quasten, *Monumenta eucharistica et liturgica vetustissima (Floril. Patrist.* VII/3; Bonn 1936). On the authenticity of *De sacramentis* see G. Morin: *JbLW* 8 (1928) 86–106.

supposed to do, but also convey the reality which they signify (*loc. cit.*: "inhalatum vobis munere sacramentorum"). This conviction also lies at the bottom of Ambrose's peculiar view that in the foot-washing after the baptismal bath, "hereditary sins (haereditaria peccata) are blotted out"; for our own sins have been forgiven by the bath of baptism (*De myst.* 6. 32). In the parallel text in *De sacr.* III 1, 5 he distinguishes expressly between the footwashing as an act of humility and as an act of healing. In regard to all these acts he says: "Do not consider the bodily figure and form, but the grace of the mysteries" (*De myst.* 2, 6; cf. also 3, 15). The senses grasp only the outer form (figura, species) of these mysteries, but it is the "gratia", the "munus" given in them which is crucial. Amongst the various acts, however, the water-bath assumes, of course, always first place, despite its simple form.[10] In order to interpret the efficacy of the water, which transcends everything sensible and visible, Ambrose makes use above all of two themes, with the connotations which they suggest. First of all is the idea of the "aquae non vacuae" (*De myst.* 4, 21): the waterfloods are "filled" and empowered to purify (4, 19), and to impart the gift of spiritual grace (4, 20) – something which does not happen "without the Spirit" (4, 19) nor without the cross (4, 20; cf. also *De sacr.* I, 5, 15). Such a hallowing is precisely the blessing of the water in the form of an epiclesis, which imparts the presence of the trinitarian God and fills the font with divine power.[11] The other theme, familiar from Romans 6, of the death and resurrection, and of that birth to new life,

---

[10] *De sacr.* I, 3, 10 (Quasten 141_{10}); cf. Tertull., *De bapt.* 2.
[11] On this point see Neunheuser, *De bened. aquae* 389–92. How concretely the water was filled by this consecration is shown, for instance, by *De myst.*

relates baptism to the death of Jesus. This is mentioned especially in *De sacr.* II, 6 and 7, where Ambrose poses rhetorically the fundamental question: "Quid est baptismum?" (II, 6, 16). His answer[12] can be given, in the terminology of Odo Casel, somewhat as follows: baptism is the sacramental type, impregnated with the reality it typifies, or it is that highest mystery-picture which happened for the first time and fundamentally in Christ's

4, 23: "in hunc fontem vis divina descendit" ("divine power comes down into this font"). Ambrose speaks unequivocally in these texts of an invocation of the Trinity. It is on the basis of these texts that we must interpret another somewhat unclear passage which became decisive for the assumption of later theologians, like Pope Nicolaus I (*Denz.* 335) and the great Scholastics (*e.g.* Thomas Aqu., *Summa th.* III, q. 66, a. 6, ad 1, 2) that there was a valid baptism "in the name of Christ" at least in the apostolic age. This passage is to be found in *De Spiritu S.* I, 3, 42–4 (PL 16, 713 B to 714 B): "Baptizati sunt in nomine Jesu Christi . . . et quod verbo tacitum fuerat, expressum est fide . . . quemadmodum in Christi nomine plenum esse legimus baptismatis sacramentum . . ." ("And so they were baptized in the name of Jesus Christ . . . and what was not spoken in a word was expressed by faith . . . thus we have read that for those who are baptized in the name of Christ the sacrament is complete . . ."). G. Bareille (*DThC* 2, 184) says "that Ambrose is speaking here not of the formula which is used in the administration of baptism, but of faith in the Trinity which is necessary for the validity of baptism". But even if Ambrose in this passage really considered a baptism administered in the name of Christ alone as valid, because the other persons were implicitly named as well (which is claimed, amongst others, by O. Faller, *Die Taufe im Namen Jesu bei Ambrosius: 75 Jahre Stella Matutina,* Feldkirch/Vorarlb. 1931, vol. 1, 139–50), this evidence would stand completely isolated and would contradict too directly the clear statements of his contemporaries and of the previous period to be able to claim any general authority. For the view of the Scholastics see below, chap. 8, note 28.

[12] Cf. for instance *De sacr.* II, 6, 19; 7, 20, 23; III, 1, 1; also *De fuga saeculi* 9, 55, 57 (ed. C. Schenkl: *CSEL* 32/2, 206$_{5-7}$, 207$_{4-6}$). The problems treated in these passages, and in other Patristic passages similar to them, are discussed extensively by O. Casel in "Mysteriengegenwart" in *JbLW* 8 (1928) 145–224, esp. 158–63. See also in *JbLW* 13 (1935) 138–40 his interpretation of further passages.

passover. By virtue of the presence of the Trinity, which is invoked, the cross and resurrection effect the death and resurrection of the candidate, who confesses his faith when he is immersed in the water-bath. He dies to sin and rises to a new life. He accomplishes the passover, that is, a "passing over from sin to life, from guilt to grace, from defilement to sanctification" (*De sacr*. I, 4, 12). Such a resurrection constitutes regeneration as a son of God.

In comparison to his full description of the mystery of baptism, Ambrose speaks rather briefly about the "signaculum spiritale" (*De myst*. 7, 42; *De sacr*. III, 2, 8). "Post fontem superest, ut perfectio fiat" ("after the font, the fulfilment is still to be accomplished", *De sacr*. III, 2, 8). The baptismal action is to close with that completion which is called by the later theology "confirmatio". "In response to the invocation of the priest the Holy Spirit is poured out." The Spirit has seven gifts: "septem quasi virtutes spiritus . . . quasi cardinales . . . quasi principales" *(loc. cit.)*. The act is called sealing (signaculum, consignari), which corresponds to the Greek words σφραγίς and σφραγίζεσθαι. Thus the original terminology for baptism is applied here to the act which terminates and crowns the entire process. The whole Trinity is at work in this final act: "God the Father has marked (sealed) you, Christ the Lord has strengthened and confirmed (confirmavit) you, and he gave the pledge of the Spirit in your heart . . ." (*De myst*. 7, 42). This imparting of the Spirit is supposed to complete the divine activity for the creature's salvation. In these terse words there is certainly an echo of the formula of the original rite. Thus the "seal of the Spirit" is clearly distinguished from the "water-bath in the Spirit" (lavacrum spiritale) as far as act and efficacy are concerned; but the two are nevertheless joined together in a unity as an "illumination" (cf. *De sacr.* III, 2, 15). This whole initiation entitles the recipient to take part in the final and highest mysteries (*De myst.* 7, 40), allows us "to approach the altar" (*De myst.* 8, 1; *De sacr.* III, 2, 15), anoints the baptized "for the (spiritual) priesthood, for the kingdom" (*De sacr.* IV, 1, 3).[13]

The peculiar problems of baptismal theology which had been raised by the errors of this period and which centered primarily around the subject of heretic baptism were, it is true, left unsolved by Ambrose. With all the more energy, then, does his famous convert, Augustine, devote himself to this task. His arguments about the doctrine of baptism are principally dictated by the necessity of dealing with the Donatists and the Pelagians. For the rest, Augustine moves entirely within the traditional framework.[14]

He does not give us, as does, for instance, Ambrose, any

---

[13] The total *initiatio* is, thus, initiation performed in such a way that the laying on of hands is the completion of this total action (*De sacr.* III, 2, 8; Quasten 153_{10}). This implies, however, that the foundation of this entire reality, even of the royal dignity of the priesthood, is already given in baptism, and more precisely in the anointing which is still a part of baptism. "Omnes enim in regnum dei et in sacerdotium unguimur gratia spiritali" ("For we are all anointed into the kingdom of God and into the priesthood with spiritual grace" (*De myst.* 6, 30, Quasten 127_{16}f.). P. Galtier has demonstrated this splendidly in *RevHist E* 13 (1912) 261–70 with regard to the Church of Milan. We cannot agree with the judgment of B. Welte (*Postbapt. Salbung* 59–64), especially since his interpretation of *De Spiritu Sancto* I, 6, 76–9 (*PL* 16, 722 D – 723 B) is not convincing. But he is correct in his remark that baptism and confirmation must be considered as a whole (*op. cit.* 63).

[14] F. Hofmann, *Kirchenbegriff d. Aug.* 354f.; cf. also the footnotes there, esp. note 78 with quotation from the *Sermo Guelferbytanus* 7 (ed. by G. Morin, "S. Augustini Sermones post Maurinos reperti" in *Miscellanea Agostiniana* vol. 1; Rm. 1930, 462).

coherent description of the act of baptism. But he speaks so often about the details that it is relatively easy to reconstruct the full rite of baptism as practised in his Church.[15]

Augustine's notion of *sacramentum,* which is important in particular for the doctrine of baptism, is no less broad than that which we meet in the period previous to him. *Sacramentum* in the broader sense means "every sensibly perceptible fact, the meaning of which is not exhausted in that which it immediately gives, but which, transcending this, points to a spiritual (perhaps more clearly, intellectual-spiritual) reality".[16] Side by side with the sacraments proper there are, therefore, *sacramenta,* for instance, Old Testament ritual rules, saving acts of God, as well as what we today call sacramentals. But Augustine is also familiar with the *sacramenta* in the narrower sense of the term. Under this head baptism and the eucharist assume what is by far the principal position. The *sacramenta* are in essence "signa", visible signs of divine things, in which invisible things are venerated.[17] God has ordered them to correspond with the needs of the various stages of salvation. As "signa" they signify "in reality not the essence of God, . . . but rather the divine economy of salvation, which has reached its climax . . . in the incarnation and saving death of Christ".[18] The pre-Christian sacraments pointed to these events, and the Christian sacraments point back to those of pre-Christian times. But the meaning of the Christian sacraments is not exhausted in this

[15] See on this point W. Roetzer, *Des Augustinus Schriften als liturgiegeschichtliche Quelle* 136–73.   [16] F. Hofmann, *Kirchenbegriff d. Aug.,* 335.
[17] Augustin., *De catech. rud.* 26, 50; *De civitate Dei* X, 5.
[18] F. Hofmann, *Kirchenbegriff d. Aug.,* 343; the supporting sources are also given there.

signification of the past: they also point to the future, to the fellowship of the elect and to the vision of God, in which there will be no need for mediation through word or sacrament.[19] The sacramental "signum" does not have a merely intellectual or symbolic relationship to the economy of salvation, that is, to the "res sacramenti". "The *signum* is more than that: it is *quodammodo* that which it signifies."[20] But Augustine does not fall here into any deification of the sign. The power of the sacrament depends in decisive manner upon the "significatio", which occurs through the "verbum".[21] But also with

---

[19] According to Augustine the sacraments of the Old Testament were "signa promissiva" or "praenuntiativa" (*Ctr. Faust.* 19, 13), which after the coming of Christ ceased to be necessary for salvation (*Ep.* 40, 6). The sacraments of the New Testament are both "signa promissiva" with regard to Christ's second coming, and "signa completiva, dantia salutem" (*Ctr. Faust.* 19, 14).

[20] F. Hofmann, *Kirchenbegriff d. Aug.,* 343; cf. *De civ. Dei* XVIII, 48.

[21] On the consecratory efficacy of the "verbum" see especially Augustine, *In Joh.* tract. 80, 3 (*PL* 35, 1840): "Accedit verbum ad elementum, et fit sacramentum ... Unde ista tanta virtus aquae ... nisi faciente verbo ... quo sine dubio et mundare possit, consecratur et baptismus" ("The word comes to the element and it becomes the sacrament ... Whence comes this great power of the water ... if not through the efficacy of the word ... with which baptism is indubitably sanctified, that it may cleanse"); or *op. cit.* 15, 4 (*PL* 35, 1512): "Take the water away, and it is not baptism; take the word, and it is not baptism"; *De bapt.* VI 25, 47: "deus adest evangelicis verbis suis, sine quibus baptismus Christi consecrari non potest" ("God is present in the words of his gospel, without which the baptism of Christ cannot be sanctified"). "The evangelica verba" are the words of the baptismal formula: cf. *op. cit.* ed. M. Petschenig: *CSEL* 51, 324$_{8-10,13}$ f: It is clear from passages like these that through the "evangelica verba", *i. e.* the names of God according to Matt. 28, 19, "baptismus" is "consecrated"; although in other phrases this "consecratio" is ascribed to Christ's blood or to his name, *e.g. In Jo. tract.* 11, 4 (*PL* 35, 1477); *Sermo* 352, 1, 3 (*PL* 39, 1551). These expressions are not mutually exclusive but rather mutually complementary. This is quite generally true of the Fathers of this period.

relation to the "verbum" it was necessary to find a solution between the extremes of an autonomy of the word on the one hand, which is the tendency if one interprets the epiclesis of the names too one-sidedly, and on the other hand the subjectivism which sees the personal word of faith as decisive. This solution Augustine seeks in the faith of the Church, behind which stand Christ and the work of the Holy Spirit. "Hic est qui baptizat" (John 1:33) is one of the biblical passages cited most frequently by Augustine. Just as the "fides ecclesiae" is responsible for the efficacy of the word of faith and therefore for the "signification", so this faith decisively influences the use of the sacraments as well. Indeed the "fides ecclesiae" is not only that which governs this subjective use, but is, in the sense of the *caritas* and the *pax* within the Church, at the same time the goal and standard of this personal sanctification.[22] With this last idea Augustine has parted definitely with Donatism's ethical understanding of the sacraments.

With this clear distinction between the palpable "signum" and the mental and spiritual "res" Augustine has removed the difficulties which arose in the controversy over heretic baptism, and has given the Church's doctrine of baptism its theological foundation and the power of penetration. And no matter how much the terminology may change in this point, this distinction is in the very nature of the matter clearly perceptible at every stage of development in Augustine's doctrine. We shall just list here the most important pairs of opposites: sacramentum tantum – virtus, effectus or usus sacramenti; sacramentum tantum – remissio peccatorum; visibile sacramentum – invisibilis unctio caritatis; visibilis baptismus – sanctificatio invisibilis; signum

---

[22] Augustine, *De bapt.* V, 20, 28; 21, 29.

118

salutis – ipsa salus; sacramentum gratia – ipsa gratia; forma sacramenti – forma justitiae; forma pietatis – virtus pietatis or radix caritatis; Christum induere usque ad sacramenti perceptionem – Christum induere usque ad vitae sanctificationem; inesse – prodesse sacramenti; perniciose habere – utiliter habere.[23] Accordingly Augustine distinguishes two ways in which the sacrament can be validly performed: its performance can be valid, but without efficacy for salvation, due to factors lying outside of the sacrament as such. And the sacrament can be validly performed and effective for salvation. If we also take into account the fact that tradition had already described baptism as *sphragis, signatio, sigillum,* then we are led logically to the conclusion that a baptism which has been administered with a certain "consecratio", and which merely by virtue of its performance is already valid, and therefore unique and unrepeatable, imparts a distinguishing mark similar to the design stamped on the face of a coin, to the mark of ownership placed on an animal in a herd, or to the "signum regale" (nota militaris, militiae character), which according to ancient custom was given to a soldier.[24] In this way Augustine hit upon the notion of "character", in order to designate the immediate effect of the "signum" and to mark it off from the actual "fructus".

It is true that the notion of character occurs occasionally only in Augustine's anti-Donatist writings. But in the nature of the

---

[23] The passages upon which this list is based are given in F. Hofmann, *Kirchenbegriff d. Aug.,* 357 f.

[24] Cf. "character" in the military sense: *De bapt.* I, 4, 5; III, 19, 25; *Ctr. ep. Parmeniani* II, 13, 29; – in the sense of a mark of ownership: *De bapt.* VI, 1, 1; *Ep.* 98, 5; *Ep.* 173, 3. There is an exhaustive treatment in N. M. Häring, "Character, Signum und Signaculum. Die Entwicklung bis nach der karolingischen Renaissance" in *Schol* 30 (1955) 481–512.

case it is the fundamental idea in his understanding of baptism. Augustine sees the essence of baptism as consisting in a "consecratio", in a cult dedication. The baptismal candidate "receives in character once and for all the form of a number of Christ; he is really incorporated into the body of Christ and obtains the capacity, the hope, and the right to receive divine grace and eternal blessedness, though he does not receive these things themselves – or at least not necessarily".[25] The baptismal character predisposes each individual for the efficacy of the grace which comes from Christ as head of the body, not merely for the forgiveness of sins which occurs in connection with the act of baptism itself, but for every subsequent forgiveness of sins as well. Because character involves only an objective sanctification, the prerequisites are also merely objective. These consist simply in the administration of the sacrament in accordance with the "regula ecclesiastica".[26] On the basis of this objective quality Augustine considers that even a baptism administered and received in jest could possibly be valid.[27]

The reason for the indestructible objectivity of the baptismal character is to be found in Christ, the author and lord of the sacrament of baptism.[28] Unlike Tertullian and also Optatus of Mileve, Augustine does not bother about an angel of baptism: the actual and ultimate minister is Christ. In order to preserve the unity of the Church, Christ did not hand over the actual authority of baptism to his servants.[29] There is thus an essential difference

[25] F. Hofmann, *Kirchenbegriff d. Aug.* 358f.
[26] Augustine, *De uno bapt. ctr. Petil.,* 11, 19 (*PL* 43, 603).
[27] *De bapt.* VII, 53, 101.
[28] Cf. *De bapt.* IV, 12, 18; *Ctr. litteras Petiliani* II, 37, 88.
[29] *In Jo. tract.* 5, 6 & 11 (*PL* 35, 1417 & 1419).

between the heretics' baptism and their doctrine, because rightly administered baptism belongs, of course, to Christ and to his bride, the Church.

Baptism can, like any material possession, be stolen from its rightful owner, without thereby losing its value.[30] He who administers or receives baptism outside of the Church commits robbery. Thus the Church's unique title to ownership is maintained, and the imprinting of the distinguishing mark remains valid, even when baptism is administered outside of the Church. "Or is it possible that the Christian sacraments are not so enduring as this (purely) bodily sign? For we certainly see that even apostates do not lose their baptism. Since baptism is, of course, not administered to them anew when they return as penitents. We conclude logically that baptism cannot possibly be lost."[31] Therefore the heretics baptize no less than others with the "baptism of the Church", that baptism "which is in every place itself sacred and which belongs properly, therefore, not to those who separate themselves, but to the (fellowship) from which they separate".[32]

Although Augustine thus admitted the validity of the sacrament in general even outside the Church, he was still very much concerned to avoid making it something automatic, and to show that apart from "caritas" the sacrament, even if validly received, was of no use. The recipient lacks "caritas" when he stands outside of the *catholica,* or when he "comes deceitfully"[33] to the sacrament by placing an obstacle in the way – "obicem oppo-

---

[30] *Ctr. Cresconium* IV, 21, 26.
[31] *Ctr. ep. Parm.* III, 13, 29.
[32] *De bapt.* I, 12, 19; cf. the entire chapter there.
[33] *Op. cit.* I, 12, 18.

nit".[34] For baptism to be effective for salvation this deception must first be done away by a "pia correctio et vera confessio".[35] Therefore, along with the "forma sacramenti" the "forma iustitiae" is necessary.[36] This consists essentially in the "conversio cordis", in a person's focusing himself morally in faith on his salvation, a process which is effected internally by divine grace and stimulated externally by the preaching of the gospel. "This attitude has no inherent dependence upon the sacrament, but rather runs parallel to it. . . . It requires completion through the sacrament, just as the sacrament must be supplemented by moral behaviour and by personal faith."[37] ". . . aliud esse sacramentum baptismi, aliud conversionem cordis, sed salutem hominis ex utroque compleri"[38] (". . . the sacrament of baptism is one thing, conversion of heart another, but man's salvation is composed of both"). In the course of time Augustine changed his opinion as to which of these components was of primary importance, which was the actual cause and which merely the "conditio" for the reception of grace. Indeed, he is not completely clear as to the meaning of the sacramental form itself. Thus, when he treats baptism of desire, he says that "faith and conversion of heart can fill up what is lacking in baptism",[39] and illustrates this with the example of the Good Thief. However, he also admits that it is difficult to say anything about the value and effect of sacramental sanctification which is carried out on the body. "But if this were not very important, then the Lord would not have received

[34] *Ep.* 98, 10. The expression "ponere obicem" is coined here for the first time. It was to achieve for the medieval theology of baptism a significance similar to that of the notion of "character".
[35] *De bapt.* I, 12, 18.   [36] *Ctr. litt. Petil.* III, 56, 68.
[37] F. Hofmann, *Kirchenbegriff d. Aug.,* 378.
[38] *De bapt.* IV, 25, 32.   [39] *Op. cit.* IV 22, 29.

122

baptism at the hands of his servant."[40] Then follows a reference to infant baptism, where faith and confession are completely impossible, "but certainly no Christian will claim that their baptism is useless".[41] According to Karl Adam[42] Augustine's opinion is something as follows: "The efficacy of the sacrament (virtus sacramenti) consists in the fact that it creates a spiritual form according to which the *res sacramenti* takes effect in the soul to the degree in which the recipient has developed the *virtus pietatis*. This efficacy consists, therefore, in the preparation of that sacramental *similitudo* which marks out and shapes the process which is accomplished in the soul by the *virtus pietatis*. It does so, however, in such a way that this process occurs in harmony with its *similitudo*. Thus this *similitudo* does indeed cause the state of grace. But it is . . . not the *causa efficiens,* but the *causa exemplaris.*"

In time Augustine came in his view of these matters to emphasize ever more strongly the objectivity of Christ's saving work and the fact that the sacramental sign was guaranteed effective despite human shortcomings. His struggle against the Pelagians and the problem of infant baptism were the occasion of this development.

In his early theological period he was especially taken up with the lack of personal faith in infant baptism. As a way out he fell back, at this time, on the expedient of considering the faith of the parents or sponsors as a substitute (*De lib. arbitrio* III, 23, 67). As early as his controversy with the Donatists the relationships become somewhat clearer to Augustine. Here both "sacramen-

---

[40] *Op. cit.* IV, 23, 30.   [41] *Loc. cit.*
[42] K. Adam, "Zur Eucharistielehre des hl. Augustinus" in *ThQ* 112 (1931) 511 f.

tum" and "conversio" are equally necessary for man's justification. If one of these two components is lacking, Augustine
presumes that God performs an act of grace. He uses the example
of the Good Thief for the case where the "sacramentum" is lacking, and that of a child who dies after baptism for the other case
where there is no "conversio". But Augustine did not continue
in this view that in the normal case full justification occurs only
when the "sacramentum fidei" is joined in a "conversio" with
the "voluntas fidei". Already in his ninety-eighth Letter from
the year 408 he continually connects the rite of baptism with
justification in the case of infant baptism. Regeneration takes
place no longer on the basis of the parents' confession of faith,
but rather by dint of the imparting of the Holy Spirit, who lives
in the Church's saints.[43] The sponsors' "confession of faith" has
a significance for the *sacramentum,* but is in no way a substitute
for the "affectus fidei". Through the sacramental "signa" infants
do have, in a certain sense, the faith to which they will later have
to accomodate themselves subjectively and ethically. In case of
death the immature child is delivered from damnation "per ipsum
sacramentum commendante ecclesiae caritate". It is no longer
the sacrament which is the prerequisite for the full effectiveness of
the "conversio". The "conversio" is the prerequisite which everyone who has attained the age of reason must have in order that
the spirit of unity in love with the Church may become fruitful.

It was natural that in the struggle against the Pelagians
Augustine's inclination to "sacramentalism" was strengthened.
The conception of infant baptism which he reached in this period
is exhaustively presented in the first book of his work, *De pecca-*

---

[43] Augustine, *Ep*. 98, 2.

124

torum meritis et remissione et de baptismo parvulorum ad Maecellinum.
The fundamental thesis of this book is the article of faith concerning the universality of original sin and the consequent necessity for all men to be saved by Christ. On the basis of these truths Augustine concludes that children who die without baptism "will be in a state of damnation, though certainly one which will be, amongst all the (possible) forms thereof, the mildest".[44] This can be expressed in positive terms as follows: "Whoever is born according to the flesh must be re-born in the spirit (spiritaliter), so that he may (thus) not only attain the kingdom of God but also be freed from sin's damnation . . . ; having been ordained to righteousness and to the eternal life of the second man, they are born again in baptism".[45] As against those who deny original sin, Augustine again and again holds up the Church's practice of infant baptism: this is meaningful only if there is in the immature child something to be washed away. "Why would it be needful to fashion the little child through baptism in the likeness of Christ's death, if it were not already fully poisoned by the serpent's bite?"[46] Faith and baptism effect a conformation to the likeness (similitudo) of Christ's death.[47] According to the Church's authority baptized children are amongst the "believers" who will not be judged. "This they attain through the power of the sacrament and the response of their sponsors."[48] "So the little ones should not be kept away from the grace of the forgiveness of sins; one does not come to Christ in any other way . . .".[49] Of course, the sacrament which he has received does not help the baptized child, "if, when he has reached the age of reason, he does not

---

[44] *De pecc. meritis* I, 16, 21.   [45] *Loc. cit.*   [46] *Op. cit.* I, 32, 61.
[47] *Loc. cit.*   [48] *Op. cit.* I, 33, 62.   [49] *Loc. cit.*

125

himself believe and keep himself from all evil desires". But when the child "passes from this life after receiving baptism and being freed from the inherited guilt which rested upon him, he is fulfilled in the light of (eternal) truth . . .".[50] There is, therefore, for children no other means of eternal salvation than baptism. Therefore "Punic Christians speak of baptism simply with the very felicitous name, salvation, and call the sacrament of Christ's body life. Whence comes that if not, as indeed I believe, from the ancient apostolic tradition, to which Christians hold fast, that apart from baptism and participation in the Lord's table no one can come either to the kingdom of God, or to salvation and to eternal life."[51] Now even Augustine becomes skeptical with regard to the baptism of desire, and would prefer to assume in the case of the Good Thief that he had been baptized previously.[52]

Thus since his struggle with Pelagius Augustine presses the "forma sacramenti" into the foreground as against the "forma iustitiae". The sacramental "similitudo" is no longer merely a co-ordinate factor, but rather the decisive factor in the process of salvation. "Baptism effects no longer, as formerly, merely a legal relationship of a mystical kind. It is a living source of strength and grace . . . . If previously the necessity of baptism was to be found in the relationship of the form to the content, and of the appearance to the essence, so now it achieves a mysterious inner value, resting in itself and efficacious of itself. It is quite simply and directly the sacrament of regeneration."[53] Augustine's neo-Platonic manner of thinking, which even in his anti-Pelagian period continues to exercise its influence, makes it

---

[50] *Op. cit.* I, 19, 25.   [51] *Op. cit.* I, 24, 34.
[52] *Retractat.* II, 44 (al. 18), 3.
[53] K. Adam, *Eucharistielehre d. Aug.,* 132, 130.

quite impossible for him to assume that the sign has any actual power to effect grace (in the sense claimed by scholastic theology). For him baptism remains merely the prerequisite for grace, even though "doubtless in the sense that the performance of the rite under the proper conditions always brings with it the imparting of grace; but not in the sense that the rite in itself is the cause of grace".[54]

Augustine's doctrine of baptism constitutes, therefore, a more profound substantiation of the fact that because of its objective and concrete nature baptism is valid in every case in which it is administered in accordance with the "regula ecclesiatica". This not merely answers the problem of heretic baptism. It also says that baptism by a layman is always valid. It is true that the layman should not baptize "without urgent necessity". Augustine says that when a layman baptizes without being compelled to do so by circumstances, "he usurps a duty not incumbent upon him". The baptism is, of course, valid. But one could in such a case "speak of illegitimate administration".[55] Augustine poses the question, whether a non-Christian can validly baptize. But he does not venture a decision of his own in this weighty matter, declaring the superior authority of a council to be competent.[56]

To seek elucidation from Augustine of the sacrament of confirmation is tantamount to enquiring into the classification of the anointing and the laying on of hands in the whole structure of rites subsequent to baptism. This is a ticklish and difficult question,[57] which can probably be solved most quickly by starting dispassionately with the evidence of the rite.

[54] J. Tixeront, *Histoire des dogmes* 2 (Pa. [11]1930) 406.
[55] Augustine, *Ctr. ep. Parm.* II, 13, 29.   [56] *Op. cit.* II, 13, 30.
[57] Cf. H. Elfers, "Gehört die Salbung mit Chrisma im ältesten abendländi-

In contrast to the Eastern liturgies, those of the African Churches, and especially the rite of Augustine's Church, place the anointing immediately after the bath of baptism, before the laying on of hands,[58] and separated from the latter by the giving of the white garment.[59]

According to Augustine baptism and the imparting of the Spirit are very closely connected with one another. Thus he says, for example, that God gives the Holy Spirit at baptism even when the minister of baptism is a murderer.[60]

Now it appears that Augustine ascribes this imparting of the Spirit – which he considers the first pouring out of the Spirit – to the anointing which takes place after the baptismal bath. We can conclude this from a mystagogic discourse in which he shows how the mystical body of Christ is prepared. "When, as catechumens, you had to wait, you were stored in the barn. You gave up your names. Then you began to be ground with fasting and exorcizings. Then you came to the water and were sprinkled with it; you were joined to the unity. Now when the fire of the Holy Spirit was added, you were baked and (thus) became the Lord's bread."[61] In another passage[62] he says clearly that this "fervour" of the Spirit refers to the chrism: "What does the fire signify, then? It is the chrism. For the oil is the sacrament of our fire, the

---

schen Initiationsritus zur Taufe oder zur Firmung?" in *ThGl* 34 (1942) 334–41, where he criticizes the views expressed in B. Welte, *Postbapt. Salbg.*
[58] Augustine, *Sermo* 324 (*PL* 38, 1447): "baptizatus est, sanctificatus est, unctus est, imposita est ei manus. Completis omnibus sacramentis assumptus est" ("he was baptized, he was sanctified, he was anointed, he had hands laid upon him. When he had completed all these sacraments, he was assumed").   [59] W. Roetzer, *Des Aug. Schr. als liturgiegesch. Quelle*, 167.
[60] *De bapt.* V, 20, 28.
[61] *Sermo Denis* 6, 1 (Morin, *S. Aug. Serm. post Maurinos rep.* 30).
[62] *Sermo* 227 (*PL* 38, 1100).

Holy Spirit." This "sacramentum chrismatis" is "within the category of visible symbols (signaculorum) as sacred as baptism itself. But it can . . . exist even in very evil men, who will not possess the kingdom of heaven".[63] What does he mean here? An action which takes place after baptism but which still belongs to baptism, or the sacrament of confirmation in our modern sense? The latter can certainly not be correct. But on the basis of the passage before us we are really not compelled to consider this action as belonging in any way at all to the confirmation which is yet to follow in the laying on of hands. This has been so compellingly demonstrated by P. Galtier that even P. de Puniet does not attempt to contradict him on this score. Rather he admits that we find even in Augustine the idea "of a first pouring out of grace which belongs properly to the anointing, and which is essentially different from the full gift of the Holy Spirit, which is reserved for the laying on of hands".[64] Notwithstanding B. Welte's attempt to demonstrate "that St. Augustine considered that the post-baptismal anointing formed a unity in meaning with the laying on of hands, and therefore that this anointing, in accordance with its symbolic significance, did not belong to baptism as such",[65] it may be taken as certain that this anointing after baptism is not to be joined with the laying on of hands in

[63] *Ctr. Litt. Petil.* II, 104, 239.
[64] P. de Puniet, *Onction et Confirmation,* 456; P. Galtier, *Consign. à Carthage et à Rome,* 358–68.
[65] B. Welte, *Postbapt. Salbung,* 68; the work is discussed by H. Elfers: *ThGl* 34 (1942) 340: it is true that for Augustine (*De trin.* XV 26, 26) there are two symbols for the Christian's reception of the Spirit: the laying on of hands and the "chrismatio". But this does not justify Welte's aboyementioned conclusion. Elfers, *Die Kirchenordnung Hippolyts v. Rom,* shows well how this situation is to be presumed for the Western Churches in general: "In the Western Church there was originally only *one* anointing

confirmation (which is also true in the cases of the old Africans, Cyprian and Tertullian), but rather that it belongs to the structure of baptism in the strict sense. It is certainly highly significant as the "sacramentum chrismatis", indeed as the "sacramentum of the Holy Spirit". This anointing within the act of baptism is intended to bring out the fact that the Holy Spirit is given here, or at least begins to be given, in order to incorporate the baptized into the unity of the body of Christ and to make each and every one of them a "Christus", one who is anointed. Moreover, this anointing is intended to grant a share in the "royal priesthood of the Church".[66]

Clearly separated from the anointing is the rite for the "impositio manuum". Augustine declares very definitely that the Holy Spirit does not descend (that is, in line with what has just been said above, he does not descend to supplement and to complete baptism) upon anyone who has not received the laying on of hands.[67] It is true, he admits, that the laying on of the pontiff's hand no longer imparts today, as in the primitive Church, the charisma. But it does "pour into us divine love

after baptism. This chrismation symbolized the sanctification of the neophyte who had been cleansed of sin in the bath of baptism. Through this union the candidate became a Christian, the anointed of the Lord; he was incorporated in this way into the royal and priestly race of the New Covenant. But the full imparting of the Spirit, on the other hand, the completion and the conclusion of the rite of initiation, was joined with the rite for the laying on of hands, which was followed by the signing on the forehead. Laying on of hands and 'signing' were reserved to the Bishop." See also O. Casel's criticism of Welte: *ArchLW* 1 (1950) no. 296f.

[66] One must interpret in this sense passages like *Sermo Denis* 6, 1 (see note 61 above), *Sermo* 227, 351, 5, 12 (*PL* 38, 1100; 39, 1548); *De civ. Dei* XVII, 4, 9 (*PL* 41, 532). For interpretation of these passages see H. Elfers, *Kirchenordnung Hippolyts*, 115–19, who takes issue with F. J. Dölger, *Sakr. d. Firmung*, 58.　　　[67] Augustine, *Sermo* 266, 3–6 (*PL* 38, 1225–7) esp. no. 6.

invisibly and in a hidden manner through the Holy Spirit which is given to us".[68] But side by side with this clear evidence stand other passages where, curiously, a lesser value is ascribed to the laying on of hands. "The laying on of hands can, in contrast to baptism, be repeated. For what else is it but a prayer (oratio) over people."[69] We ask in astonishment: is the same laying on of hands meant here as that which we today term "confirmation", so that Augustine would thus have claimed that this is repeatable? P. de Puniet would like to solve this problem by means of the assumption that there is a difference between the laying on of hands performed in confirmation and that used for the reconciliation of heretics.[70] We could evade this problem if we could agree with B. Welte in seeing in the anointing administered after baptism an essential element of confirmation. But since this is hardly possible we may just have to assume that Augustine – in contrast to the Roman Church, in particular – had not yet progressed to a clear recognition that this laying on of hands cannot be repeated.[71]

As we look back upon the practice of baptism as shown up to this time, and upon the doctrine of baptism expounded by Augustine and by those who prepared the way for him, and supplementing this doctrine by evidence from still other theologians of this period, we must observe above all that what a later period practised as two clearly separate sacraments, baptism and confirmation, constituted then a single structure of sacred acts –

---

[68] *De bapt.* III, 16, 21.   [69] *Loc. cit.* Cf. also V, 23, 33.
[70] P. de Puniet, "Confirmation" in *DACL* 3/2, 2540 ff., F. Cabrol, "Hérétiques" in *DACL* 3/2, 2540 ff., F. Cabrol, "Hérétiques" in *DACL* 6 2253 ff.
[71] F. Cabrol, *Hérétiques* 2254. A survey of the various solutions is given by B. Welte, *Postbapt. Salbung,* 2 f.

one single act of initiation, which is called "baptisma" in the most comprehensive sense of this word. It imparts fellowship with Christ, with his death and resurrection, and therefore regeneration. The dependence of baptism on the death and resurrection of Christ (cf. Rom. 6) is mentioned again and again by the Fathers.[72] The ancient idea of new birth leads to the conception of the baptismal water as a mother's womb at birth. Thus Leo the Great says: "At the new birth of each one of us the baptismal water becomes the mother's womb. For the same Holy Spirit which filled the Virgin fills the font as well, so that sin, which in her case was eliminated by her sacred conception, is here blotted out by a mystical washing."[73] From that point it is no longer very far to an express statement that the water is consecrated, or that it is filled with power which gives it its spiritual efficacy.[74] These effects are impressively summarized in the words of Leo the Great: "The sign of the cross makes kings of all those who have been regenerated in Christ; but the anointing of the Holy Spirit ordains them to priests, and, apart from the special ministry of our office, all religious and spiritual Christians should know themselves to be members of a royal race and partakers of the priestly obligation."[75] A total view of Christian

[72] For instance Leo M., *Sermo* 63, 6; *Ep.* 16, 3 (*PL* 54 ,357 B; 698 C). Hieronymus, *Dial. ctr. Lucif.* 7 (*PL* 23, 162 D).
[73] Leo M., *Sermo* 24, 3 (*PL* 54, 206A); cf. also Zeno, Tract 30–2 (*PL* 11, 477 f.); Pacianus, *De bapt.* 6 (*PL* 13, 1093 A); Niceta Rem., *Explan. symboli ad competentes* 10 (*PL* 52, 871 C).
[74] Hieronymus, *Dial. ctr. Lucif.* 6 (*PL* 23 161 A) speaks especially clearly of such a "purification of the water". For further evidence see B. Neunheuser, *De bened. aquae,* 387–400.
[75] Leo M., *Sermo* 4, 1 (*PL* 54, 149 A). That baptism is meant here and not already the beginning of confirmation is stated forcefully by P. Galtier (*RevHistE* 13, 1912, 472); according to him the Western tradition was

initiation similar to that given here by Leo is presented also by Pacian of Barcelona (died ca. 390). New birth can take place "only in virtue of the sacrament of the water-bath, of the anointing with chrism, and of the bishop's act of the mysteries. For by the water-bath sins are washed away; by the anointing with chrism the Holy Spirit is poured out from on high; but we pray for both by the hand and mouth of the bishop. And so the whole man is re-born and renewed in Christ."[76]

One of the most important forward steps in the baptismal theology of this period was the clarification of the question as to the minister, together with the development of the notion of a baptism which is validly received, but which remains without fruit. This provided the first beginning of the subsequent doctrine of the "character sacramentalis". It is clear that the sacrament of confirmation is equated with the laying on of hands described in Acts 8. But it has not yet proved possible to draw a clear line of demarcation between the efficacy of confirmation and the positive effects of baptism. And only in a later period will the recognition ripen that the laying on of hands, being, as it is, the second rite of initiation, shares with baptism the characteristic of not being repeatable.[77]

---

unanimous on this point. P. de Puniet had come to a different conclusion (*op. cit.* 453). H. Elfers, *Kirchenordnung Hippolyts*, 125, footnote 26, agrees with Galtier's opinion.

[76] Pacian., *De bapt.* 6 (*PL* 13, 1093 B).

[77] O. Casel refers to the unity of the act of initiation in *JbLW* 7 (1927) no. 224, p. 265, 267 (reviewed by J. Coppens, *L'imposition des Mains*). Even in Rome no final clarity had been reached with regard to the impossibility of repeating the laying on of hands for the imparting of the Spirit: see the remarks of Innocent I, *Ep.* 24, 3, 4 (*PL* 20, 550) and Leo M., *Ep.* 166, 2 *ad Neonem* (*PL* 54, 1194 B) amongst others, whom O. Casel brings forward against Coppens. The matter was decided only in the time of Pope

The order of the individual rites is that which has been customary in Africa and Rome since antiquity: water-bath and
anointing with chrism, laying on of hands followed by *consignatio*
without any anointing.[78]

Vigilius: " . . . quorum tamen reconciliatio non per illam impositionem
manuum, quae per invocationem Sancti Spiritus fit, operatur, sed per illam,
qua paenitentiae fructus acquiritur et sanctae communionis restitutio per-
ficitur" (". . . whose reconciliation is effected not through that imposition
of hands which is done through invocation of the Holy Spirit, but by the
imposition of hands by which the fruits of repentance are acquired and
re-admission to Holy Communion is achieved") (*Ep. ad Profuturum Bracar.
(Ps.-Eutherium)* 3: *PL* 69, 18 B).
[78] For the third century see P. Galtier in *RevHistE* 13 (1912) 474, with
whom P. de Puniet agrees. For Augustine himself see the text quoted in
note 58 above.

Chapter Six

BAPTISM AND CONFIRMATION IN THE EAST

IN THE FOURTH AND FIFTH CENTURIES

BIBLIOGRAPHY: J. Ernst, *Die Ketzertaufangelegenheit in der altchristl. Kirche* (v. chap. 4 above). G. Bareille, "Baptême d'après les pères grecs et latins" in *DThC* 2, 178–219. P. de Puniet, "Baptême" in *DACL* 2, 251–346. O. Casel, "Neue Zeugnisse für das Kultmysterium" in *JbLW* 13 (1935) 109–26, 150–4 (on Theodore of Mopsuestia). M. Jugie, *Theologia dogmatica Orientalium ab Ecclesia catholica dissidentium,* vols. 1–5 (Pa. 1926–35). M. Lot-Borodine, "Initiation à la Mystique sacramentaire de l'Orient" in *RevScPhTh* 24 (1935) 664–75; 25 (1936) 299–330. H. Elfers, *Kirchenordnung Hippolyts v. Rom.* W. de Vries, "Der 'Nestorianismus' Theodors von Mopsuestia in seiner Sakramentenlehre" in *OrChrPer* 7 (1941) 91–148; "Sakramententheologie bei den Nestorianern" (*OrChrAnal.* 133; Rm. 1947). J.–C. Didier, "Le pédobaptisme au IVe siècle. Documents nouveaux" in *MelScRel* 6 (1949) 233–46.

WHILE the Roman view with regard to heretic baptism came in the West to predominate, the Oriental Churches shared the position put forward by the Council of Nicaea in its nineteenth Canon: the followers of Paul of Samosata who returned to the Catholic Church should under all circumstance be "re-baptized" (ἀναβαπτίζεσθαι).[1] Later, when the Roman practice became do-

---

[1] *Denz.* 56; J. Ernst, *Ketzertaufangelegenheit,* 58–63.

minant in the whole Church, the attempt was made to remove
the contradiction contained in this canon by claiming that the
disciples of Paul of Samosata had falsified the formula of baptism.
This is urged, for instance, by the remark of Innocent I: "They
do not baptize in the name of the Father and of the Son and of
the Holy Spirit."[2] But this is contradicted by the testimony of so
weighty an authority as Athanasius, who, as a member of the
Council of Nicaea, would certainly have been better informed
as to the grounds for the rejection of this sect's baptism. And he
reckons the Samosites as belonging to the heresies, "which merely utter the names of the divine Persons, without thinking rightly
about them".[3] Still, the Council did not by any means adopt
"the extreme view of Cyprian and Firmilian, who rejected in
principle all baptism outside the Church".[4] This is shown by a
comparison of two of the Nicene Canons, numbers 19 and 8.
The latter orders that the Novatian clergy who returned to the
Church "are, after receiving the laying on of hands, to remain in
the clerical state",[5] without laying down anything with regard to
Novatian baptism. In all probability, therefore, the Council
wanted to leave this question undecided. This would have been
quite in keeping with the existing practice in the Orient at that
time, where, according to the testimony of St. Basil, various
regulations were in force with regard to this matter.[6] Basil was
not disturbed by this lack of uniformity, for he held this to be

---

[2] Innocentius I, *Ep.* 17, 10 *ad Rufum* (*PL* 20, 533 B); similarly Augustine,
De haeres. 44: "unde credendum est eos regulam baptismatis non tenere"
("wherefore it must be held that they do not keep the rule of baptism")
(*PL* 42, 34).
[3] Athanasius Alex., *Oratio* II *ctr. Arianos* 43 (*PG* 26, 237 BC); cf. J. Ernst,
Ketzertaufangelegenheit, 18 ff., 59 ff.
[4] J. Ernst, *op. cit.* 9 f.   [5] *Denz.* 55.   [6] J. Ernst, *op. cit.* 9.

not a matter of dogma, but a question of the ecclesiastical discipline prevailing in each case.[7]

But as far as the baptism of genuine heretics was concerned, the Orientals continued for a long time to come to hold to the opinion of Cyprian and Firmilian. Thus Athanasius doubts the validity of Arian baptism.[8] Similarly Basil, appealing to "the ancients", says that it is the practice of the Church, "to declare the baptism of the heretics fully invalid, but to recognize that of the schismatics, since they were, of course, still part of the Church".[9] This "recognition" must be understood in the sense mentioned above, as being purely a matter of ecclesiastical discipline. It is therefore quite possible that the practice of the individual Churches varied. Basil's insistence upon "re-baptism" is decisively influenced by "the rule of the ancients, to recognize only that baptism which does not deviate in any point from the faith.[10] This view corresponded completely to the fundamental principles laid down at Nicaea, and it dominated the general practice of the East in the period following. A Christian sect's baptism was judged by the degree to which it accepted the Nicene doctrine of the Trinity.[11] Because so many theologians of the Eastern

[7] *op. cit.* 5; cf., for instance, Basilius M., *Ep.* 188 *ad Amphilochium (Ep. can.* 1) (*PG* 32, 663): ". . . each land should follow its own custom"; there are still further texts in Ernst, *op. cit.* 3–6.

[8] Athanasius Al., *Or. II ctr. Arianos (PG* 26, 236 C – 273 A): "For if the fulfilment is given in the name of the Father and of the Son, but they do not mention the true Father, . . . is that which they give . . . not completely empty? For the Arians do not give (baptism) in the (name) of the Father and of the Son, but in the (name) of the creator of the created . . ." Cf. J. Ernst, *op. cit.* 18–22.

[9] Basilius M., *Ep.* 188 *ad Amphil. (PG* 32, 665 B, 668 A); cf. J. Ernst, *op. cit.* 22–32.

[10] *Loc. cit.* (*PG* 32, 665 B); J. Ernst, *op. cit.* 25.

[11] That is shown, amongst other things, by a letter of the Church of Con-

Church considered the baptism of the Anti-trinitarians to be invalid or at best doubtful, it was felt to be necessary "in order to safeguard the sacrament" to admit such a repetition of baptism. The East did not recognize that faith in the Trinity could be safeguarded when baptism was administered quite simply in accordance with the usage of the Church. The Church in the West had deeper insight in this respect, and thus it gave the theology of baptism a further and decisive development.[12]

The evidence which goes back to Cyril of Jerusalem deserves to be placed at the head of all the pieces of testimony which will be discussed in this chapter. We have him to thank for the most impressive picture of the liturgy of baptism and for giving us at least the basic lines of the baptismal theology of one of the most important ecclesiastical centers of the East, which may be taken as more less typical for the initiation mysteries of this period in the East in general.[13]

stantinople to the Patriarch Martyrius of Antioch (459/71), which "constitutes a testimony for the practice of at least a large part of the Oriental Church at the beginning of the first century". In this letter the individual sects are separated in detail with regard to the recognition or non-recognition of their baptism. Arian baptism was considered valid, but not the baptisms of the Eunomians (who baptized with one immersion only), the Montanists, the Sabellians, and other heresies. Strange as this classification may seem in a number of points, it is in fact the position taken by the heresies with regard to faith in the Trinity which is decisive. This doctrine was taken over by the Synod of Trulla (692) as Canon 92 and thus attained legal force for the entire Greek Church. (On this whole question cf. J. Ernst, *Ketzertaufangelegenheit* 64–6.)

[12] For a dogmatic assessment of the results see J. Ernst, *op. cit.* 86–94.

[13] The *Mystagogic Catechisms* of St. Cyrill of Jerusalem are quoted here from the edition of J. Quasten, *Monumenta eucharistica et liturgica vetutissima*, Pars II (*Florileg. Patrist.* 7/2; Bonn 1935); the other catechisms are taken from *PG* 33, 332ff. On the significance of Jerusalem in the framework of the liturgy see A. Baumstark, *Vom geschichtlichen Werden der Liturgie* (FbB.

There are twenty-four catechisms which bear Cyril's name. The first of these, the προκατήχησις, is an introductory lesson about the magnitude and importance of baptismal grace. Eighteen Κατηχήσεις φωτιζομένων follow, in the main, a continuous explanation of the baptismal creed of the Church of Jerusalem. Cyril used these nineteen catechisms to prepare his baptismal candidates in Lent of the year 348. But after the reception of baptism these νεοφώτιστοι were to be initiated more deeply into the mysteries of the sacraments, which had to remain closed to the non-baptized. This is the task of the five following catechisms, which on this account are called *Mystagogic Catechisms.* It is true that Cyril's authorship of these least catechisms is disputed. W. J. Swaans, Th. Schermann and others would like, on the basis of manuscript evidence, to ascribe them to Cyril's successor, John of Jerusalem (386–417).[14] But the assumption of S. Salaville[15] and others seems to be better justified. This view maintains that the text presents us with notes taken within the circle of Cyril's hearers, and, in fact, a comment in the manuscript indicates this. So Cyril is very likely the author of these *Mystagogic Catechisms,* but he did not himself write down the text which has been preserved to us.

Forty days were provided for the preparation for baptism. During this time the candidate had to confess his sins, receive

1923) 41–4. On the baptismal liturgy and theology of the East in this period see J. Daniélou, "Die Symbolik des Taufritus" in *LitgMöncht* 3 (1939) 45—68 (French in *DieuV,* 1945).

[14] W. J. Swaans, "A propos des 'Catéchèses mystagogiques' attribuées à S. Cyrille de Jérusalem" in *Mus* 55 (1942) 2ff. Th. Schermann in *ThRev* 10 (1911) 577.

[15] S. Salaville, "Une question de critique littéraire. Les catéchèses de Saint Cyrille de Jérusalem in *EchOr* 17 (1915) 531–7.

exorcism, and attend the catechetical sessions. This was all supposed to serve to cleanse his soul.[16] The act of baptism was introduced by the ceremony in which Satan was renounced. For this purpose the candidates were made to take their places in the baptistery, facing west, because this direction was a symbol for the region of darkness, the kingdom of Satan.[17] Then the candidates turned towards the east, as a sign that the paradise of God was now their goal. Then they all confessed: "I believe in the Father and in the Son and in the Holy Spirit, and in a baptism of repentance."[18] Afterwards they went into the inner part of the baptistery and took off their clothes to express their desire to put off the old man and to become like Christ, "who had been laid bare there on the cross, and had thereby laid bare the dominions and powers, triumphing over them openly on the cross"[19]. The candidate's body was then anointed with exorcized oil from head to foot. That was supposed to signify that the candidates became partakers of the pure oil of Christ, that is, of his strength. Men and women were separated for this ceremony. Then the candidates were led to the sacred bath, as Christ was taken from the cross to the grave. Each one of them was questioned individually about his faith in the three divine Persons, and immersed three times in the water.

The heart of the baptismal act is the water-bath, the three-fold immersion accompanied by the "saving confession" of the divine Persons. The interpretation of this essential core is,

---

[16] Cyrill. Hier., *Procat.* 9 (*PG* 33, 348f.); cf. *Cat.* 1, 2 (*PG* 33, 372 B) where the theme of putting off and putting on clothes (from Eph. 4:22ff.; Col. 3:9f.) determines the moral effort of preparation. See also *Cat.* 1, 5 (*PG* 33, 377).   [17] *Cat. myst.* 1, 4 (Quasten 6_1–7_2; *PG* 33, 1068f.).
[18] *Op. cit.* 1, 9 (Qu. 11_{17-21}; *PG* 33, 1073).
[19] *Op. cit.* 2, 2 (Qu. 13_{16-21}; *PG* 33, 1077).

therefore, one of the first questions which must be posed with regard to Cyril's theology of baptism. The immersion in the water and the emergence signify death and resurrection. As Christ remained three days and three nights inside the earth, so the baptized have died and been buried in the immersion, and coming up they are born again (*Cat. myst.* 2, 4). But the Christian's dying and rising in baptism does not take place ἀληθῶς, that is, physically, in historical fact, but in an image (ἐν εἰκόνι), in imitation (μίμησις). For the Christian the relationship of the Lord's real, actual, historical suffering to the order of grace is such "that, having become partakers of his suffering through imitation, we attain salvation in truth".[20] Christ suffers painfully, we effortlessly; we are granted salvation through participation in his pain (2, 5). Baptism is the image (ἀντίτυπον) of Christ's passion. But since Cyril's thought is stamped with Platonism, there is no μίμησις, μέθεξις, or κοινωνία without what is reproduced being made present. Applied to baptism this means that since it is an ἀντίτυπον the original image which is reproduced must also be present in baptism. The natural, historical reality is the original, of which the sacramental reality is the image. The believer shares through the image in its original, and thus becomes a partaker of the natural and historical reality of the original. Of course, this must not be understood as impugning the unique unrepeatable nature of the original image's natural reality. But the reproduction of the original enables the believer really to experience for himself

---

[20] *Op. cit.* 2, 5 (Qu. 17₇₋₁₀; *PG* 33, 1081): "We did not truly (ἀληθῶς) die, we were not truly buried. We have arisen, without having been really crucified. The imitation is accomplished rather in an image; but salvation is in truth."

God's saving act, and to receive a share in the divine life. This life is a genuine reality, and not merely a figure of it.

Cyril finds this idea of baptism as a symbolic μίμησις of the passion and death of Christ expressed also in the words of St. Paul (Rom. 6:5): "If we have been planted in the likeness of his death . . .". For in Christ the true vine has been planted, and "we are planted with him by the participation in his death which ensues in baptism. Mark the Apostle's words carefully. He does not say: if we were planted in death, but, in the likeness of his death . . . . As far as we are concerned passion and death are, however, mere likeness. But our redemption is not likeness, but reality" (2, 7).

Thus baptism conveys, according to Cyril, a peculiar participation in Christ's passion, which "is fulfilled in us first of all in figurative, symbolic forms, which, however, are not merely images, but which are filled with the reality of the new life imparted to us by Christ. This peculiar participation in Christ's life, partly symbolical, partly actual, is called by the ancients 'mystical'. It is a mean between the mere external image and the pure reality."[21]

Basically Cyrill does not go beyond tradition. But he was the first to emphasize the fellowship in Christ's passion as well as to assemble an abundance of related theological notions, of which the words αἰνίττομαι, εἰκών, μίμημα, μίμησις, ὁμοίωμα, ἀντίτυπον are the best examples.

[21] O. Casel, *Das christliche Kultmysterium* (Rg. 1932) 32. On the whole problem at issue here see G. Söhngen, *Symbol und Wirklichkeit im Kultmysterium (Grenzfragen zw. Theol. u. Philos.* 4; Bonn 1937) 96 f.; same author, *Wesensaufbau d. Myst.* 82 f.; Casel's answer to Söhngen is in *Glaube, Gn. u. Myst.* 253–69; Casel's final translation and interpretation of this passage from Cyril is to be found in *ArchLW* 1 (1950) 140 f.

Alongside this idea, treated in the *Mystagogic Catechisms* alone, appears another: the notion of an element in baptism which is "filled with power". It is already present behind the image of "the waters which bear Christ, which exhale a sweet smell".[22] But we find it expressed very clearly in the words[23]: "Do not look upon this water-bath as upon ordinary water; look rather upon the grace of the Holy Spirit which is given with the water. For . . . the pure, plain water, when it has received the epiclesis of the Holy Spirit, of Christ, and of the Father, (obtains) power for holiness." The water is in itself powerless. But, since it has in the epiclesis received power to sanctify, we should "not regard the poverty of the element, but rather expect salvation from the power of the Holy Spirit" (*Cat.* 3, 4). To establish the connection between the water of baptism and grace Cyril refers to Christ's words in John 3:3, as well as to man's constitution from flesh and spirit, which requires a cleansing of the body and of the spirit. It is not clear from his words whether the water receives its sanctifying power from the mere naming of the three divine names, or from a separate consecration of the water.[24]

No less important than the interpretation of the baptismal water is that of the chrism. The act of baptism is brought to a close with the giving of the chrism. "In accordance with your baptism you have been judged worthy to be crucified and buried

---

[22] Cyrill. Hier., *Procat.* 15 (*PG* 33, 357 A).

[23] *Cat.* 3, 3 (*PG* 33, 429 A).

[24] Cf. B. Neunheuser, *De bened. aquae* 371 f. See also Cyril's discussion of the significance of water in Old Testament typology: *Cat.* 3, 5 (*PG* 33, 433 AB); there is a reference to the "sanctification" of baptism by Jesus in Jordan and the connection of this "descent" with Jesus' death in *Cat.* 3, 11–12 (*PL* 33, 441 A – 444 A).

with him in a figurative manner, and with him to rise again. This is also true with regard to the chrism. He was anointed with the spiritual oil of joy, that is, with the Holy Spirit . . . . But you have been anointed with myrrh and have thus become partners and comrades of Christ" (*Cat. myst.* 3, 2). "As partners of Christ you have been rightly named χριστοί. But you became χριστοί when you received the ἀντίτυπον of the Holy Spirit; and it all happened to you figuratively (εἰκονικῶς), since you are images (εἰκόνες) of Christ" (3, 1). Continuing this image-theme, Cyril now proceeds to connect the baptism of Christ in Jordan and the descent of the Holy Spirit upon him on the one hand with, on the other hand, the immersion-bath, the emergence from the font and the giving of chrism, which he calls "the image of that with which Christ was anointed. But this is the Holy Spirit" (3, 1). The oil or myrrh used at this anointing does not remain in its ordinary state after the epiclesis,[25] "but has become Christ's gift of grace (χάρισμα) and the instrument (ἐνεργητικόν) of his Godhead through the presence of the Holy Spirit. Now the body is anointed with this visible myrrh, but the soul is sanctified with the Holy and invisible Spirit" (3, 3).

So the water-bath and the myrrh play corresponding rôles: the one is the ἀντίτυπον of Christ's passion, the other the ἀντίτυπον of the Holy Spirit. In both cases we have an image based upon Christ's saving act, the purpose of which is to give the initiate in this "figurative" form the reality of the original which the image represents. Taken all together this amounts to dying and

---

[25] As an example of the consecratory prayer of such an epiclesis see the prayer for the consecration of the oil by Serapion of Thmuis in Egypt (middle of the fourth century) in F. X. Funk, *Didascalia et Constitutiones Apostolorum*, vol. 2 (Pb. 1906) 186f.

rising again with Christ, being filled with the Holy Spirit together with him, in order, with Christ, to be a *christus*, one anointed. The two symbolic acts supplement each other and only together do they produce the complete Christian: "only after holy baptism and mystic chrism have you put on the full armament of the Holy Spirit . . ." (3, 4). Cyril seems also to be familiar with the summary description of the entire act of initiation with the word "baptism". It is, of course, not only forgiveness of sins, liberation, regeneration, but also "imparting of the gift of the Holy Spirit" (2, 6). And the custom of terming the entire action *sphragis*[26] points in this same direction. But it is clearly recognized in the third *Mystagogic Catechism,* which is devoted to the chrism, that the anointing with chrism which forms the closing climax of his action is something quite independent.[27]

Cyril defends the necessity of baptism for salvation as a tradition of the primitive Church. "There is no salvation for

---

[26] F. J. Dölger, *Sphragis,* 186 f. gives abundant source material.

[27] We hear nothing of a laying on of hands, however, although Cyril in *Cat.* 16, 26 (*PL* 33, 956 C) refers to biblical examples of the imparting of the Spirit through the laying on of hands. Nevertheless H. Elfers is probably correct when he says: "The evidence seems to show that even in the Eastern Church a laying on of hands was not lacking in the administration of confirmation." If this is not mentioned, the reason is "probably that in the Eastern Church the *sphragis* with myrrh was considered to be so important that the sacrament of confirmation took its name from this rite" (*Kirchenordnung Hippolyts,* 141). There are sporadic cases where confirmation is called, even in isolation, *"sphragis",* for instance *Cat.* 18, 33 (*PG* 33, 1056 B); cf. F. J. Dölger, *Sphragis,* 187 f. This is not so clear in other passages, as, for instance, *Procat.* 17 (*PG* 33, 365 A). There we read: "May God grant you . . . the seal of the Holy Spirit which is indelible for all ages." But it appears from the context that it is the act of initiation as a whole which is meant here, without distinction of individual acts. Thus the passage would say that the acts included in this basic initiation, taken as a whole, imprint an "indelible seal", a thought which – together with the further idea that

145

him who does not receive baptism."[28] He does not seem otherwise to recognize either infant baptism or the baptism of
desire as a way of salvation, but only martyrdom, to which
he does, however, attach the highest value. The martyrs can
inherit the kingdom without water, they have received the
baptism of blood: "When the Saviour redeemed the world on
the cross, there flowed from the wound in his side blood and
water, so that he who lives in time of peace may be baptized in
water, while he who perishes in an age of persecution may
receive baptism in his own blood. Indeed, even the Saviour
terms martyrdom a baptism. For he says (Mark 10:38): Are
you able to drink the cup that I drink, and to be baptized with
the baptism which I receive?" (*Cat.* 3, 10).

Cyril does not offer any systematic dogmatics in his catechisms, but speaks as a pragmatist. Right here, however, it
becomes obvious just how deep was the knowledge of the
mystery of baptism to which the simplest believers in Jerusalem were led.

We see in the other great Fathers of this period primarily
witnesses for the tradition. Even the list of names which they
coin for baptism is impressive.[29] It is frequently the relationship
between the moral conduct of the individual and what happens
in the sacrament which forms the object of the discussion,

(validly) administered baptism could not be repeated (cf. *Procat.* 7 /*PG*
33, 345 AB/) – was to be of great importance for later theology. On the
theme of the "indelible" and "unbreakable" seal see esp. F. J. Dölger,
Sphragis, 126–40.
[28] *Cat.* 3, 10 (*PG* 140); cf. also *Cat.* 3, 4 (*PG* 33, 432).
[29] See, for instance, Gregorius Nazianz. *Or.* 40 *de bapt.* 3 (*PG* 36, 361 B);
4 (*loc. cit.* 361 D); Gregorius Nyssenus, *Or. catech. magna* 32 (*PG* 45, 84 A);
Johannes Chrysost. *Ad illuminandos catech.* 1, 2 (*PG* 49, 223 ff.).

especially, for instance, in the case of Basil[30] and of Gregory of Nyssa.[31] Gregory emphasizes the personal preparation for the sacrament in an attempt to counteract an excessively concrete conception. The minister of baptism is also for the Fathers of the East irrelevant, since baptism derives its power from the epiclesis of the divine names. Gregory Nazianzen illustrates this well with the example of a signet ring, the seal of which is always valid, regardless of the material in which it is imprinted.[32]

Infant baptism finds an advocate in Gregory of Nyssa. He emphasizes that it is necessary in a case of imminent danger of death. Apart from this, however, he advises a delay of about three years.[33] But the practice of infant baptism was in this period still far from universal. Indeed, Gregory Nazianzen, obviously in the zeal of his struggle against the postponement of baptism until life's end, an abuse which stands in contradiction to infant baptism, even denies the validity of the baptism

---

[30] Basilius M., *De Spiritu S.* 12, 28 (*PG* 32, 117 BC): faith and baptism are "two kinds of salvation, related to one another and indivisible. Faith receives its completion in baptism, but baptism is founded in faith .... The confession of faith which leads us to salvation preceeds; then follows baptism and seals our assent in conclusion". With regard to Gregor. Naz. see *Or.* 40, 32 (*PG* 36, 405 A).

[31] Gregor. Nyss., *Or. cat. magna* 40 (*PG* 45, 104 B).

[32] Gregor. Naz., *Or.* 40, 26 (*PG* 36, 396 D). The following sentence, "so you should admit anyone as minister of baptism – provided only that he is formed by the same faith", betrays, of course, the attitude to heretic baptism which was peculiar to the Eastern Churches. See also *Or.* 33, 17 (*PG* 36, 236 BC).

[33] Gregor. Naz. *Or.* 40, 28 (*PG* 36, 400 AB): "It is better to be sanctified unconscious than to pass from life without sealing and fulfilment." He also refers to the danger that the child dying without baptism, although not damned, will not be admitted to glory (*op. cit.* no. 23, *PG* 36, 329 C).

of desire.[34] The baptismal bath and the imparting of the Spirit were still considered as a unity, but in such a way that the latter remained clearly the conclusion and the completion of baptism.[35]

But the principal contribution of these Fathers is that they bring out the two themes used to interpret the essence of baptism: baptism in Jesus' death, in accordance with Romans 6, and the filling of the water with a sanctifying power.

The theme of baptism in Christ's death is testified to in many places.[36] And the Fathers were fond of trying to draw up a description of baptism in technical terms on the basis of this interpretation. Thus according to Basil a μίμησις, an imitation of Christ takes place in baptism. The water is in this connection the image (εἰκῶν) of death. Through the epiclesis of the Godhead and the presence of the Spirit which this epiclesis effects

[34] *Op. cit., Or.* 40, 23 (*PG* 36, 329 C). On this whole question cf. J.-C. Didier, *Pédobaptisme,* 233, 46.
[35] As, for instance, in the passage from Gregory Nazianzen (*Or.* 40, 4, *PG* 36, 361 D), who calls baptism "gift, grace, (bath of) baptism (anointing with) chrism, illumination, robe of immortality, water-bath of regeneration, seal . . .". Cf. also *op. cit.* nos 38 and 40 (*PG* 36, 413 A–C, 420 C). Nevertheless, that confirmation is a proper conclusion within the total framework is shown by Cyril of Alexandria, when he speaks of the anointing with oil as the "conclusion and fulfilment for those who have been justified in Christ through baptism" (*In Joel.* 32, on 2, 21–24, *PG* 71, 373 B).
[36] Basilius M., *De Spir. S.* 15, 35f. (*PG* 32, 132 AB); cf. also 12, 28; 14, 32 (*PG* 32, 117 A, 125 A); *Hom.* 13 *exhort. ad bapt.* 1 (*PG* 31, 424 C); Gregor. Naz., *Or.* 40, 9 (*PG* 36, 369 B); Joh. Chrys., *In Rom. 6 hom.* 10, 4 (*PG* 60, 480); see also *In Jo.* 3, 5 *hom.* 25, 2 (*PG* 59, 151): "Divine symbols are . . . accomplished: burial and mortification and resurrection and life, and that all happens together. For when we submerge our head in the water as in a grave the old man is buried; and as he submerges deeply he is completely hidden. But then, when we emerge again with the head, the new man arises." Cyril. Al., *In Lc.* 2, 22 (*PG* 72, 497 BC). On Gregor. Nyss. see footnotes 38 and 39.

"the image (τύπος) of death is figuratively created (ἐξεικονισθῇ)".[37] This interpretation is to be found with special fullness in the case of Gregory of Nyssa.[38]

For the purpose of salvation it is necessary to produce an "affinity and likeness" between Christ and the faithful. This happens figuratively (ὁμοίωμα) through imitation (μίμησις). "We portray" the three-day death of Christ and his resurrection "in imitation, by pouring the water three times and emerging again from the water".[39] What has once happened to Christ is thus subsequently performed upon the faithful; and they are able in this way "with Christ to achieve salvation". Therefore baptism imparts also the foundation for the future accomplishment of this salvation, namely the resurrection. The resurrection on the last day has its beginning and its cause here.[40] When Gregory, then, following these ideas, which are in line with the general teaching of the Church, adds that the unbaptized will be purified "in the fire in which our universe is finally restored",[41] he is following in this point the special opinion of his master, Origen.

John Chrysostom has also pointed expressly to the significance of the "image of death" in baptism and to the fact that baptism "leads to the cross", and constitutes a fellowship in Christ's crucifixion.[42] But the Fathers prefer to treat the second theme: whence does the water achieve such power to convey grace? "Not in virtue of the water's nature, but in

---

[37] Basilius M., *De Spir. S.*, 15, 35 (*PG* 45, 84 A – 92 D).
[38] Gregor. Nyss. *Or. cat. magna* 32–6 (*PG* 45, 84 A – 94 D).
[39] *Loc. cit. PG* 45, 89 D); O. Casel (*JbLW* 14 1938 211) adopts the reading ὑποκρινόμεθα, not ἀποκρινόμεθα as in Migne.
[40] *Op. cit.* (*PG* 45, 88 A, 92 A).   [41] *Op. cit.* (*PG* 45, 92 BC).
[42] Joh. Chrys., *In Rom.* 6 *hom.* 10, 4; 11, 1 (*PG* 60, 480, 485).

virtue of the Spirit's presence."[43] Gregory of Nyssa gives this answer still deeper significance by juxtaposing the insignificance of the external action with its tremendous effects: not only the water, but also prayer, epiclesis, indeed even faith achieve their power to impart grace only through the "presence of the divine power", which causes these effects.[44]

Gregory tries, more almost than anyone else, to describe the indescribable. As once the Jordan at Christ's baptism received "the firstfruits of sanctification and blessing",[45] so now the water of baptism is for everyone "his Jordan", going out from Christ into the entire world.[46] Any water can become baptismal water, "provided that it finds faith on the part of the recipient and blessing from the sanctifying priest".[47] Thus the water of baptism is filled with a mysterious power by the advent of the Spirit, or through the εὐλογία of the "sanctifying priest". Even if this event had to be interpreted in connection with the baptismal formula alone (that is, with the epiclesis of the divine names) and this connection can at any rate not be excluded – we are led inevitably to the conclusion that the baptismal water is somehow changed, and filled, even if only temporarily, with a new power. But Gregory seems to account for the change which takes place in the water by assuming a separate con-

---

[43] Thus Basilius M., *De Spir. S.*, 15, 35 (*PG* 32, 129 D); cf. Gregor. Naz., *Or.* 40, 8 (*PG* 36, 368 B); Cyrill. Al., *Ctr. Iulian.* 7 (*PG* 76 880 B); *In Jo.* 3, 5 (*PG* 73, 244 D – 245 A).

[44] Gregor. Nyss., *Or. cat. magna* 33 (*PG* 45, 84 D); cf. 34 (*PG* 45, 85 B).

[45] Gregor. Nyss., *In bapt. Christi* (*PG* 46, 592 D); on the underlying idea see B. Neunheuser, *De bened. aquae* 466–73.

[46] Gregor. Nyss., *Adv. eos qui differunt bapt.* (*PG* 46, 420 CD).

[47] *Op. cit.* (*PG* 46, 421 D).

secration; for he tries to make the effect of this consecration clear by comparing it with analogous consecrations. Just as a plain stone becomes the Holy Table of the altar through a Logos-consecration, or through a "eulogia", or as ordinary bread becomes the body of Christ, so "we conclude that the water, although it is certainly (in itself) nothing else but mere water, renews man in spiritual regeneration, after it has received the blessing of the grace which comes down from above".[48] From this parallel with the other acts of consecration one can see just how strongly Gregory of Nyssa wants to emphasize that the act in which the element of water is hallowed is crucial. The greatness of baptism's effects is achieved in the power of him who is invoked in the consecrating epiclesis, who is present and fills the water with his power.

The development of the two themes already mentioned is, moreover, the basic concern of the rich, but singular, contribution made by Ephraim the Syrian (died 373) in his hymns, and especially in those composed for the feast of the Epiphany.[49] This connection with Epiphany presupposes that baptism was administered principally on this day, which commemorates Christ's baptism in Jordan. This circumstance, coupled with what is said in Matt. 3:11, leads Ephraim to conceive of baptism as being in a special manner "baptism in the Holy Spirit and in fire".[50]

---

[48] *In bapt. Christi* (*PG* 46, 581 B–584 C); cf. here B. Neunheuser's illustrations, *De bened. aquae*, 374–6. The footnotes there are unfortunately printed in the wrong order.
[49] We quote here from the edition of Th. J. Lamy, *S. Ephraemi Syri Hymni et Sermones* vol. 1 (Mechliniae 1882), save where another edition is mentioned. Cf. here P. Krüger, "Das Taufgeheimnis in der ältesten syrischen Liturgie" in *PhilJB* 55 (1942) 45–57.   [50] Cf. *Hymn.* 5, 4 (Lamy 1, 52).

In analogy to what took place at Jesus' baptism in Jordan, the Spirit of God descends upon the water in Christian baptism as well. Whether this occurs in a separate consecration of the water is not said. But at any rate the water is filled with the Spirit. This conception is supplemented by the thought that "God mixes with the water his 'fermentum', which raises those who have been formed from dust and unites them with God".[51] This "fermentum", this element of life, joins the "servant with the master's family".[52] These two ideas are behind the statement that the candidates, when they are immersed in the baptismal water, both "put on our Lord and are blended into his fellowship", and "put on the Holy Spirit and are placed amongst the spirits that serve God" or are "incorporated into the flock of the Good Shepherd".[53] Both these ideas are joined in the sentence: "You have become sons of the Holy Spirit; your head is Christ, you are his members."[54] Thus the Lord and the Spirit belong most intimately together. They work together, to "transform the waters in baptism". "The Holy Spirit broods over the waters of baptism"; "Jesus has mingled his power with the waters . . . . Not only our bodies are to be washed in the water-bath, but also our souls. The visible waters should be perceived by the body, but the hidden power by the soul, so that what is hidden and what is manifest fulfil one another."[55]

A reminiscence of another line of thought, which is grounded

---

[51] *Hymn.* 4, 5 (Lamy 1, 46); cf. *Hymn.* 6, 1 (L. 1, 54).
[52] See P. Krüger, *Taufgeheimnis,* 49; "family" is in the Latin. The translation is given as "stirps, familia, cognatio, prosapia".
[53] *Hymn.* 4, 1; 5, 1; 6, 6 (Lamy 1, 44, 50, 58).
[54] *Hymn.* 9, 1 (Lamy 1, 90).
[55] *Hymn.* 8, 20; 8, 16; 9, 5 (Lamy 1, 88, 86, 92).

152

in Romans 6, is contained in the reference to the fact that "Christ's sheep . . . put on in the water the symbolic figure of the glorious and living cross".[56] And a number of other passages, for example stanzas 2–4, 9–11 and 15 of Hymn 10, can be taken in this sense, inasmuch as they bring out the fundamental relationship of the life which is to be gained in baptism to the saving work of Christ, and in particular to his death and resurrection. To this general theme belong also Ephraim's words about the "source of life which proceeds from the side of Christ".[57]

The oil has a special place in Ephraim's thought. He even celebrates its great importance in special hymns.[58] The third hymn for the feast of the Epiphany expresses most clearly the connection of the oil with baptism. The later Syrian baptismal rites provide for the singing of this hymn during the anointing of the candidate's entire body with olive oil: "Christ and the oil come together; the inner anointing is joined with the outer. The new spiritual sheep are anointed exteriorly with oil, interiorly by Christ" (*Hymn* 3, 1). In fact, the hymn even goes on: "(The flock) is conceived by the oil and born in the water" *(loc. cit.)* so that "weak man, wrapped in water and oil, may stand before the highest majesty" (8, 3). It seems almost as if the oil imparts fire to the water, so that in this way "fire and spirit" are given "in the true baptism" (5, 4; cf. 8, 4–6), and "all sins are washed away by water with oil" (5, 5). We may see in this high evaluation of the anointing with oil and of its close relationship to the water-bath an attempt on the part of the Syrian liturgy to show the riches of the "regeneration in

---

[56] *Hymn.* 7, 3 (Lamy 1, 64); cf. P. Krüger, *Taufgeheimnis,* 51.
[57] *Hymn.* 5, 14 (Lamy 1, 54).
[58] *Hymn.* 25–8 *de oleo et oliva* (Lamy 2, 786–806).

153

water and the Holy Spirit" by means of one coherent total action, consisting of, first, an anointing with oil, and then the water-bath. And this is confirmed by the evidence from the baptismal liturgy itself, as presented to us, for instance, by Theodore of Mopsuestia. To be sure, it is not from Ephraim, but from other sources, such as Theodore of Mopsuestia and Cyril of Jerusalem, that we learn that baptism is followed by a "signatio", which in turn is joined with an anointing. Doubtless such an anointing (with chrism, myrrh) would easily have found a place in Ephraim's theology superior to the position of the oil with baptism.[59]

Finally, we have evidence for the richly developed baptismal theology of this period in the "Explanations of the Mysteries of Holy Church", which comes to us from the area of the Antiochene Church, from the pen of Theodore of Mopsuestia.[60]

Theodore's theology of baptism can be characterized sum-

---

[59] A confirmation anointing can hardly be assumed in the cases of Ephraim and Theodore of Mopsuestia. Cf. the reservations which W. de Vries ("*Nestorianismus*" *Theodors* 132–5) makes with regard to Theodore. In the same vein: H. Elfers, *Kirchenordnung Hippolyts,* 141–6. Ephraim's text on Joel, which Elfers (*op. cit.* 132) quotes (cf. also A. Merx, *Die Prophetie des Joel und ihre Ausleger,* HaS. 1879, 144), is likewise not a proof for any such anointing. It seems to us, rather, that it must be referred, in line with our arguments above, to the total action of baptism.

[60] First edition by A. Mingana, *Commentary of Theodore of Mopsuestia on the Lord's Prayer and on the Sacraments of Baptism and the Eucharist* (*Woodbrooke Std.* 6; CbE. 1933) (Syr.-Eng.). We now have as well: R. Tonneau – R. Devreesse, *Les Homélies Catéchétiques de Théodore de Mopsueste. Reproduction phototypique du MS. Mingana syr.* 561 (*ST* 145; Vt. 1949) with a valuable introduction by R. Devreesse. The attached French translation is even more literal than that of Mingana. A literal German translation (only provisional, however, and published against his will) is supplied by O. Heiming in O. Casel's article in *JbLW* 13 (1935) 109–54. The translation of the passages considered in this article was made from the Syrian.

154

marily as follows:[61] "Baptism is, like the Eucharist, the memorial of the death and resurrection of Christ. It is the image of
our death, of our burial, of our resurrection or second birth,
of our introduction to the good things to come. The liturgical
action will . . . bring this out and present it symbolically in the
development of its ceremonies." The interpretation of the words
"memorial" and "figure-sign" is important here. These notions
occupy a central position in Theodore's sacramental theology.
"In every mystery invisible and ineffable things are made
known ("ātā", *i.e.* σημεῖον, σύνθημα, σύμβολον, γνώρισμα)."[62]
Just what importance do this symbol which signifies and this
mystery have? "In baptism a type of new birth is effected; for
you will receive the new birth in reality, as it will then actually
be, when you arise from the dead."[63] Baptism contains the
type of this birth: "as in a sign we take part, through baptism,
in this birth";[64] indeed, as a type baptism is called simply
"second birth".[65]

Then baptism is described also, and in dependence on
Romans 6, as a type of the death and resurrection of Christ.
". . . we are baptized because we wish from now on to have a
share in his death, in the hope that this participation may also
enable us to rise from the dead in the same manner in which
he has risen. Therefore, when I am baptized and immerse my
head, I receive the death of our Lord, of Christ, and I wish to
receive his burial: moreover, I thereby confess truly the resurrec-

---

[61] R. Devreesse, in Theodor. Mops., *Hom. cat.* (ed. Tonneau) XXVIII.
[62] Theodor. Mops., *Hom.* 12, 2 (Tonneau 325).
[63] *Hom.* 14, 2 (Tonneau 405).
[64] *Hom.* 14, 4 (Tonneau 411).
[65] *Hom.* 14, 3 (Tonneau 407).

tion of our Lord. For I think that when I ascend from the water, I have, in a sort of type, already risen."[66]

We have, therefore, a "typos", an image, a sign; that is, not yet the full, entire reality. But on the other hand, the expression means certainly something more than "mere image": "We use not merely empty signs, but realities, which we confess and which we see without doubt."[67] This "sign-reality" is a genuine reality; not yet the final perfection, to be sure, but still a beginning, a foundation, a pledge. "You fulfil the type of this genuine second birth (which, as such, will achieve its full realization only in the resurrection) in such a way that, when you have been elevated by these signs, you are able to participate in the reality which lies behind them."[68] The baptismal type is a symbolic act and presents us thus with a peculiar reality which lies midway between Christ's saving act and its final result for us, which will be achieved only in the resurrection. It makes us partakers in this saving act while still leaving us to hope for the coming fulfilment of this participation.[69]

---

[66] *Hom.* 14, 5 (Tonneau 413).   [67] *Hom.* 14, 6 (Tonneau 413).
[68] *Op. cit.* (Tonneau 415).
[69] These points are very well presented by R. Devreesse in Theodor. Mops., *Hom. cat.* (ed. T. XXVIII: "A cette transformation de l'homme, à ce passage de la vie naturelle à l'état surnaturelle, de la catastase terrestre à l'immortalité, nous sommes acheminés par l'usage des sacrements, qui sont 'l'indication en signes et symboles de choses visibles et ineffables'. Arrêtons-nous un instant à cette définition pour en bien saisir les termes et l'ampleur, et nous aurons d'emblée toute la ligne du développement qui suit, un exemple inattendu, certes, de l'emploi de la 'typologie' par l'auteur que l'on croyait le plus hostile à son usage, ou le moins habile à son maniement. Le sacrement emprunte donc des contingences de la vie de l'humanité, plus strictement encore de l'histoire et des gestes opérés par le Christ, toute la matière des signes requis par son institution; d'autre côté, il contient la figure et les assurances du monde à venir, en même temps que les prémices

A reality of this magnitude, even if it is still a mere beginning, is made possible by the power of the Holy Spirit. Theodore brings out this thought most forcefully in his reference to the blessing of the water.

"You then descend into the water which has been hallowed by the pontiff's blessing. For it is certainly not in ordinary water that you are baptized, but in water of the second birth; because it cannot become what it is save by the advent of the Holy Spirit. The pontiff must first . . . pray God, that the grace of the Holy Spirit may come upon the water, making it capable of regeneration in this sublime birth, and that he may make of it the womb of a sacramental birth. . . ."[70]

In a number of passages it seems as if all effects of this kind are ascribed to the Holy Spirit alone, and that the water-bath is

de l'Esprit-Saint et sa grace; enfin, la liturgie, qui est l'expression visible des signes et des figures, affermit en nous la conviction de leur réalité et l'espoir de leur efficacité." ("We approach this human metamorphosis, this transition from our natural existence to a supernatural state, from the earthly condition to immortality, by use of the sacraments, which are 'the guide, through signs and symbols, to things visible but ineffable'. If we pause for a moment over this definition to grasp fully its terms and scope, we shall have from the outset the complete line of development which follows: an unexpected example, to be sure, of the use of 'typology' by an author whom one would expect to be its strongest opponent and most unskilled in applying it. Thus the sacrament borrows from the contingencies of human life, or more exactly from history and from the acts performed by Christ, all the material for the signs necessary for its institution. On the other hand, it contains the symbol and the pledges of the world to come, as well as the first-fruits of the Holy Spirit and his grace. Finally, the liturgy, which is the visible expression of signs and symbols, confirms us in the conviction of the reality of these signs and symbols and in our hope that they will be effective.") Cf. also W. de Vries, *"Nestorianismus" Theodors* 91–148 and his later work, *Sakramententheologie b. d. Nestorianern,* in which the judgments are, in our opinion, more moderate and better weighed.
[70] *Hom.* 14, 9 (Tonneau 421).

a "mere" sign. The reason for the graces really imparted in baptism is not the "nature of the water" but the "efficacy of the Spirit". Therefore, "the pontiff... uses formulas of consecration and blessing, and prays that the grace of the Holy Spirit may descend upon the water".[71] We must conclude as follows: the "typoi" (dmūtā), the symbolic signs ('ātā), the mysteries ('rāzā), impart, in the power of the Holy Spirit, a genuine participation in the saving act of Christ. This they do in such a manner that they are an earnest of that which will be given in full reality only in the final resurrection.[72] Moreover, Theodore's arguments show that baptism cannot be administered a second time,[73] that God is the real cause and not the priest,[74] and finally, they tell us what the effects of baptism are.[75]

Then there is also a very brief report of the "signing" (signatio). "The pontiff approaches, signs you on the forehead and says: N. is signed in the name of the Father and of the Son and of the Holy Spirit." The text which follows, if considered impartially, makes it appear as certain that according to Theodore the act of baptism is concluded with what we today call confirmation.[76] Despite a few references to an anointing with oil we cannot really be so certain that there was an anointing in connection with the confirmation. Like the other Syrians, Theodore was probably familiar with a preparatory anointing before the baptismal bath.[77] This is a "little beginning of the mystery" and is "the

---

[71] *Hom.* 14, 10 (Tonneau 425).
[72] *Hom.* 14, 12 (Tonneau 427; cf. the indices of the Greek and Syrian words in Tonneau, pp. 609–17).
[73] *Hom.* 14, 13 (Tonneau 429).   [74] *Hom.* 14, 15 (Tonneau 433f.).
[75] *Hom.* 14, 25 (Tonneau 455).   [76] *Hom.* 14, 27 (Tonneau 457f.).
[77] *Hom.* 13, 17 (Tonneau 397), save for an anointing of the whole body with oil which follows at this point: *Hom.* 14, 8 (Tonneau 419).

sign that from now on you are marked as Christ's lamb, as a
soldier of the heavenly king".[78] But in contrast to this express
mention of the oil *before* baptism, the report of the "signatio"
after baptism contains not a word about a rite of anointing;
probably this post-baptismal rite consisted only of the "signing"
(and the laying on of hands). This signing is said to impart the
Holy Spirit – at least in the sense that the Spirit from now on
abides permanently with him who has been so signed. We may
see in this ceremony not merely the sign which announces that
the Spirit has, in a sense, already been given in baptism. The
unusual brevity with which this rite is treated, and the circumstance that Theodore speaks from now on of the "mystery-birth"
which has taken place in baptism as something which is completely finished,[79] and after which the candidate "may approach
the food of immortality", do not entitle us to overlook the value
of "confirmation" in its own right. It is here, of course, as in all
earlier pieces of evidence, combined with water-baptism in a
larger, more comprehensive unity.[80]

In the *Catechetical Homilies* of Theodore of Mosuestia we see
clearly once again what was the great contribution of the

[78] *Hom.* 13, 18 (Tonneau 397 f.): identified with a "mark", an "imprint".
[79] *Hom.* 14, 29 (Tonneau 461).
[80] W. de Vries: *"Nestorianismus" Theodors,* 132–5 and *Sakramententheologie
b. d. Nest.,* 182–9 says quite rightly that there is no anointing here. Still it
seems that he attaches too little importance to the special value of the
"signing" in this place. For instance, he says – formulating his words very
carefully, to be sure: "The rites which we have from the Nestorians cannot
with certainty be interpreted as confirmation" (*Sakramententheol.* 188); or,
"When all is said and done we must probably say that the Nestorians did
not clearly recognize a sacrament of confirmation separate from baptism,
and that there are no rites in use amongst them which would be fully
adapted to the administration of this sacrament" (op. cit. 189).

Patristic theology of the East to the interpretation of baptism. It is the fundamental application and type of Christ's saving word, and in particular of his death and resurrection, which occurred once in Christ, and which will one day happen openly to us. Further, baptism is very specially a work of the Holy Spirit, who in blessing fills the palpable element of water.

Chapter Seven

THE CLOSE OF THE PATRISTIC PERIOD

BIBLIOGRAPHY: P. de Puniet, *Baptême, Études sur les Ordines baptismi* in *DACL* 2, 1 (1910) 251–346; same author, *Apertio aurium, op. cit.* 1, 2 (1907) 2523–37; same author, *Catéchuménat*: *op. cit.* 2, 2 (1910) 2579–631. Th. Spačil, "Doctrina theologiae Orientis separati de sacramento baptismi" in *OrChr* 6 (1926) 181–263. Ph. Oppenheim, *De fontibus et historia ritus baptismalis (Inst. syst.–hist. in s. litg.* II 2, vol. 1; Tn. 1943) with extensive bibliography. A. Dondeyne, "La discipline des scrutins dans l'Église latine avant Charlemagne" in *RevHistE* 28 (1932) 5–33, 751–87.

THE EPOCH in which the theology of baptism reached the highest and richest flowering of its development is without doubt the period of the great Fathers of the fourth and fifth centuries. The central points of the dogma have already been worked out; they have found concrete expression in the liturgy of the sacraments of initiation, which was cast simultaneously in the same essential form that is still the foundation of the present rite. Now that we have reached the late Patristic time, let us see how the sacrament of regeneration is reflected in its entire fulness in basic forms of the fully developed liturgy of baptism and in the testimony of the last great church Fathers.

161

It is, of course, impossible to mention in detail here everything of profit for the history of dogma which is yielded by the development of the various liturgies of baptism. We must content ourselves with the selection and treatment of the baptismal liturgy of those Churches of East and West which are historically most important.

For the East it is the baptismal liturgy of the Greek-Byzantine Church which will form the basis for our consideration. And we shall follow here a ninth century text, which, we can safely assume, reproduces in its essential points a significantly older usage.[1]

After a "Prayer for the Preparation of the Catechumens" with

---

[1] F. C. Conybeare – A. M. Maclean, *Rituale Armenorum* (Ox. 1905) 399–408 gives a first-rate critical edition of the Greek ritual of baptism from the Barberini MS. There is good older edition by J. Goar, *Euchologium sive Rituale Graecorum* (Pa. ²1730) 274–96. The rite in use today, which agrees in its essential characteristics with the above-mentioned older witnesses, is to be found in *Euchologion to mega* (Rm. 1873), the official edition of the Uniate Church, pp. 147–61, and in A. Maltzew, *Die Sakramente der Orthodox-Katholischen Kirche des Morgenlandes* (Bln. 1898) 1–89; L. v. Rudloff, *Taufe und Firmung im Byzantinischen Ritus* (Pb. 1938) gives a translation. – From this point we could feel our way back to the *Didascalia,* the work underlying the first six books of the *Apostolic Constitutions* and its later supplements, especially Book VII (ed. F. X. Funk, *Didascalia et Constit. Ap.*); cf. here B. Altaner, *Patrology* (Ed. Ld. 1960) 47–52, and D. van den Eynde, "Baptême et Confirmation d'après les Constitutions Apostoliques" VII, 44, 3 in *RechScRel* 27 (1937) 196–212. From such a study we discover that the external structure of the baptismal celebration is: catechizing, renunciation, confession of faith, consecration of the oil, anointing with oil, consecration of the water, the act of baptism, consecration with myrrh. (Next to chaps. 39–45 (Funk 440_{12}–52_{10}) it is chiefly chap. 22, 2 (Funk 406_{6-10}) which is important. It helps to clarify the relationship between water-bath and the anointing with myrrh.) Theologically we find the two general themes confirmed which are characteristic of the baptismal teaching of the classical Fathers: implantation in the image of death (VII, 39, also III, 17, 1–3 [Funk 442_{14-22}; 211_{18}ff.]) and consecration of the water in a special consecratory prayer (VII 43 [Funk 448_{14}ff.]).

several exorcisms and the renunciation as well as prayer in litany form, the actual act of baptism begins with the great prayer for the blessing of the water and that for the blessing of the oil. The litany itself says what is expected in baptism: the sanctification of the water by the descent of the Holy Spirit; baptism is understood as illumination. The candidate becomes a son of light, an heir of eternal goods, and is planted in the death and resurrection of Christ. The water is supposed to be for him the bath of regeneration, the forgiveness of sins, and the garment of incorruptibility. The prayer for the blessing of the water asks that God manifest himself over the water, and joins to this similar thoughts about the water's effects, which have already made themselves heard in the litany.[2] There follows the blessing of the oil (τοῦ ἐλαίου). We find here the following words, amongst others: "Bless also this oil by the power and effect and overshadowing of thy holy *pneuma;* may it thus become the unction of incorruptibility, the weapon of righteousness, the renewal of soul and body, and a defence against all the works of the devil . . .".[3] The consecrated oil is used to sign the baptismal water, and then the candidate himself is anointed on several places, and finally on the entire body. Then follows the baptism proper: "N. is baptized in the name of the Father and of the Son and of the Holy Spirit. At each invocation (προσρήσει) the candidate is immersed and raised up again."[4] In this ninth century rite the candidate is then clothed. But in the older texts this is not mentioned at all.

---

[2] *Rit. Armen.* (Conybeare 401); *Euchol.* (Goar 289).

[3] *Rit. Armen.* (Conybeare 402).

[4] *Op. cit.* (Conybeare 404). The rubric must be taken, in accordance with the oldest witnessses, as meaning that the immersion is performed at "each invocation", *i.e.* at the invocation of each of the three divine Persons, or thrice.

Instead, the anointing with myrrh follows the water-bath imme-diately. This is performed with the words: "Seal of the gift of the Holy Spirit."[5] The intimate unity in which, in the consciousness of the Eastern Church, the two actions, water baptism and the anointing with myrrh, were joined is shown by the fact that only now,[6] in conclusion, do we find sung the words: "All you who have been baptized in Christ have put on Christ, alleluia", following which two lessons were read: Rom. 6:3–11 and Matt. 28:16–20. The concluding rubric[7] corresponds to the oldest usage: "The Divine Liturgy is to be celebrated at once."[8]

As far as the baptismal liturgy of the Western Church is con-cerned, the sources – which, it must be admitted, have been pre-served for us more or less by chance – provide information about the form of baptism in the period of the transition from adult to infant baptism. These sources are, essentially, the *Sacramentarium Gelasianum*[9] and the *Ordo Romanus,* which Mabillon reckons to be the seventh and which M. Adrieu more recently described as Ordo XI.[10] In these two books, then, we

---

[5] A number of manuscripts give a special formula for each anointing of the individual senses; cf. *Rit. Armen.* (Conybeare 405a) and A. Dmitrijewski, *Beschreibung der liturg. Handschriften in den Bibliotheken des orthodoxen Orients* (Russian), vol. 2: *Euchologia* (Kiew 1901) 209, 3.

[6] Thus in the manuscript given by J. Goar, *Euchol.* 291.

[7] *Rit. Armen.* (Conybeare 406).

[8] To be sure, the official Roman edition does not have this (*Euchol. to mega* 159); it simply brings the celebration to a conclusion at this point. Several manuscripts given by A. Dmitrijewski, *Beschreibg. litg. Hss.* 3 and L. v. Rudloff, *Tf. u. F.* 39 are different.

[9] Edited by H. A. Wilson, *The Gelasian Sacramentary. Liber Sacramentorum Romanae Ecclesiae* (Ox. 1894).

[10] M. Andrieu, *Les Ordines Romani du haut Moyen Âge*, vol. 1 (*Spicil. S. Lovan.* 11; Lv. 1931) 8; vol. 2: *Les textes* (*op. cit.* 23; 1948) 363–447. M. Andrieu comes to the conclusion that the *Gelasianum* is still familiar with the discipline of holding three examinations of adults on the Sundays

find the oldest form of the baptismal liturgy in the Roman Church which is preserved in the present rite for adult baptism.[11]

It is worthy of note that even here an extended period of solemn preparation for baptism is still customary, which extends from the third Sunday in Lent to Holy Saturday, and which is joined with the rite of "signing", with the administration of salt, with exorcism, catechizing about the faith, etc.[12] During the actual celebration of the Easter Vigil a procession goes to the font. The texts for the blessing of the baptismal water which now follow emphasize almost exclusively the theme of regeneration. The font gives birth to the new people; "the pure maternal womb of the divine font receives sanctification, and thus there arises from this font a heavenly race, regenerate as a new creature". The theme of the passion is heard faintly and just once, in the reference to the fact that Christ "made the water to gush forth together with blood from his wounded side". There is an express direction that the chrism be poured into the baptismal water.[13] The *Sacramentarium Gelasianum* supplies in a completely

in Lent; but that the form of the examination before Palm Sunday which is given in the *Gelasianum* (Wilsin 45–9) is an accomodation to the new usage which had meanwhile been recorded in *Ordo XI* (Andrieu 2, 404f.). This Ordo, which was written in the seventh century or perhaps already in the second half of the sixth century, constitutes an accomodation of the liturgy of baptism to the custom of infant baptism. The old form of examination has been abandoned, and seven assemblies have been made from the previous three. The acts of these assemblies take on primarily a value as sacramental symbols (Andrieu 2, 405). The above-mentioned form of examination in the Gelasianum before Palm Sunday is given by *Ordo XI* in compressed form. For the order of baptism given in *Ordo XI* cf. A. Dondeyne, *La discipline des scrutins* . . . .
[11] With regard to the development of this form into the present rite for the baptism of children cf. Ph. Oppenheim, *De font. et hist. rit.* bapt., 91ff. 103–9.   [12] *Ordo XI* (Andrieu) no. 3–6, 10–28, 38, 39–75, 76–78.
[13] *Op. cit.* no. 94.

archaic manner an extensive description of the usage in connection with the actual act of baptism. The candidate is asked: Do you believe in God the Father . . .? "I believe", etc. "Deinde per singulas vices mergis eum tertio in aqua. Postea cum ascenderit a fonte infans signatur a presbytero in cerebro de chrismate his verbis: Deus omnipotens . . . qui te regeneravit ex aqua . . ."[14] ("Then you immerse him three times in water. When the child has come up from the font he is signed by the presbyter on the forehead with chrism with these words: Almighty God . . . who has regenerated you in water . . ."). It is quite clear that we still have here a description of the threefold immersion, which is carried out with the naming of the divine names, reinforced by the candidate's confession of faith, exactly as reported in what is probably the oldest witness for the Roman usage, the *Apostolic Tradition* of Hippolytus.[15] In the *Gelasianum* there follows immediately: "Deinde ab episcopo datur eis Spiritus septiformis. Ad consignandum imponit eis manum in his verbis: Deus omnipotens . . . qui regenerasti . . . Postea signat eos in fronte de chrismate dicens: Signum Christi in vitam aeternam."[16] ("Then the seven-fold Spirit is given by the bishop. For the signing he lays his hand on them with these words: Almighty God . . . who hast regenerated . . . Afterwards he signs them on the forehead with chrism, saying: The sign of Christ for eternal life.") Thereupon the bishop returns to his throne and intones the Gloria of the mass.[17] In *Ordo* XI the crucial change of place prior to the administration of the "confirmatio" is even more strongly marked: "Pontifex vero egreditur a fonte, habens compositam

---

[14] *Sacr. Gelas.* no. 44 (Wilson 86).
[15] Cf. p. 3f. above.   [16] *Sacr. Gelas.* (Wilson 86f.).
[17] *Op. cit.* (Wilson 87); *Ordo* XI (Andrieu 2, 446₂₁) no. 103.

sedem in ecclesia." ("The bishop now leaves the font, since he has a seat prepared in the church.") He first distributes presents here to the neophytes, who have put on their clothes again. Only after this does the "confirmatio" follow. The rite of the *Ordo* and also its terminology are at this point later than in the *Gelasianum,* which retains its archaic basic form here.[18] Nevertheless the final remark of the Gelasianum is significant: "et hoc omnino praecavendum est ut hoc non neglegatur, quia tunc omne baptismum legitimum christianitatis nomine confirmatur" ("and this is all to be observed and not to be neglected, because every legitimate baptism is confirmed with the name of Christianity"). Thus in the later form as well there remains the consciousness that the two acts, immersion-bath in water and confirmation, belong intimately together.

So the basic structure for the administration of baptism in the most important Churches of the East and West at the close of the Patristic period harmonizes to a very large degree. It is not difficult to see how, in this matter, even in liturgical families of quite different kinds, the same, single fundamental faith has found its appropriate liturgical expression. There is to be found in all these liturgies a careful instruction of the catechumens prior to baptism, a blessing of the elements, first of water, then also of the oil, or of the chrism, as the case may be. And finally we find always, and as the central action, a decidedly simple form of immersion-bath in water. The accompanying prayers show that baptism is understood as the work of God's Spirit, present in virtue of the epiclesis, and that what the Spirit does primarily is to impart new birth. In the liturgies of the East the effects of

[18] Cf. *Ordo XI* (Andrieu 2, 404).

baptism are grounded in the fact that the sacrament is implantation in the death of Christ, and participation in this death, as well as in Christ's burial and resurrection. Even the Roman rite of baptism is not intended to be understood in any other sense, even if the reason for baptism's effects are not always expressed clearly in the liturgical prayers. Of course, one cannot expect that the language of the liturgical prayers will supply directly any theological interpretation of what it means to be implanted. And finally, all these liturgies show clearly that at this time the water-bath of baptism and the anointing with chrism, or the laying on of hands and the "consignatio" (confirmatio) were still, despite a clear differentiation between them, joined together in a total action, and further that this total action is supposed to lead into the celebration of the Eucharist.

What is thus attested by the liturgy is confirmed by the doctrine of those Fathers who stand at the end of the Patristic period. It is true that they are no longer so creative as their predecessors in the fourth and fifth centuries. Their principal merit consists in the fact that they rescued their rich theology of baptism and carried it into the new age which was dawning, with all its tremendous upheavals. In this way they provided the foundations for a later systematic theology.

We must mention here first the theologian who has come down in history under the pseudonym, "Dionysius the Areopagite".[19] He is a witness for the Syrian liturgy of baptism at the

---

[19] Cf. J. Siflmayr, "Die Lehre von den Sakramenten und der Kirche nach Ps.-Dionysius" in *ZKTh* 22 (1898) 146–303, esp. 260–7, 282–91, and 301–3. The passages about baptism and myrrh in Ps.-Dionysius Areopagita are to be found in *De ecclesiastica hierarchia* cap. 2 and 4 (*PG* 3, 392 A – 404 D, 472 D – 485 B).

turn of the fifth and sixth centuries. But he is of incomparably greater importance for the history of dogma in his capacity as a theological interpreter, whose teaching, thanks to his claim to be a disciple of the apostle St. Paul, enjoyed for centuries the highest regard and gained in the Latin West an influence on the development of theology.

Pseudo-Dionysius builds right into his system the "mystery of illumination" (μ. φωτίσματος). The acts of consecration serve the "conformation to and union with God"[20]. This is achieved by "acts of love" and "cult acts". At the beginning is the act which "forms the attitude of our souls to complete reception of the other sacred words and sacred acts, the preparation of the way for our ascent into the peace of heaven above, the giving of our sacred and divine regeneration". The whole is "the unutterable effecting of our divine state of being (ἡ τοῦ εἶναι θείως ἡμας ἀρρητοτάτη δημιουργία)"[21] God himself has come down to us, "in order to conform to himself that which is united to him as in fire, according as this serves to make what is united divine. For he gave them power to become the children of God".[22] Prayers, questions, confession of guilt, exhortation, laying on of hands and sealing with the sign of the cross initiate the newcomer. After disrobing he renounces Satan, facing west. Facing east, he pledges himself to Christ. After renewed acts of confession and getting completely undressed and receiving the laying on of hands, the entire body is anointed with oil. At the font, the μήτηρ τῆς υἱοθεσίας (the mother of adoption), the prelate blesses the water by epiclesis and by pouring myrrh three times in the form of a cross. Then

---

[20] *De eccl. hier.* 2, 1 (*PG* 3, 392 A).
[21] *Op. cit.* (*PG* 3, 392 B).   [22] *Op. cit.* 2, 2 § 1 (*PG* 3, 393 A).

he immerses the candidate thrice, invoking the three divine Persons as he does so.[23] After he has put on his clothes the candidate is finally signed with consecrated myrrh by the prelate, is sealed (σφραγισάμενος) and is thus made capable of participation in the Eucharist.

Pseudo-Dionysius supplements this presentation of the rite as the "mystery of illumination" by theological considerations. "The sensible holy acts are images of spiritual things (ἀπεικονίσματα τῶν νοητῶν), the accompaniment and way thereto. But the spiritual things are the beginning and the (foundation for the) understanding of the sensible holy acts."[24] In this sense every single act has its mystagogic meaning. Each act constitutes a sacred reality which at the same time points to something higher; and these acts demand a corresponding manner of life for the future.[25] Having been summoned to moral battle, he who has been perfected follows "the divine path through the goodness of him who is the first amongst the fighters and powers. For through baptism he dies in this way with Christ, mystically speaking, to sin".[26] The three-fold immersion in water is an imitation (μιμεῖσθαι) of the "thearchic" death of Jesus, the giver of life, and of his three-days' rest in the grave, "as far as this divine imitation is attainable for men".[27]

The picture of Christian initiation thus painted corresponds completely with tradition, even if the language used, due to its neo-Platonizing, philosophizing colouring and its overloaded, clumsy diction, strikes us as peculiar. The formu-

---

[23] *Op. cit.* 2, 2 § 7 (*PG* 3, 401).   [24] *Op. cit.*, 2, 3 § 2 (*PG* 3, 397 C).
[25] *Op. cit.* Cf. esp. *loc. cit.* § 5 (*PG* 3, 401).
[26] *Loc. cit.* § 6 (*PG* 3, 104 A).
[27] *Loc. cit.* § 7; cf. 4, 3 § 10 (*PG* 4, 404 B; 484 B).

170

lations to be found in pseudo-Dionysius have actually been used previously, even if less explicitly – by Origen and by Augustine, for instance – to interpret the peculiar middle position of the act of baptism between the saving act of Christ and the salvation of the individual Christian. Dionysius is by no means new or creative. But the system in which he brings forth such doctrines, and the authority which was ascribed to him, certainly had their consequences for the further development of doctrine.

It is also noteworthy how closely the link still is in pseudo-Dionysius between what we would nowadays call confirmation and baptism. Within the framework of his system the pseudo-Areopagite has no chapter for "confirmation" on its own, but merely one for the "consecration of the myrrh" (μύρου τελετή).[28] This act of consecration,[29] "the sacrament of myrrh, is surrounded on the whole with just as rich a wreath of symbols, gradations, and sacred words as the Eucharist".[30] The emphasis which other church Fathers, such as Gregory of Nyssa, have already on the filling of the element with sanctifying power, is magnified here to such a degree that the consecration of the myrrh assumes a place, as the sacrament of myrrh, alongside that of the Eucharist as the sacrament of the body and blood of Christ. The myrrh is considered to be the antitype of that oil with which Christ was anointed in his human nature.[31] Even if this interpretation does lie in the

---

[28] Complete title (*PG* 3, 472 C): περὶ τῶν ἐν τῷ μύρῳ τελομένων καὶ τῶν ἐν αὐτῷ τελειουμένων.

[29] *Op. cit.* (*PG* 3, 472 D, 476 C): ἱερουργία, τελετουργία or τελεσουργία.

[30] J. Siglmayr, *Lehre v. d. Sakr.*, 285.

[31] Cf. *PG* 3, 484 C and the parallel with Cyril of Jerusalem, *Cat.* 21, 3 (*PG* 33, 1092 A). Cyril does not force this view as violently as pseudo-Dionysius.

general line of theological development, it cannot be found anywhere else in such systematically exaggerated form. The myrrh, which has already a transcending importance in its own right, and which is, as such, made the subject of an entire chapter, now becomes necessary as the "divinely efficacious" basis[32] of all sacred consecration, as for instance the consecration of the baptismal water and the τελειωτικὴ χρῖσις, the anointing of the candidate which concludes the baptismal act itself. This anointing is the "completion of the divine birth, and (it) unites him whom it completes with the divine *pneuma*".[33] But it is not only in the sealing unction of confirmation that the pseudo-Dionysius sees the myrrh as constituting the completion and seal of regeneration. In another passage he ascribes the identical effect to the pouring of the myrrh into the baptismal water as well.[34] And it is on the basis of this mixture of the baptismal water that he sees in both the actual baptism itself as well as in the anointing with myrrh which follows it an imparting of the Spirit. Furthermore, pseudo-Dionysius mentions also the fact that myrrh is necessary for the consecration of an altar, making it thus the point of departure for all further sanctification which is given to the Christian.[35]

The evidence of St. John Damascene (died 749) is of quite another kind. He was, in a certain sense, "the first and at any rate the last great dogmatic theologian of the Greek Church".[36]

---

[32] *De eccl. hier.* 2, 2 § 7 (*PG* 3, 396 D): θεουργικώτατον.
[33] *Op. cit.* 2, 3 § 8 (*PG* 3, 404 CD).
[34] *Op. cit.* 4, 3 § 10f. (*PG* 3, 484 BC).
[35] *Loc. cit.* § 12 (*PG* 3, 484 C – 485 B). Cf. J. Stiglmayr, *Lehre v. d. Sakr.,* 290f.
[36] G. Rauschen – J. Wittig, *Grundriß der Patrologie* (FbB. ⁹1926) 455; his tractate *De fide orthodoxa* (Part III of the πηγὴ γνώσεως) "became during

This not because he achieved anything great or systematic on his own – he was in many respects a compiler, as he himself admits.[37] But he had a flair for summarizing succinctly the teaching of earlier Fathers, so that posterity, even in the Latin West, evaluated his work highly.

His discussion of baptism[38] contains nothing essentially new. But it does stress strongly baptism's relationship to the death of Christ so that everything else is derived from this relationship. " . . . baptism makes the Lord's death manifest ($\delta\eta\lambda o\tilde{\iota}$). It is through baptism that we have been buried with the Lord." From the uniqueness of Christ's death John concludes that baptism cannot be repeated. But when someone "has not been baptized in the holy triplicity" he must be "re-baptized". The Apostle's words in Rom. 6:3–4 do not justify baptism merely in the name of Christ. The passage means simply that baptism is the type of Christ's death. "In its three immersions baptism signifies the Lord's three days' rest in the grave."[39]

the Middle Ages the classical textbook of dogmatics for the Greek and Slavic Orthodox Churches – and has remained in use to some extent up until modern times" (B. Altaner, *Patrologie* [²1950] 474). For the subsequent influence of this work see M. Grabmann, *Die Geschichte der scholastischen Methode,* vol. 1 (FbB, 1909) 108–13, and P. Minges, "Zum Gebrauch der Schrift De fide orthodoxe des Johannes Damascenus in der Scholastik" in *ThQ* 96 (1914) 225–47. How frequently St. Thomas Aquinas makes use of this chapter of John Damascene can be seen if one looks in the index of quotations in, for instance, the *Deutsche Thomas-Ausgabe,* vol. 29 (1935) 568.

[37] Johannes Damasc., *Fons scientiae,* prolog. (*PG* 94, 524 C – 525 A).
[38] Baptism is treated by John Damascene in *De fide orthodoxa* chap. 82 (= lb. IV c. 9 according to the Western tradition) under the title: "Of faith and baptism" (ed. E. M. Buytaert, *Saint John Damascene: De fide orthodoxa. Versions of Burgundio and Cerbanus,* Franciscan Institute Publications, Text Series no. 8; St. Bonaventura N. Y. 1955) 292–8; *PG* 94, 1117–25.   [39] *Op. cit.* (Buyt. 293$_{19}$f.; *PG* 94, 1117 B – 1120 A).

The passion of him who became incarnate, and in particular Christ's pierced side, is the source from whence the water of baptism and the blood of the eucharist proceed. The command to baptize was conditioned by consideration of man's physical and spiritual nature, for which baptism was supposed to signify "cleansing by water and the Spirit". In this connection the water was to constitute the image of death, while the Spirit was to give the pledge of life.[40] The meaning of the baptismal water is illustrated by references to water miracles in the Old Testament, where water also served as a means of cleansing: "for the visible is the symbol of the invisible (τῶν νοουμένων)".[41] Baptism takes place in the name of the Holy Trinity, "because the candidate needs the Holy Trinity for his foundation and preservation".[42] John sums up the effect of baptism in these words: "Through baptism we receive the gift of the Spirit's firstfruits, and regeneration becomes for us the beginning of another life, a *sphragis,* a (shield of) defence, and illumination."[43] From these gifts there grows up the obligation to strive to keep one's self in the future "from falling again into sin's slavery".

John of Damascus places baptism within a quite broad redemptive framework. He has eight different baptisms: the Flood, the "Red Sea", the cloud (in the wilderness), the cleansing ablutions of the Law, John's baptism of repentance, the Lord's baptism in Jordan, the hard baptism of penance and tears of contrition, the blood-baptism of martyrdom, and the

[40] *Op. cit.* (Buyt. 294₄₃f.; *PG* 94, 1121 A).
[41] *Op. cit.* (Buyt. 294₅₁f.; *PG* 94, 1121 B).
[42] *Op. cit.* (Buyt. 295₆₅ff.; *PG* 94, 1121 D).
[43] *Op. cit.* (Buyt. 295₅₇ff.; *PG* 94, 1121 C).

punitive "baptism" of hellfire.[44] Thus we have here, presented side by side, typical prototypes, the actual type, namely Christ's baptism in Jordan, the possible New Testament substitute forms of baptism, and finally the baptism of hell which is actually no baptism at all. There is no mention of Christian baptism itself as a variety in its own right. It is just the fulfilment of all prototypes and the highest form of related kinds of baptism that are possible even today. There is an especially impressive reference to Christian baptism in the explanation of the baptism in Jordan: the Lord was not baptized because he had any need of baptism, but "in order to crush the heads of the dragons in the water, in order to shut up sin and to bury the whole old Adam in the water, . . . to serve as type and image of our own baptism".[45] Christian baptism is a baptism "by water and the Spirit". If Christ baptizes "with fire" that is because he has given his apostles the grace of the Spirit in the form of firey tongues.

He tells us very little of the anointing with oil. The oil "is added to baptism because it demonstrates (μηνύον) our anointing and makes us χριστούς, anointed ones, and proclaims to us the mercy of God through the Holy Spirit".[46] It is true that he attributes here an independent efficacy to the anointing with oil. But on the other hand this anointing appears combined in the strongest way with the water-bath to a total action, to the one "regeneration", without there being any clear final separation of the Spirit's efficacy in the water-bath and the anointing with oil.

[44] *Op. cit.* (Buyt. 295$_{69}$–297$_{95}$; *PG* 94, 1124 A–D).
[45] *Op. cit.* (Buyt. 296$_{77-83}$; *PG* 94, 1124 B).
[46] *Op. cit.* (Buyt. 297$_{102}$–298$_{105}$; *PG* 94, 1125 B).

If we look for witnesses for the baptismal theology of the West at the end of the Patristic period we must turn first of all to the towering figure of Gregory the Great. Of course, we cannot expect any scholarly presentation from him; his strength lies in the practical cure of souls, and it is only from this standpoint, when the concrete pastoral case makes it expedient, that he comes to speak of baptism. Thus he does so not systematically, but merely occasionally, in his letters and in his exegetical writings.

The Church's baptism stands in the framework of other "baptisms": its Old Testament prototype and counterpart were mere faith, or the power in which a sacrifice was offered, or, finally, the circumcision as well.[47] The immediate predecessor of the Church's baptism was that of the Baptist, which was, however, not capable of taking away sin. Christian baptism must be followed by the baptism of the conscience with tears of contrition.[48]

The baptism commanded by Christ is unconditionally necessary for salvation. The harshness with which Gregory applies this doctrine to the fate of children who die unbaptized occasioned a number of people to reckon him as among the "tortores infantium". In order that children may not be deprived of salvation Gregory warns against waiting for the solemn administration of baptism, in case of danger, and admonishes that the mother and her newborn child be baptized at once.[49]

With regard to heretic baptism Gregory represents the Latin

[47] Gregorius M., *Moralium* lib. IV, 3 (*PL* 75, 635 B).
[48] *Hom. in Evgl.* 7, 3; 10, 7 (*PG* 76, 1101 A, 114 B).
[49] *Moral.* IX, 21 (*PL* 75, 876 D – 877 A); *Registrum Epist.* XI, 64, 10 (*PL* 77, 1194 AB).

practice completely. Heretics who have been baptized in the name of the Trinity are received again into the Church by anointing with chrism or the laying on of hands or by the mere confession of faith. Only those to whom this condition does not apply – Gregory reckons the Bonosians and the Kataphrygians as belonging to this number – must be "re-baptized"; and Gregory is aware that this mode of expression is actually incorrect. In cases of doubt baptisms, confirmations, as well as consecrations of churches are to be "repeated".[50]

In accordance with the practice of his Church Gregory maintains the threefold immersion, but he has also nothing against baptism with a single immersion. He mentions reasons of a symbolical nature for both usages: the first form symbolizes the three days' rest in the grave and can also be thought of as a veneration of the Trinity; the second form is also justified, since the Trinity is, of course, at the same time in unity.[51] Thus he recognizes here for the traditional usage practically only a pure "symbol" value. The primary time for baptism is the great feast of Easter. But where it would cause difficulties to wait until this time, a forty-day period of penance and abstinence is to be arranged, and then baptism is to be administered on a Lord's Day or on another great festival.[52]

In connection with adult baptism Gregory presses strongly for previous repentance and change of life, which, however, are not to be taught the candidates "by force" but rather "by goodness (and the persuasive strength) of the preaching"[53].

[50] *Reg. Epist.* XI, 67; XIV, 17 (*PL* 77, 1205 B – 1207 A, 1325 D).
[51] *Op. cit.* I, 43 (*PL* 77, 497 C – 498 A).
[52] *Op. cit.* VIII, 23 (*PL* 77, 925 A).
[53] *Op. cit.* I, 47 (*PL* 77, 510 AB); *Regulae pastor.* lb. III, 30 (*PL* 77, 112 AB).

Baptism wipes out all past sins, similarly to the manner in which in the typical prototype, the passage through the Red Sea, all the enemies of the people of God were destroyed.[54] But just as new enemies arose for the people in the wilderness, so new difficulties will arise in the life of the baptized; and on this account he should remain mindful of his baptismal vow.[55]

Gregory's accounts of confirmation are even scantier. It is nevertheless possible to ascertain that he considers confirmation to be an action separate from baptism and to possess an independent value. He gives it equivalent rank along with baptism and the consecration of a church in issuing a decree that, when there is doubt about the validity of a "baptism or confirmation or the consecration of a church", the "faithful are to be baptized and confirmed and the churches are to be canonically consecrated".[56] Bishops are the only really proper ministers of confirmation. But in case of necessity ordinary priests also receive authority to anoint the baptized on the forehead with chrism.[57]

The testimony of Isidore of Seville (died 636) with regard to the doctrine of baptism is of a different order from that of Gregory the Great. Whereas Gregory offers only casual remarks about baptism, occasioned merely by the immediate pastoral situation, Isidore when dealing with the ecclesiastical states in his encyclopaedic work, includes a short but still quite significant and systematic chapter on baptism. Its material is taken from the Fathers of the early period.[58]

[54] *Reg. Epist.* XI, 45 (*PL* 77, 1162 BC).
[55] *Hom. in Evgl.* 29, 3 (*PL* 76, 1215 A).
[56] *Reg. Epist.* XIV, 17 (*PL* 77, 1325 D).
[57] *Op. cit.* IV, 26 *PL* 77, 696 B).
[58] Isidor. Hispal., *De ecclesiasticis officiis*, lib. II: *De origine ministrorum* (*PL* 83, 777 D – 826 B). On Isidore's significance and later influence cf. B. Al-

First of all Isidore speaks (from chapter 21 on) about the "order of those who are coming to the faith", that is about the catechumens, the "competentes", the baptized. Chapter 25 is dedicated to baptism itself. Baptism is seen first of all against the background of its Old Testament preparation, and is then divided into water-baptism, which is the actual bath of regeneration, blood-baptism, and the baptism of repentance. The water of baptism proper flowed forth from the side of Christ on the cross. "Therefore we who are baptized in Christ are made regenerate in him, that as men who have been purified we may be made alive."[59] Baptism's gifts of salvation possess their foundation in the three divine Persons (*De eccl. off.* II 25, 4); therefore it is essential that the trinitarian formulary be complete. Children dying unbaptized remain excluded from Christ's kingdom; but the baptism of infants is possible because others can make the confession of faith for them (II 25, 7). The fact that baptism cannot be repeated is illustrated by a nice reference to the uniqueness of Christ's death; "In his image (in cuius imaginem) we are immersed through the mystery of the sacred font, so that, dying to this world, we may be buried with Christ and may emerge from the same water in the image of the resurrection (in forma resurrectionis)" (II 25, 6). Isidore's judgment as to the validity of baptism which is administered by heretics or by men of bad morals is completely in line with the ecclesiastical tradition. The proper minister is the priest, but in case of necessity it can be a deacon or layman.

---

taner, *Patrology* (1960) 550, 594, and J. R. Geiselmann, *Die Abendmahlslehre an der Wende der christlichen Spätantike zum Frühmittelalter. Isidor v. Sevilla und das Sakrament der Eucharistie* (Mch. 1933) 1–4, 230 ff.

[59] *De eccl. off.* II, 25, 3 (*PL* 83, 821 A).

Following the doctrine of baptism comes, in chapter 26, *De chrismate,* and in chapter 27 *De manuum impositione vel confirmatione.* Despite their brevity these two chapters are important because they show how clearly the double action of anointing and laying on of hands is viewed as an independent rite of importance, to be distinguished from the act of baptism. Two chapters are devoted to the act of confirmation, since in chapter 26 the symbolic meaning of the chrism is explained not merely for the realm of confirmation but also for its further use as well. In chapters 25 through 27 are to be seen already the basic lines of the future tractate about baptism and confirmation[60].

[60] A fellow countryman of Isidore, St. Ildefons of Toledo (died 669), has given, in quite similar fashion, a brief preview of the medieval tractate on baptism: *Adnotationes de cognitione baptismi.* He also desires to offer nothing of his own, but merely the words of the Father (*PL* 96, 112 B). All the same it is remarkable how in the relatively broad description of the miraculous properties of the baptismal font (chaps. 105–7, *PL* 96, 150 D – 156 D) the baptismal water is assessed in an exaggerated form. Cf. also P. Glaue, *Zur Geschichte der Taufe in Spanien: I. Isidor v. Sevilla, Ildefons v. Toledo und Justinian v. Valencia* – "Über die Taufe" *in SBHeidelbAk* Phil.–hist. Kl. (1913) no. 10; *II. Nachrichten über die Taufsitten bis* 711: *Konzilsbestimmungen und Schriftsteller-Zeugnisse: op. cit.* (1927) no. 2.

Chapter Eight

THE DOCTRINE OF BAPTISM AND CONFIRMATION
IN THE CAROLINGIAN PERIOD
AND IN EARLY SCHOLASTICISM

BIBLIOGRAPHY: J. Bellamy, "Baptême dans l'Église latine depuis le VIIIᵉ siècle" in *DThC* 2, 1 (³1923) 250–96. F. Brommer, *Die Lehre vom sakramentalen Charakter in der Scholastik bis Thomas von Aquin inklusive (Forsch. z. chr. Lit. u. Dogmengesch.* 8/2; Pb. 1908). J. Kürzinger, *Zur Deutung der Johannestaufe in der mittelalterlichen Theologie (Aus der Geisteswelt des Mittelalters,* vol. 2; Mst. 1935) 954–73. A. Landgraf, "Kindertaufe und Glaube in der Frühscholastik" in *Greg* 9 (1928) 512–29. H. Weisweiler, *Die Wirksamkeit der Sakramente nach Hugo von St. Viktor* (FbB. 1932). L. Ott, *Untersuchungen zur theologischen Briefliteratur der Frühscholastik unter besonderer Berücksichtigung des Viktorinerkreises (Beitrag z. Gesch. d. Phil. u. Theol. MA.* 34; Mst. 1937). K.F. Lynch, *The Sacrament of Confirmation in the Early-Middle Scholastic Period* (vol. 1, Lv. 1957).

A CERTAIN impression of the ideas current in the Carolingian period on the subject of the sacraments of Christian initiation can be gained from the answers to the questionnaire concerning the significance of the individual actions in the baptismal liturgy which Charlemagne sent out to the bishops and theologians of his realm.[1] Certainly we should not expect to find any profound

---

[1] *PL* 99, 892 A–D; the references (in the *Patrologia Latina*) for the answers that are preserved are given briefly by Ph. Oppenheim, *De font. et hist. rit. bapt.,* 13.

theology here. But still, the answers of men like Alcuin, Theo-dolph of Orléans, Amalar of Trier, and Leidred of Lyons do show how the outlines of the future tractate on baptism were slowly becoming more distinct, with the help of collected Patristic testimony, in a process similar to that which we have already observed in the cases of Isidore of Seville and Ildefons of Toledo. The relationship of faith to baptism is being discussed;[2] there are lists of the various kinds of baptism, but with the assertion that there is always but "one faith, one baptism";[3] for, after all, baptism is nothing but an "image of Christ's death and burial" according to Romans 6. The threefold immersion is being inter-preted, with an appeal to Gregory the Great (*Reg. epist.* I, 43), as signifying Christ's three days' rest in the grave; but at the same time it is emphasized that the crucial point is the "invocation of the Trinity". Worthy of note in this connection is the answer of Theodolph of Orléans, who devotes an entire chapter to the "sacrament of baptism", that is, to the actual act of baptism itself: "Thus we die to sin when we renounce the devil . . . ; we are buried with Christ when, with the invocation of the Holy Trinity and the threefold immersion in the font, we descend as into a grave; we rise with Christ when, freed from all sins, we come up from the font as from a grave."[4] Equally matter-of-fact is Theodolph's presentation of the traditional teaching that the descent of the Spirit imparts healing powers to the water: "For

[2] Leidradus, *De sacramento baptismi,* 5 (*PL* 99, 860 C): "sine ista fide si quis ad baptismum accedit, ipse contra se ianuam indulgentiae claudit" ("if anyone approaches baptism without this faith, he closes the doors of forgiveness upon himself"). Cf. also *op. cit.* chap. 10: De infantibus vel his qui pro se respondere non possunt (*PL* 99, 868 A–C).

[3] *Op. cit.* chap. 6 (*PL* 99, 962 B–D).

[4] Theodulph. Aurelian., *De ordine baptismi,* 13 (*PL* 105, 232 D).

through this visible element that invisible reality (res) is represented in an image, so that, as the body is outwardly cleansed by water, the soul may be secretly purified by the Holy Spirit in the power of this mystery."[5]

There is a clear distinction made between the anointing with chrism after baptism and the bishop's anointing on the forehead at the laying on of hands. In answer to the question as to the difference between the various activities of the Holy Spirit which these anointings suggest, Leidrad of Lyons says: "We must know that the Holy Spirit is given in many ways, not only in baptism, but also after baptism."[6]

Even these few pieces of evidence show how in the early Middle Ages a quite simple theology of baptism is being built up, which, thanks to the fact that it is closely linked with the doctrine of the Fathers, displays a certain uniformity. This process of development becomes clearer in connection with the flowering of scholarship which characterized early Scholasticism, in the period, that is, following the close of the eleventh century. Some idea of the liveliness of this process is afforded by the corpus of theological letters which is so important for this period.[7]

The old questions, handed down by the Fathers, have turned into problems once again. Thus, for instance, there is the question of the efficacy of baptism, mentioned in the letter of Walter of Mortagne (died before 1144) to the monk Wilhelm;[8] or the question as to the proper time for the beginning of the baptismal obligation and the problem of how far water baptism

---

[5] *Loc. cit.* (*PL* 105, 232 A).
[6] Leidradus, *De sacr. bapt.,* 7 (*PL* 99, 864 D).
[7] Cf. L. Ott. *Untersuchgn. z. theol. Brieflit.*
[8] *Op. cit.* 146 ff.

can be replaced by the desire for it, both mentioned in the letters of Bernard of Clairvaux to Hugh of St. Victor.[9] A letter of Theoduin of Liége[10] raises the question of infant baptism. And other similar material may be found elsewhere. L. Ott uses this material in order to build up a commendable picture of the views of other contemporary authors, as, for instance, the school of Anselm of Laon, Abelard, Hugh of St. Victor and his circle, Master Simon and others.[11] We must limit our consideration of this period essentially to Hugh of St. Victor.

His principal theological work, *De sacramentis christianae fidei*,[12] constitutes what is actually one of the first major attempts to interpret baptism within the larger framework of systematic theology. He raises the question of baptism's essence (lb. II, pars 6, c. 2), of the place (c. 3) and the time (c. 4) of its institution, of its relationship to the circumcision (c. 5), of the time when the baptismal obligation becomes binding *(loc. cit.)*, of the difference between Christian baptism and that of John (c. 6), of its necessity for salvation (c. 7), of the mystic meaning of the individual rites (c. 8–12), of re-baptism (c. 13), of the necessity of water for baptism (c. 14), and finally, with the help of Old Testament prototypes, the question of baptism's form. Following this (pars 7), he treats confirmation in six short chapters. In answer to the question as to which of the two sacraments has precedence, he writes (c. 4): "Both are great . . . , and both are so joined in respect to the effecting of salvation that, except in the case where delay would entail danger of death, they may under no circumstances be separated." Thus even here, where,

---

[9] *Op. cit.* 499 ff.   [10] *Op. cit.* 12.   [11] *Op. cit.* 156–61.
[12] *Lib.* II pars 6 (*LP* 176, 441 D – 460 C).

because of the systematic treatment, the two sacraments must be discussed separately, they remain joined in the closest way, in accordance with their liturgical performance.

He testifies to the threefold immersion with the naming of the three divine Persons, in accordance with Matthew 28, and relates these actions to faith in the threefold God and to our "being buried with Christ in his three days' death" (c. 11). But he is familiar also with a parallel moral interpretation: "Trina immersio est trina cogitationis, locutionis et operationis emundatio" ("The threefold immersion is a threefold cleansing of thought, word, and deed"). After administration of the "sacramenta baptismi" the forehead is anointed with chrism, which Hugh interprets as meaning "that he (the baptismal candidate) is, by participation in the Spirit of Christ, properly called a Christian from now on, after he has become a fellow heir of the kingdom and of the glory through this sacred anointing" (c. 11).[13]

Hugh's definition of the essence of baptism places the *causa materialis* in the foreground: "Baptismus est aqua diluendis criminibus sanctificata per Verbum Dei" ("Baptism is water sanctified by the Word of God for blotting out sins").[14] This definition gives at first the appearance of a static understanding of the sacrament, rooted in the matter. But the arguments which follow show that Hugh, going back to the Augustinian distinction between "elementum" and "verbum", is developing a very dynamic conception: it is only in the act of washing in order to

---

[13] (*PL* 176, 457 D). It is clear that this anointing is still a part of baptism; the "confirmatio", "in which the Christian is sealed by means of the anointing with chrism, through laying on of hands on the forehead" (*PL* 176, 460 D), is treated separately in the following seventh part (*op. cit.* 459 D – 462 C).   [14] *Op. cit.* II, 6, 2 (*PL* 176, 443 B).

blot out guilt that the water can be sanctified by the "verbum" which accompanies the action, namely the baptismal form. This form imparts to the water, in addition to its natural power as a symbol of cleansing, the potency to transmit grace. We find very strong expressions, which emphasize inordinately, as St. Thomas Aquinas later states critically,[15] the efficacy of the element of water (after it has been filled with divine power) – for example: "Elementum . . . ex sanctificatione contineat gratiam" ("May the element contain . . . grace for sanctification"). Hugh conceives of the sacrament's signification and efficacy as being almost identical: the greater a sacrament's symbolical power, the greater is its efficacy. Compared with the things which led up to baptism, the payment of tithes, sacrifices of the "lex naturalis", and the circumcision of the "lex scripta", baptism itself possesses an incomparably greater signification and correspondingly greater efficacy for the purging of sins. As a water-bath it embraces the entire man, not merely one of his members or merely his outward possessions.

Behind the efficacy of the external sacrament for salvation stands not the merit of the minister, but the "power of the sanctifying God".[16] The sacrament "does not belong to him by whom or through whom it is administered, but to him in whose name we have received it".[17] The symbolism alone indicates that it is primarily Christ's passion which sanctifies baptism.[18]

In Hugh's thought the notions "sacramentum – res sacramenti", which he takes over from Augustine, have achieved

[15] Thomas Aqu. *Summa theol*. III, q. 66 a. 1 cp. and ad 2.
[16] Hugo de St. V., *De sacram*. II, 6, 11 (*PL* 176, 457 D).
[17] *Op. cit*. II, 6, 13 (*PL* 176, 458 D). Cf. here L. Ott, *Untersuchgn. z. theol. Brieflit.*, 158.   [18] Hugh de St. V., *De sacram*. II, 6, 3 (*PL* 176, 448 C).

already what might be called a technical meaning, as for instance, when he says that in the baptism of John the sacrament alone was administered in the immersion, but that in the baptism of Christ there is added to this the "res", the inner reality of the sacrament as well. "Thus the sacrament was in both cases identical, as far as the external form is concerned; but with regard to the effect, it was not the same, since in the first case there was the 'sacramentum solum', since there was no forgiveness of sins. But in the second case the (external) form of the sacrament (sacramenti forma) is produced, and at the same time the (inner) power (virtus sacramenti) is given with it for the forgiveness of sins."[19] It remained, however, for the *Summa Sententiarum*,[20] written in dependence upon Hugh, to work out fully these Augustinian themes by distinguishing between the mere (external) sacrament, the sacrament which is filled with inner reality (sacramentum et res), and the inner reality alone apart from the sacrament.

Once the discussion had reached this stage, a whole series of questions, with which the theologians of the time were very much concerned, was opened up dealing with the relationship between the objective efficacy of the sacrament (which was assured from tradition) and man's subjective co-operation. In complete allegiance to Augustine the theologians were not willing to renounce the crucial importance of faith. This led at first, to the difficulties regarding the baptism of children who were minors.

---

[19] *Op. cit.* II, 6, 6 (*PL* 176, 451 D).
[20] *Summa Sententiarum* Tract. V, 5 (*PL* 176, 130 C – 133 A). On the *Summa Sent.* in general see A. M. Landgraf, *Einführung in die Geschichte der theologischen Literatur der Frühscholastik* (Rgb. 1948) 75f.; the most important of the more recent literature on this subject is also to be found there.

A solution was attempted by means of the Augustinian thesis, that the faith of the sponsors constituted the way in which the faith of the Church came in to represent the children, until such time as they could supply the faith themselves. But it is only the "recognition of 'infused virtue' which led to a clarification. The presence of faith in infant baptism is produced by the infusion of the virtue of faith which takes place in baptism."[21] We meet the same problem seen from the opposite side in the question whether baptism can be replaced by the desire for it. Bernard of Clairvaux treats this problem extensively in a letter to Hugh of St. Victor.[22] The theologians of this period generally consider that martyrdom, the so-called baptism of blood, is a valid substitue for baptism with water. But it remained disputed "whether the faith which is bound up with the desire for the sacrament, the *votum sacramenti,* can substitute for the sacrament".[23] Chief amongst those who answered this question negatively was Abelard.[24] Hugh, on the other hand, and Bernard with him, tried hard "to ground the baptism of desire in scripture and in tradition (primarily in Augustine)".[25] It is, furthermore, the *Summa Sententiarum* which broadens the material used by Hugh to substantiate his arguments and which also takes up a number of contrary opinions from the Fathers.[26] The relationship be-

---

[21] A. Landgraf, *Kindertaufe,* 453; cf. also L. Ott, *Untersuchgn. z. theol. Brieflit.,* 152.

[22] Bernardus abb. Claraevall., *Ep.* 77 *seu Tract. de baptismo aliisque quaest. ad Hugonem de S. Vitore* (opusc. 10) (*PL* 182, 1031 A – 1046 A); cf. here L. Ott, *Untersuchgn. z. theol. Brieflit.,* 5–7–27.   [23] L. Ott, *op. cit.* 510.

[24] Petrus Abaelardus, *Sic et non* 106 (*PL* 178, 1495 C – 1501 A); cf. also c. 107–14 (*PL* 178, 1501 A – 1513 B). See here L. Ott, *op. cit.* 511.

[25] Hugh de S. V., *De sacram.* II, 6, 7 (*PL* 176, 452 A – 454 C); cf. L. Ott, *op. cit.* 515.

[26] *Summa Sent.* tract. V, B (*PL* 176, 131 C – 132 C); cf. L. Ott, *op. cit.* 516f.

tween faith and baptism, as Hugh sees it, leads him to the conclusion that baptism can be a valid sacrament only when the minister is inwardly committed to the confession of trinitarian faith, which is proclaimed outwardly in the baptismal rite. The exterior integrity of the baptismal formula can be spoiled by human insufficiency; but with the interior faith of the minister the sacrament remains valid. Thus Hugh's view stands in a certain opposition to the fundamental principle of post-tridentine theology, which makes the correct sign of crucial importance, and in case of necessity demands from the minister merely the intention of doing what the Church does, in order to safeguard the validity of the sacrament as far as possible against dependence upon the interior state of the minister, which cannot be properly ascertained. The position which he takes on this question determines his view of heretic baptism as well. He knows of but one condition: the correct trinitarian faith of the minister. Therefore in the case of a heretic who returns to the Church he is opposed to a repetition of baptism, and speaks only of a laying on of hands for the imparting of the Spirit.

The baptismal teaching of Peter Lombard (died 1146) is not as independent as that of Hugh. He depends very much upon the *Summa Sententiarum*. He is important nevertheless, since the division of material in his work on the Sentences was to be authoritative for the period following: he became the Master *par excellence*. His work was the basis for the commentaries of the great masters of High Scholasticism.[27]

[27] On the numerous textual editions of the Magister Sententiarum cf. A. M. Landgraf, *Einf. in die Gesch. d. theol. Lit. d. Frühschol.;* the best edition is that of the large Bonaventura edition, vol. 4 (Quaracchi 1889). The chapter divisions in this edition have been adopted in the quotations

Peter Lombard treats baptism under four viewpoints: quid sit – forma – quando institutus – causa institutionis. His definition of the essence of baptism is based squarely upon an understanding of baptism in terms of its act: "Baptismus dicitur intinctio, id est ablutio corporis exterior facta sub forma verborum praescripta" ("Baptism is a dipping, that is, an exterior washing of the body, carried out under a prescribed form of words" *Sent.* IV, dist. 3, 1). The element (or the action which is performed with the element) and the word (which is described as the "forma") form together the substance of the sacrament; everything else belongs merely "ad sollemnitatem (externam)" – to the sacrament's (external) solemnity. The word, which "consecrates" baptism, consists of the name of the Trinity, more precisely in the word's "inwardly abiding power", which, according to the well known passage from Augustine, *In Jo. tract.* 80, 3, is given on the basis of faith. It is therefore immaterial whether all divine Persons are expressly invoked or merely one of them, with tacit inclusion of the others.[28] The same freedom

here. The baptismal theology of Peter Lombard is contained in *Sententiarum* lib. IV, dist. 2–6 (*PL* 192, 841–55).

[28] The Master as well as the other theologians of his day base this opinion on the text from Ambrose, *De Spiritu S.* I, 3, 42–4, mentioned in chapter 5, note 11 above. This opinion had been concurred in by a Council of Friaul in 791 (*Mansi* 13, 838) and by Pope Nicolaus I in his *Answer to the Bulgarians* (*Denz.* 335). On the interpretation and the dogmatic value of this answer see J. Bellamy in *DThC* 2, 272f. The great theologians of the thirteenth century had, in contrast to the overly generalized conclusions of Peter Lombard, already made essential limitations. They said that this usage was valid only for the Apostolic age, on the basis of "a special revelation of Christ". Thus Thomas Aqu. *Summa theol.* III, q. 66 a. 7 ad 1 (for the statements of the other theologians see the work by Bellamy, *loc. cit.*). The view of these scholastics is supported, in this text from Ambrose, by very doubtful authority. Moreover, they did not understand

applies with regard to the number of immersions, "pro vario more Ecclesiae" ("according to the various usage of the Church"). Basing his argument upon St. Ambrose, he develops the same doctrine as Hugh, that even a baptism with an imperfect form can effect the "plenum sacramentum" if accompanied by full interior faith in the Trinity.

At Christ's death the law of circumcision was repealed and replaced by the obligation of baptism. Peter Lombard considers that the actual moment of baptism's institution was Christ's baptism in Jordan. On this occasion there was a self-revelation of the Trinity, and at the same time the water, which is the "elementum sacramenti", experienced by contact with Christ's body an abiding sanctification. He calls various effects of grace, such as "the interior purity" and the "renewal of the spirit", the "causa institutionis". Behind all these effects lies justification (justificatio). This is the "res", the inner reality, the reason why baptism was instituted.

The sacrament can be received in three ways, differing according to their consequences: some receive the "sacramentum et rem", others the "sacramentum et non rem", and still others the "rem et non sacramentum" (D. 4). Those who have already been justified by the baptism of desire and then come subsequently to water-baptism, "already sanctified in spirit, with faith and love", are placed, through their baptism, under the "iudicium Ecclesiae", whereas they had previously stood merely under

the terminology of holy Scripture, which in speaking of "baptism in the name of Jesus" in distinction from the baptism of John means simply a baptism which is performed in the name of Jesus and in obedience to his command (see p. 9 above). Cf. also the German commentary on Thomas Aquinas by D. Winzen: *Die Sakramente. Taufe u. Firmung (Dtsch. Thomas-Ausg.,* vol. 29) 432f., footnote 117.

the "iudicium Dei". They are also "absolved of the duty of out-ward satisfaction" and receive such an increase of grace and virtue that they may be considered henceforth as new men (c. 5). Thus baptism becomes, even for someone who has already been justified, a genuine sacrament, the inner reality of which (res) has already preceded the baptismal rite. It is true that Peter Lombard does not say expressly in any passage that baptism imparts a "character" in the sense of later theology.[29] But this doctrine is, in germ, already there, as is shown by his arguments about the fact that baptism cannot be repeated or lost, and about the "sacra-mentum" and "res". And he gives quite deliberately the name of "character" to baptism which is administered with the proper form (D. 6 c. 2).

Good and evil men can baptize with equal validity (D. 5 c. 1). For the ministers have merely the ministry (ministerium), but not the power (potestas) over baptism (c. 2). The Master leaves at bottom undecided the question whether the Lord could also have given his servants the "power" to effect interior forgiveness of sins. He contents himself with the answer that the Lord effects sanctification "through invisible grace, the servant through the visible sacrament" (c. 3). The "servants" who are legitimately entitled to baptize are priests alone. But the validity of baptism remains unaffected, even it if is administered by a deacon, a lay-man, a heretic, a schismatic, or a criminal. The prerequisite is merely that the form handed down from the time of Christ be

[29] Cf. F. Brommer, *L. v. sakram. Charakter,* 5–8, 19; Brommer demon-strates quite correctly that the passage in Dist. 6, 2 ("quod qui etiam ab haereticis baptizati sunt, servato charactere Christi, rebaptizandi non sunt") must be taken as referring to the formula of baptism, and trans-lated: "for even those who have been baptized by the heretics, with the form provided by Christ, are not to be re-baptized" (*op. cit.* 5f.).

used (c. 2). It is, of course, true that baptism received outside the Church does not lead to salvation. In order that the external form for administering baptism may be observed, it is necessary to have the "intentio", upon which Peter Lombard lays great emphasis (c. 5). In order, in the case of infant baptism, to maintain baptism's character as the "sacramentum fidei" the sponsors' vicarious confession of faith is essential (c. 6).

How the doctrine of baptism of the early scholastics as formed primarily by Hugh of St. Victor, led up to the later scholastics can be seen in the *Summa theologica* of Alexander of Hales (died 1245).[30] This work brings together what was known about baptism in the mediaeval period up to this time, shaping it according to a uniform and methodical principle. First of all the existing definitions of baptism are considered and classified in accordance with Aristotle's fourfold conception of "cause". Thus Hugh of St. Victor's definition is seen as formed chiefly with a view to the "causa materialis" (even though there is in the words "diluendis criminibus" a suggestion of the "causa finalis" as well). The "causa formalis" is perceived in those definitions which proceed from the immersion and the verbal formula which accompanies it (as is the case with the definitions of Peter Lombard and of Augustine). This Halensian *Summa* finds the "causa finalis" expressed in the definition of the pseudo-Areopagite. A subdivision of this cause appears in the "causa efficiens", for which Alexander cites the definition of John of Damascus, in which baptism is conceived of in terms of the Holy Spirit and described as the principle of supernatural life. All these traditional definitions of baptism must complement each other, as Alexander

[30] The baptismal doctrine of the *Summa* is contained in Pars IV, qu. 8 membrum 1–12.

explains, and thus form a total conception. It is evident that in this kind of systematization the positive value of individual definitions is really too constricted.

It is especially noticeable that Alexander's *Summa* also applies these four causal categories to the history of baptism's institution, and thus passes from an historical to a systematic consideration, as is shown by comparison with the work of Hugh of St. Victor. According to Hugh the institution of baptism took place in stages, historically, each stage signifying a steadily growing importance. The immediate preliminary outline is the baptism of Jesus; baptism is first urged in the conversation with Nicodemus, and it is universally instituted in the baptismal command issued to the apostles. Alexander of Hales, on the other hand, ignores this historical process entirely and conceives of the baptism of Jesus in Jordan as the "causa materialis", the baptismal command as the "causa formalis", the conversation with Nicodemus (which speaks of entrance into the kingdom of heaven) as the "causa finalis", and the words of Jesus in Mark 16:16 ("He who is believed and is baptized will be saved") as the "causa efficiens".

It is in the doctrine about the minister of baptism that we can see most clearly the advance of the history of dogma since the period of the early scholastics. Whereas Hugh considers the minister's intention and faith as belonging together, the position adopted in Alexander's *Summa* is fundamentally different. It is true that here too "fides" is the principle of the sacrament, but it is no longer the minister's "fides", but rather the "fides Ecclesiae". It suffices that the minister have the "intentio faciendi quod facit Ecclesia" ("the intention of doing what the Church does"). It is the Church alone which guarantees the faith necessary for the administration of baptism. "Duo, fides et intentio, requiruntur ad hoc ut aliquis baptizetur, sed non in eodem; requiritur enim fides Ecclesiae et intentio baptizantis" ("Two things, faith and intention, are specifically required in order that someone may be baptized. But they are not required in the same person. For faith is necessary for the Church and intention for him who baptizes"). Thus we have here a change of emphasis from the personal to the instrumental conception of the minister of baptism. He baptizes not "in persona sua" but "in persona ministri Ecclesiae". Therefore even a heretic, in fact, even an unbaptized person can become the "minister Ecclesiae" and baptize by intending to do "quod intendit Ecclesia". Beneath this altered conception of the minister of baptism lies a change in the notion of the Church. Hugh conceives of the Church in wholly concrete terms. It is the perfectly plain and obvious ground upon which the minister of baptism lives and stands, so that it is impossible to distinguish between his faith and that of the Church. In Alexander's *Summa,* on the other hand, the Church is thought of in much more abstract and institutional terms, more as a general principle which exists over against the minister of the sacrament, as an individuum to its species. The minister, as the "minister Ecclesiae", performs merely the external sacrament, which is the occasion for God alone to effect the inner sacrament, in which there is no human co-operation. In the same way the Church's intention in the administration of baptism is described substantially as "abluere exterius, ut Deus abluat interius" ("to wash outwardly, in order that God may wash inwardly", membr. 5).

The twin concepts of matter and form have in the *Summa* found their way completely into the doctrine of the sacraments. According to Alexander the baptismal formula must be trinitarian because it restores to man the shattered image of the trinitarian God, and because the whole Trinity is the author of saving grace. The baptismal water, which is the matter of the sacrament, has received "potentialiter" the power to baptize through the sanctifying contact with Christ's body which occurred to the element of water at the baptism in Jordan. This potency is translated into act each time baptism is administered.

Alexander's *Summa* requires that the adult candidates for baptism have, along with "fides" and "intentio", "contritio" as well. Without contrition the candidate's will would still be abiding in sin, which is tantamount to "ponere obicem" ("placing an obstacle" in the way), and which makes him incapable of receiving baptism (membr. 7). In the case of immature children, on the other hand, neither intention nor faith are necessary. As they have been afflicted with original sin without their co-operation, so they also become partakers of Christ's grace without their co-operation.

In his discussion of the effects of baptism Alexander expatiates upon the baptismal character, taking up a traditional notion which was, in this form, recent, but already quite widely known. What the concrete occasion for the rise of this doctrine actually was, we do not yet know. Among its first representatives we may probably reckon the canonist Huguccio (died 1210) and his pupil, later to become Pope Innocent III. Huguccio distinguishes in baptism, along with the water and the washing, a "character quidam dominicus" ("a certain dominical character"), which is a "qualitas dominica" ("a dominical quality"), "an identifying mark, in virtue of which a man is called a Christian or a baptized person . . . or a soldier of Christ, or one who has been marked". The "signaculus" clings to him "inseparably forever", and is the reason why baptism cannot be administered again even to someone who has been baptized in heresy.[31] Similarly Innocent III says that the "sacramental act (of baptism) imprints a character", so long as the recipient (he is talking about people who are asleep or mentally distracted) has not previously manifested his opposition.[32] Alexander of Hales proceeds from an alleged passage in pseudo-Dionysius: "Character est signum sanctum communionis fidei" ("Character is the sacred sign of the communion of faith"). He interprets this character as the "assimilatio" and "configuratio" with Christ. It is a "habitus", and specifically a "qualitas spiritualis", which disposes to final perfection through grace. It is not itself grace, but has a "similitudo" to grace. This character impresses upon the soul an image which serves principally its power of cognition, and on account of which character is also called "quoddam lumen spirituale" ("a certain spiritual light"), in dependence upon the Patristic description of baptism as φωτισμός. Alexander tries to prove the indelibility of this character by analogy with the indissolubility of the union of natures in Christ: "Sicut illa unio naturarum est perpetua et redemptio quae secuta est incarnationem, semel facta et perpetuo, sic character perpetuus est, qui ex virtute mediatoris per passionem creatur" ("Just as that union of natures is perpetual, and as the redemption which followed the Incarnation was performed once for all, so is that character perpetual which is created by the power

---

[31] Huguccio, Manuscript Commentary on Dist. IV, De consecr., in F. Gillmann, "Der 'sakramentale Charakter' bei den Glossatoren Rufinus. Johannes Faventinus, Sikard von Cremona, Huguccio und in der Glossa ordinaria des Dekrets" in *Kath.* 90 = IV, 5 (1910) 306.
[32] Innocentius III, *Ep. ad Ymbertum archiepisc. Arelat.* (end of 1201) (*Denz.* 411); see also F. Brommer, *L. v. sakram. Charakter,* 13.

of the Mediator through his passion"). The character expresses our possession by Christ and becomes thus the sign of distinction. The fact that it is attained only through water-baptism, and not through the baptism of desire or of blood, shows its relationship to the visibility of the Church. Alexander is familiar with a confirmation character, parallel to that of baptism. The two are distinguishable according to the sacramental grace to which they dispose: baptismal character disposes to the "gratia credendi", confirmation character to the "gratia militandi in militia Christi".

Chapter Nine

THE THEOLOGY OF BAPTISM IN HIGH AND LATE SCHOLASTICISM

BIBLIOGRAPHY: Apart from the works mentioned in chapter 8: J. Strake, *Die Sakramentenlehre des Wilhelm von Auxerre (Forsch. z. chr. Lit.- u. Dogmengesch.* 13/5, Pb. 1917, 57–115. D. Winzen, (Kommentar zu) Thomas von Aquin, *Die Sakramente. Taufe und Firmung (Dtsch. Thomas-Ausgabe,* German-Latin edition of the *Summa theologica,* vol. 29; Szb. 1935). H. Schillebeecks. *De sacramentele heilseconomie. Theologische bezinning op. S. Thomas' sacramentenleer in het licht van de traditien van de hedendaagse sacramentsproblematiek* (Ant. 1952). N. Sanders, "Duns Scotus over het character sacramentalis" in *StdCth* 23 (1948) 39–42.

IN PASSING from early to High Scholasticism, theology, and in particular the doctrine of the sacraments, takes the path of ever greater systematization. In his work on the Sentences Peter Lombard has given the traditional doctrine a systematic summary which became the basis for the commentaries on the Sentences in which the masters of High Scholasticism developed the doctrine further. They follow in the main the same arrangement of the material. But a few questions, such as the problem whether, and in what way, baptism is a cause of grace, are relegated, in connection with Distinctions 1 and 2, to the tractate *De sacramentis in genere,* which is gradually becoming broader in scope. Let us obtain first a general view of the principal doctrinal material of this period before we take up the consideration of its principal representatives.

First of all, with regard to the symbolism, that is the signification of the (exterior) sacrament, it is established that the sacrament of baptism is a water-bath, an immersion of the candidate in water, accompanied by invocation of the Trinity. This overall structure is a tangible confession of faith far more explicit than anything which takes place in the other sacraments.[1] With all the emphasis placed upon the fact that the "res", the sacramental reality, proceeds from the Trinity, as the administrator of grace, and from the merits of Christ's passion,[2] great importance is still attached at this point to the candidate's faith as well. He is the one who alone makes these ultimate sources of strength effective. For children who are not yet capable of faith the "faith of the Church" intervenes in baptism. The

[1] Bonaventura, *Sent.* IV, d. 3 p. 1 a. 1 q. 3 concl. (ed. Collegii S. Bonaventurae (Quaracchi 1899) 69): "in hoc sacramento magis explicite est professio fidei quam in aliquo alio Sacramento, . . . in actu est professio fidei passionis, scilicet per immersionem, sed in verbo professio fidei Trinitatis. Unde et maior efficacia est in hoc Sacramento quam in aliquo alio" ("There is in this sacrament a more explicit profession of faith than in any other sacrament, . . . in act there is a profession of faith in the passion, namely through the immersion; but in word there is a profession of faith in the Trinity. Wherefore there is a greater efficacy in this sacrament than in any other").

[2] Within, naturally, the proper framework afforded by the general soteriological presuppositions, and with the corresponding distinctions, which are represented, for instance, by Bonaventure and the young Thomas on the one hand and the Thomas of the *Summa* on the other hand. Cf., for instance, Bonaventura, *Sent.* IV, d. 5 a. 3 q. 1 concl. and q. 2 concl. (Quaracchi-Ed. 128, 130); also Thomas Aqu., *Summa theol.* III, q. 64 a. 1, 3, 4; and *Sent.* IV, d. 5 q. 1 a. 1–3.

adult cannot, of course, receive the grace of the sacrament without personal faith.[3] From these facts everything else follows with complete consistency. Anyone can be the minister, since he who actually baptizes inwardly is, of course, Christ.[4] Baptism can be administered once only; a repetition would "crucify the Son of God afresh", since baptism draws its efficacy "from the one passion of Christ".[5]

The fact that baptism – when administered with the correct intention – is always valid, even when it is received unfruitfully, and that it may not therefore be repeated, supplies an occasion for treating the baptismal character. This doctrine, which we have already met in the work of Alexander of Hales, is set forth extensively first of all by William of Auvergne (died 1294)[6] and by William of Auxerre (died 1231).[7] For the former the baptismal character is one of the decisive reasons why

---

[3] Bonaventura, *Sent.* IV, d. 3 p. 1 a. 1 q. 3 obi. 3 (Quar. 68): "fides est illud, secundum quod manet adhuc passio, quia creditur" and *loc. cit.* concl. (69): "Attamen sicut baptismus est Sacramentum non singularis hominis, sed Ecclesiae; sic efficaciam habet a fide Ecclesiae, et hoc per unitatem sponsae et columbae" ("But just as baptism is the sacrament not of the individual man, but of the Church, so it has its efficacy from the Church, and so through the unity of the bride and the dove"). Similar expressions are to be found elsewhere, for instance Thomas Aqu., *Sent.* IV, d. 6 q. 1 a. 3 sol. 2 ad 3: "non requiritur fides personalis offerentium puerum ad baptismum, . . . sed solum fides ecclesiae militantis" ("the personal faith of those who present the child for baptism is not necessary, . . . but only the faith of the Church militant") or of the adults (*loc. cit.* sol. 1).

[4] The interpretation of this process is here also dependent upon the soteriological presuppositions of the individual theologian; cf. the texts in note 2 above.

[5] Bonaventura, *Sent.* IV, d. 6 p. 1 q. 6 concl. (Quar. 146).

[6] Cf. K. Ziesché, *Die Sakramentenlehre des Wilhelm von Auvergne* (Wn. 1911) 24–7.

[7] Cf. J. Strake, *Sakramentenlehre des Wilh. v. Auxerre,* 28–39, 75 f.

baptism cannot be repeated. He calls the character "an impersonal, objective gift of grace",[8] "sanctitas" in the improper sense, "sanctitas prima" as distinguished from "sanctitas secunda", the actual grace of the sacrament, which is a kind of consecrating sanctity that brings grace itself in its train without actually being its cause.[9] William of Auxerre tries to trace his interpretation of character back to the authority of the Church Fathers, especially to the definition of baptism put forward by John of Damascus and the pseudo-Areopagite.[10] He calls character a sign of distinction. He subsequently finds a happier expression for it: sign of distinction and sign of dignity. He places character – as Huguccio has already done – in the category of quality, in the third species thereof, as a "passio" or a "patibilis qualitas". It is only character and washing together which form the sacrament, because both elements, although different from one another in essence, signify the same sacramental grace. "Character, being a sign of grace, can also be called a sacrament."[11] The Commentary on the Sentences by Hugh of St. Cher (died 1263), who takes over William of Auxerre's arguments almost word for word, takes a decisive further step at this point by interpreting the baptismal character for the first time as "sacramentum et res".[12] The use of this terminology, the elements of which stem from Augustine, builds a bridge between the old tradition and the new teaching

[8] K. Ziesché, *Sakr.-L. d. Wilh. v. Auvergne,* 25.
[9] *Op. cit.* 25–7; cf. F. Brommer, *L. v. sakr. Charakter,* 35–44.
[10] See pp. 169 and 172 above; cf. F. Brommer, *op. cit.* 50, note 2; 58, note 2.
[11] Thus F. Brommer, *op. cit.* 56; the text of Wilhelm of Auxerre is at *loc. cit., note* 3.
[12] *Op. cit.* 56f.

with regard to character. Light is thrown upon the relationship between character and grace by the sentence: "baptismus qui est character est causa gratiae" ("baptism which is character is a cause of grace").[13] This is based upon the Areopagite's definition of baptism and is intended to say only that character "disposes the soul for the reception of grace, that is, that it is the material cause".[14]

The great masters of scholasticism all go back to the same doctrinal foundations, even if their actual point of departure for their teaching about character is in each case different. Albertus Magnus begins with the term "character", which the Master has used in Dist. 6 cap. 2, though he does not have the technical meaning in mind. Bonaventure leaves the word on one side and begins with the problem itself, that is, with the fact that baptism cannot be repeated, because of the character which it imprints.[15] Thomas Aquinas, however, treats the question in connection with Distinction 4, mentioning the decisive word right in the title of the first Question: "Primo de effectu quo est in baptismo sacramentum et res, scilicet de charactere" ("First, the effect by which 'sacramentum' and 'res' in baptism are caused, namely character"). Little was actually known of the inner essence of character in the various sacraments. There was an awareness that this was virgin territory in theology. What is probably the most fruitful start in the interpretation of character is afforded by Thomas Aquinas' *Commentary on the Sentences* (D. 4 q. 1 a. 1 sol.). He says there that character comes closest to being a "potentia", citing the Areopagite as his

---

[13] Text *op. cit.* 58, note 1.
[14] *Op. cit.* 60; cf. what follows there as well.
[15] Bonaventura, *Sent.* IV, d. 6, conspectus quaestionum (Quar. 136).

authority. It is true that he is mistaken in his statement that "the tradition with regard to character came to us first from Dionysius", but objectively his presentation is, in itself, and as an interpretation of the pseudo-Areopagite's definition of baptism,[16] a masterpiece: " . . . this sign is nothing other than a certain potency in respect of hierarchic actions, namely administering and receiving the sacraments and what otherwise pertains to the faithful." This "potentia" is, in the case of baptism, "an intellectual potency, a passive potency, as it were, by which man is made capable of receiving spiritual acts; . . . one who is not baptized could not, of course, receive the effects of the other sacraments at all, and is therefore incapable of transmitting them to others" (D. 4 q. 1 a. 4 qc. 3 sol. 3).

St. Thomas presents the same teaching even more definitely and clearly, although no more exhaustively,[17] in the *Summa theologica,* doing so, however, not this time within the framework of the tractate on baptism, but as part of the doctrine of the sacraments in general. This rearrangement may be justified on systematical grounds. But for the development of the doctrine of baptism and of sacramental teaching in general it was not a good step. The external sacrament lost the Christological and ecclesiological basis upon which it rests. The fact that baptism, through its character, forms the foundation for Church and cult was obscured. There arose the danger that theological interest would concentrate too narrowly on personal sanctification by means of the "gratia gratum faciens" and so

[16] Cf. p. 169–70 above; also F. Brommer, *L. v. sakr. Charakter,* 58, 69–77.
[17] F. Brommer, *op. cit.* 147–69.

would neglect the ecclesiastical and cult consecration of the baptismal candidate by means of the "gratia gratis data". Nevertheless, St. Thomas is no more to blame for this development than the other theologians of his time. They left the doctrine of character in its traditional place, within the tractate on baptism, but treated it as if it were outside of this context. St. Thomas at any rate did not overlook the ecclesiological significance of character, since he understands it in his *Summa theologica* as a spiritual power which participates in the priesthood of Jesus Christ and is thus esteemed as a cult grace.

There is prevailing agreement with regard to the decisive and actual effect (res) of baptism: "As the authorities say and the masters together demonstrate, all guilt is expunged in the sacrament of baptism, when its efficacy and value for salvation are fully received, and man is restored, as far as concerns his soul, to original innocence."[18] Every satisfactory punishment (poena satisfactoria) is also expunged,[19] but not "the lust of the flesh against the spirit, death, and similar penalties (poenalitates)".[20] The positive gift of grace is of various magnitude in the several recipients, since this depends upon the varying degrees in which the candidates unite themselves with Christ's saving act.[21] In connection with various traditional definitions of baptism St. Thomas notes as the positive effects of baptism that it bestows grace, increases virtues, incorporates in Christ, opens up the way into the kingdom of God (*Sent*. IV, d. 4 q. 2 a. 2 qc. 1–6). There is unanimous agreement that the origin of these gifts

---

[18] Bonaventura, *Sent*. IV, d. 4 p. 1 a. 1 q. 1 concl. (Quar. 95).
[19] Thomas, *Sent*. IV, d. 4 q. 2 a. 1 qc. 2 sol. 2.
[20] *Loc. cit.* sol. 3; cf. Bonaventura, *loc. cit.*
[21] Albertus M., *Sent*. IV, d. 4 a. 10 ad 2.

is to be attributed to Christ's passion, as witness the following passage from St. Thomas:

"Through baptism man is baptized in Christ's death, dies with him and is buried with him, as is said in Romans 6; therefore baptism, as far as this depends on baptism, brings (influit) upon the candidate the entire efficacy of the passion" (*Sent.* IV, d. 4 q. 2 a. 1 qc. 2 sol.). "Baptism works in virtue both of the passion as well as of the resurrection and ascension, insofar as man is conformed with Christ in his passion by the immersion, in which he is in a certain sense buried with Christ; furthermore, he is conformed with Christ in his resurrection, in respect of the lustre (of purity) which the water imparts; and finally he is conformed to Christ in his ascension into heaven, in respect of the fact that the candidate is led up out of the sacred font" (*loc. cit.* d. 4 q. 2 a. 2 qc. 6 sol.).[22]

Having pursued up to now the development of the doctrine of baptism as we find it in the commentaries on the sentences, let us now turn to those works which present the doctrinal material about baptism separately and in terms of their own system. This is done with suggestive brevity in the *Breviloquium* of St. Bonaventura (Pars VI, cap. 7). In contrast with the predominantly abstract and metaphysical method of his teacher, Alexander of Hales, Bonaventure's doctrine of baptism is treated more from the soteriological point of view, as well as with greater religious fullness. His view of the sacraments as the Church's vital organs leads him to consider them in two ways, corresponding with their double purpose, which is to heal the

[22] Of course, we must presuppose here the interpretation of the "instrumental" cause, which differs with each theologian, and which for St. Thomas differs from the *Commentary on the Sentences* to the *Summa theologica*.

consequences of original sin and to promote the life of grace. In the first sense, as "medicamentum", baptism is the foundation of all the other sacraments, since it takes away the guilt of original sin itself. In the second sense, in accordance with which the individual sacraments are related to the three supernatural virtues and to the four cardinal virtues, baptism is, in its character as "sacramentum fidei", just as much the "ianua sacramentorum" as "fides" in its turn is the "ianua virtutum".

Baptism is constituted "as required by its power, by our salvation and our sick condition". The "virtus reparans" is "the power of the whole Trinity", or else "the power of Christ's passion"; therefore, the express mention of the Trinity is necessary (apart from the presumed special case in the primitive Church of baptism "in the name of Jesus"). He demands further that the act of baptizing be mentioned in the baptismal formula, and that baptism – at least "de congruitate" – be performed by three-fold immersion, "as an expression of Christ's death and burial and of his resurrection after three days". Our salvation must be founded "by regeneration or renewal in the essence of a grace which imparts spiritual being". Man's "sick condition" consits in original sin with its consequences, which are counteracted by baptismal grace as "gratia regenerans, rectificans, purificans". The candidate must bring faith and contrition to baptism; for the immature child, who is not yet capable of that, a "fides aliena", "a faith from elsewhere", suffices, "such as we find in the Church universal".

With the distinction that baptism is to be understood not as a sacrament of the individual man but as a sacrament of the Church, and that it therefore obtains its efficacy from the Church's faith, Bonaventure brings the concept of the "fides

207

Ecclesiae" into the foreground. Corresponding on God's side to the "fides Ecclesiae" is the "pactio divina", "quae ipsum opus operatum ordinavit ad gratiam percipiendam" ("which instituted this very *opus operatum* for the obtaining of grace"). This "pactio" is a purely objective principle of the sacrament's efficacy, whereas the "fides Ecclesiae" can be described as a subjective-objective principle.[23]

Aquinas also treats the same material in the third part of his *Summa theologica* (Quaestio 66–71). At the same time, this tractate displays the result of development in the history of dogma. He first of all applies to baptism the well-known categories: "sacrament only", "reality and sacrament", and "reality only". The "sacrament alone" comes about actually not "in the water, but in the application of the water to man, and that is in the washing . . . ; 'reality and sacrament', however, is the baptismal character (character baptismalis), for this is the reality signified by the external washing and (at the same time) the sacramental sign of inner justification. This (justification) is the 'reality only' of this sacrament, namely what is signified and not that which signifies".[24] Taking the "sacrament only" as meaning the external symbolic act, St. Thomas interprets this consistently with the help of the twin Aristotelian concepts of "materia" and "forma". The application of the material elements, which was called "immersion-bath" by the ancients, is now termed by him – as it has already been by Peter Lombard – "ablutio",

---

[23] Bonaventura, *Sent.* IV, d. 3 p. 1 a. 1 q. 3 (Quar. 69). For the vicarious importance of the "fides Ecclesiae" cf. H. Berresheim, *Christus als Haupt der Kirche nach dem hl. Bonaventura* (Bonn 1939) 282–8.
[24] The translation is our own, and is published in Thomas von Aquin, *Summa theologica*, Deutsche Thomas-Ausgabe vol. 29.

washing. This more neutral term corresponds better to the practice of the time. Apart from the fact that the Church had at all times recognized baptism by pouring, baptism by immersion had come, in the course of time, perhaps already in the eighth century, but at any rate since the twelfth century, to be replaced in the West more and more by pouring, which from the fifteenth century on supplanted immersion almost completely.[25] St. Thomas recognizes that immersion is not at all necessary or essential. Baptism in the form of sprinkling or pouring stands on an equal footing with immersion. But immersion has the advantage of symbolizing more clearly Christ's death, which is the original image of baptism (q. 66 a. 7).[26] All the more, of course, is the nature and the number of immersions unessential (q. 66 a. 8). The baptismal formula given by St. Thomas is the trinitarian one customary today, based upon Matt. 28:19. By means of this formula baptism is consecrated, and therefore it mentions the principal cause, the Trinity, and the instrumental cause, the minister (in the words "I baptize thee", q. 66 a. 5). The naming of only *one* of the names of the Trinity, with merely mental inclusion of the other names would not suffice for validity, since a "tangible form" is essential for the sacrament. St. Thomas makes an exception only for the case of baptism "in the name of Jesus" in the primitive Church (q. 66 a 6). Along with water baptism St. Thomas lists also the "other baptisms", which are familiar from the Church's tradition: baptism of blood and of the Spirit

---

[25] From the eighth century, according to H. Leclercq, *Immersion* in *DACL* 7/1, 305–8; from the twelfth century, according to J. Bellamy, *Baptême* in *DThC* 2/1, 254–6.

[26] Cf. also D. Winzen, *Kommentar z. Dtsch. Thomas-Ausg.* vol. 29, 433, notes 119 and 120.

(q. 66 a. 11–12). Martyrdom and conversion to God accomplished in the power of the Holy Spirit have, of course, been recognized in the Church from time immemorial as extraordinary forms of participation in the saving work of Christ.

St. Thomas follows tradition in his demonstration as well. In baptism man is conformed in Christ's passion and experiences the efficacy of the Holy Spirit. Man attains the first effect in martyrdom. He attains the second, "inasmuch as his heart is impelled by the Holy Spirit to faith and to the love of God and to contrition for sins. Therefore we speak also of the baptism of penance" (q. 66 a. 11). Of course, baptism of blood and of penance are not sacraments (a. 11 ad 2); nevertheless baptism of blood has precedence over water baptism, "not as a sacrament, but in respect to the sacrament's effect" (a. 12 ad 1).

St. Thomas grants to laymen, without regard to sex, the right to baptize in case of necessity: "so that no one may be deprived of his salvation because he has not come to baptism" (q. 67 a. 3). "It is at bottom (always) Christ who baptizes .... But in Christ there is neither man nor woman" (a. 4). St. Thomas is no longer embarrassed with regard to an unbaptized minister of baptism, as Augustine was in his day (see above p. 127). Official doctrinal statements had appeared in the intervening period and gave support to his words: "The person who baptizes performs a merely external ministry; but it is Christ who baptizes inwardly. He can use everyone however he wants to" (q. 67 a. 5 ad 1).

All are obliged to be baptized since baptism alone incorporates man into Christ and thus leads to salvation. But St. Thomas places the necessary limitation upon this teaching by referring to baptism of desire. A man can be saved without baptism "if he lacks the sacrament in reality (re), but not in will (voto) . . . on account of the desire for baptism" (q. 68 art. 2). By means of the underlying faith in this case, "God sanctifies the man inwardly, since his power is not bound to the visible sacraments" *(loc. cit.)* If this attributes a certain primacy to "invisible sanctification", the sacrament's prior position is still safeguarded, as in the statement (a. 2 ad 3):"We term the sacrament of baptism necessary for salvation, inasmuch as man's salvation is not possible without possession of baptism at least in will." What is decisive for entrance into eternal life is the "absolution from all guilt and punishment". But this is imparted only "in the reception of baptism and in martyrdom". After baptism of desire one does not at once enter into eternal life, but must first "pay the penalty for past sins" (a. 2 ad 2).

With these considerations we stand right in the middle of the problem of the relationship between objective and subjective sanctification.[27] The much used expression that baptism is the "sacrament of faith" seems to bind both areas into one. From the point of view of the redemptive process St. Thomas teaches (q. 68 a. 1. ad 1) that faith was necessary at all stages in the unfolding of redemption, although it was expressed in each period by a different sign. Even circumcision is assessed as such a sign, indeed it is called a "sacrament" (q. 70 a. 1 ad 2). Circumcision even mediates grace, though only "insofar as it was a sign of faith in Christ's future passion" (q. 70 a. 4 corp.); whereas on the other hand, "in baptism grace is imparted through the power which baptism itself possesses as an instrument of Christ's passion which has already occurred". But baptism is in addition

[27] See *op. cit.* 520f.; also C. v. Schäzler, *Die Lehre von der Wirksamkeit der Sakramente ex opere operato* (Mch. 1860), esp. 436–503.

211

always a sign and revelation of "living faith, which is efficacious through love". Therefore baptism cannot mediate salvation "if the will to sin endures, since this excludes the soul of faith (fidei formam)" (q. 68 a. 4 ad 3). Consequently the will or intention of the candidate is essential for the valid reception of baptism (a. 7 corp.).[28] The case is somewhat different with regard to faith. Of course, for *fruitful* reception of baptism, for attainment of grace, the correct faith is indispensable, as stated in Rom. 3:22. However, baptism can be received *validly* without this correct faith, inasmuch as it imprints an indelible mark, the character. The prerequisite is merely that "everything else is present which necessarily pertains to the sacrament. For the sacrament is accomplished not by the righteousness of him who administers or receives the sacrament, but by the power of God" (q. 68 a. 8 corp.). The objection that infants are incapable not only of having faith, but that they cannot even have the intention of receiving the sacrament is met by St. Thomas at first with the argument that if it is possible for infants to contract original sin already in Adam, they can "far sooner receive grace through Christ" (a. 9). St. Thomas then develops a solution on the basis of the child's special way of salvation, which D. Winzen[29] describes in the following terms: "What is peculiar to the child, however, is that it is not yet independent, but is, as it were, a member of its parents, and especially of its mother, who feeds it. So the child's own independent intention or its own faith is supplanted by the faith of its parents who present it, or by the faith of the Church."

[28] S. D. Winzen, *op. cit.* 446. note 162; there is also a brief reference there to the interpretation of the baptism "for the dead" mentioned by St. Paul in 1 Cor. 15:29.
[29] *Op. cit.* 520.

212

Faith and intention are, however, by no means the cause of salvation, but merely mediate it. To a certain degree they form the connection with Christ who acts in the sacrament. The baptismal formula, the "verbum fidei", or the act of baptism itself, which takes the place of faith, is the mediatory, that is, the instrumental cause of the sanctifying power which proceeds in the last analysis from Christ, from God.[30] From the fact that man "is incorporated by baptism (according to Rom. 6:3f.) into Christ's death" and "that Christ's death has sufficiently satisfied for sins", St. Thomas concludes that no work of satisfaction may be imposed upon the candidate for his previous sins. For "that would not be doing justice to Christ's passion and death, as if they were not sufficient for full satisfaction . . ." (q. 68 a. 5 corp.).

The primacy of Christ's work of salvation, in the sense of man's incorporation into Christ's passion and death in accordance with Romans 6 (q. 69 a. 2 corp.), the theme which pervades the entire tractate on baptism anyway, is brought out with particular beauty in Quaestio 69, which treats the effects of baptism. "Everyone who is baptized obtains fellowship in Christ's passion as the means of salvation, as if he himself had suffered and as if he himself had died" (q. 69 a. 2 corp.). From this fact the individual effects proceed with logical consistency.

It is true that everything which has been said applies only to the actual act of baptism, the "washing". But in his concentration on this, however, St. Thomas did not lose sight of the total act in which baptism is administered. He distinguishes between "actions which belong to the sacrament of necessity, and actions which belong (merely) to a certain solemnity of the sacrament"

[30] *Op. cit.* 448, note 168.

(q. 66 a. 10 corp.). The latter are not superfluous; they belong to the "bene esse sacramenti" (*loc. cit.* ad 4). Quaestio 71 speaks in the same sense of baptismal instruction and of the renunciation.

With respect to content and form the doctrine of baptism reaches, for the time being, a climax in this tractate of St. Thomas and achieves a certain conclusion. The theological assimilation of the Patristic material is completed by its incorporation into a closed system of sacramental theology. St. Thomas went back diligently to Patristic sources, and in particular to Greek sources like pseudo-Dionysius and John of Damascus. He introduces a terminology which has been sharpened by Aristotle, and joined the fundamental concept of the "sacred sign" or symbol (sacramentum) on the one hand, with the no less fundamental notion of the instrumental cause on the other. In this way the baptismal theology which he presented achieved a form which, despite the fact that a few purely formal elements are conditioned by their medieval background, summarizes the Church's belief in a classic form which maintains its validity up until our day.

Among St. Thomas' disciples are to be found some who stood in very close connection with him and passed on his teaching about baptism, men like Hannibal de Hannibaldis (died 1272 or 1273) and William Petrus de Godino (died 1336). Other Dominican theologians display a considerable degree of independence from their master and criticize him, as for instance, John Quidort of Paris (died 1306) who, among other points of criticism, does not recognize the reason advanced by St. Thomas in his *Commentary on the Sentences* for the passive form of baptism used by the Greeks.[31] Hervaeus Natalis (died 1323) devotes the most

[31] Johannes Quidort of Paris, *Sent.* IV, d. 3 a. 2 (*Cod. lat. Paris* 889, fol. 77v).

extensive Quaestio in his tractate on baptism to the doctrine of sacramental character, which he describes as a spiritual potency and which he defends against the criticism being brought forward against the doctrine of character as well as against the concept of the sacraments' instrumental efficacy. This controversy seems to have been started by Henry of Ghent (died 1293), although in those of his writings which have been preserved, arguments about this subject are lacking. This controversy is carried further by the Dominican school of Jacob of Metz at the beginning of the fourteenth century. The position taken by Durandus of S. Porciano, the most important representative of this school, shows clearly where the opposition to the instrumental efficacy of the sacrament and to the ontologically real mediation of grace leads. In a demonstration of the sacrament's power to take away punishment Durandus explains: "intrantibus novum statum non imputantur eis ad poenam commissa secundum statum pristinum . . . Baptizatis non imputatur ad poenam aliquid quod commiserint secundum conversionem pristinam" ("the things done in their original state are not imputed to those entering a new state . . . . Nothing which they have done in their previous life is imputed to the baptized as ground for punishment").[32] The text suggests that the removal of guilt and punishment which is an effect of baptism, be understood merely in the sense that no account is taken of guilt and punishment. But Durandus is far from bringing forward the doctrine of "homo simul iustus et peccator".

At this time, when differences of opinion had already become

---

[32] Durandus de S. Porciano, *Sent.* IV, d. 4 q. 3 (ed. Parisiis 1508, fol. 340.

perceptible within the Thomist camp, there arose outside an opponent who compelled the Thomists to hard theological battle: John Duns Scotus. In many points Duns Scotus' doctrine of baptism remained true to tradition. Worthy of note is his definition of baptism, which goes into great detail:[33] "Baptismus est sacramentum ablutionis animae a peccato, consistens in ablutione hominis viatoris aliqualiter consentientis vel libero arbitrio nunquam usi, facta in aqua elementari fluida, cum prolatione verborum, actum et suscipientem et ministrum cum invocatione Trinitatis designantium, ab alio simul abluente, et verba ista proferente et intendente facere quod facit ecclesia christiana" ("baptism is the sacrament in which the soul is washed from sin, consisting of the washing of a man in his earthly pilgrimage with his consent or of one who has never had the use of free will, performed with natural water in a fluid state, whereby words designating the action, the recipient, and the minister are spoken, together with invocation of the Trinity, by another, who washes and at the same time speaks those words, and who intends to do what the Church does"). In opposition to Peter Lombard (*Sent.* IV, d. 3 c. 5) and to St. Thomas (*Summa th.* III, q. 66 a. 2 corp.) he maintains that Christ did not institute baptism at his baptism in Jordan but at some other time, about which the Gospels are silent, but which in any case was prior to the baptismal activity of the disciples (*Op. Oxon.* IV, d. 3 q. 4 n. 2). With respect to the matter of baptism he distinguishes between the "materia remota", the water, and the "materia proxima", the "ablutio", which may be administered in the form of "perfusio", "aspersio", or

---

[33] Johannes Duns Scotus, *Opus Oxoniense* IV, d. 6 q. 11 n. 5–6; cf. *op. cit.* d. 3 q. 1 n. 3.

"immersio" with equal validity. He gives, however, to the twin concepts of matter and form a different meaning than that which is customary elsewhere in Scholastic teaching. Whereas elsewhere the sensible sign is related to the words of institution as matter is related to form, Scotus takes the matter to consist of the entire foundation of a sacramental act, that is, of all elements which come into play in connection with its administration, both signs and words. He takes the form, however, to be the sign's particular mode which makes of it precisely this sacrament, that is, the special purpose in which the elements find their unity. According to him the words can be called at most a secondary form of the act, inasmuch as they determine the act.[34]

For Scotus baptism is, as are all the sacraments, a symbol which when applied externally affords the occasion, because of divine institution, for God to grant the grace which corresponds to, and is signified by, this symbol.[35] Scotus thus takes a position contrary to that adopted especially clearly by Hugh of St. Victor, according to which the sacraments are directly efficacious in the production of grace. However, the underlying attitude of the *Doctor subtilis,* which comes to light here, must be dealt with in connection with the dogmatic history of the doctrine of the sacraments in general.

Amongst the effects of baptism, as set forth by Scotus, his doctrine of character deserves special mention. By "character" he understands, as do the other theologians of his day, "quoddam

---

[34] *Op. cit.* d. 3 q. 2 n. 3; d. 3 q. 3 n. 2.
[35] *Op. cit.* d. 1 q. 2 and 4 and 5; d. 6 q. 9 n. 18; cf. Hieronymus de Montefortino, *Ven. Ioannis Duns Scoti Summa theologica ex universis operibus eius concinnata iuxta ordinem et dispositionem Summae S. Thomae Aqu.* vol. 5 (Rm. 1903) 579–81.

spirituale donum impressum a Deo in anima suscipientis sacramentum non iterabile" ("a certain non-repeatable gift impressed by God on the soul of him who receives sacrament"). Character is neither grace nor virtue, since both of these can, of course, be destroyed. In virtue of the baptismal character there is accomplished in the candidate an "induere Christum" (a "putting on of Christ"). He becomes a Christian, a member of Christ's family and a member of the Church. This is true even when baptism is received unworthily. In such a case, character also effects the forgiveness of pre-baptismal sins if there is subsequent repentance. Though Scotus thus takes over the doctrine of sacramental character and incorporates it into his system, he does not adopt the traditional proofs customarily advanced in his day. He criticizes them sharply and comes to the conclusion that neither Holy Scripture, nor the authority of the saints, nor even the nature of the sacrament would compel acceptance of a character, and that it is merely the authority of the Roman Church which decides the issue here.[36] Naturally Scotus does not mean by this that the Church's teaching magisterium affirms the doctrine of character without any evidence in Scripture or tradition, but merely that this evidence is, in itself, not sufficient for proof. He is also at pains to produce himself at least reasons of congruence for the existence of character.[37]

The extent of baptismal grace is, according to Scotus, different from person to person, and that not merely in the case of adults, because of the more or less good disposition of their souls, but also in the case of immature children, to the extent that the moral

[36] *Op. cit.* d. 6 q. 9.
[37] *Op. cit.* d. 6 q. 9 n. 15 ff.

218

attitude of their parents, of the minister, and of other persons who take part in the baptism enters in some way into the divine order of grace.[38]

William of Ockham impressed the stamp of his spirit on late Scholasticism. His nominalism gave philosophy and theology a new direction, which is, as the "via moderna", set in opposition to the "via antiqua" of the Thomists and Scotists. It is symptomatic for him and his followers that they commented comprehensively the first book of the *Sentences,* which offered rich opportunity for their philosophic interests, while giving quite scanty treatment to the purely theological tractates of the other books, and thus to the doctrine of baptism as well. Of the fourteen Questions in the fourth Book of his *Commentary on the Sentences* only two are concerned with baptism. In the question of sacramental causality Ockham reveals himself as an opponent of instrumental causality and adopts the pact theory of Duns Scotus. For him the sacrament is merely a "causa sine qua non" for the dispensation of grace. His definition of baptism is purely nominalistic. He denies all reality to baptism: "baptismus non habet quid rei" ("baptism has no reality", q. 2 a. 1). Baptism is a mere name for that which the word "baptism" designates: the washing of a *homo viator* who offers no actual or habitual opposition to the reception of this washing, which is carried out with natural water, . . . accompanied by utterance of the words ordained by Christ, "I baptize thee . . .". Ockham's position with regard to the doctrine of character is identical with that of Scotus. he adopts this doctrine solely on the authority of the Church's magisterium. He also proposes himself a few reasons of congru-

---

[38] Cf. Hieronymus de Montefortino, *I. Duns Scoti Summa* 5, 723 ff.

ence, for instance, that the reception into the family of Christ which always takes place in baptism – whether it has been received fruitfully or not – makes it seem fitting that there be a permanent sign of distinction. The signification of the character is based upon divine institution, in accordance with the Scotist conception of sacramental efficacy. Baptism effects a "generatio in vitam spiritualem" ("a birth into spiritual life"). This takes place in accordance with the principle: "In generatione qualibet per inductionem formae omnis forma contraria expellitur, etiam dispositio ad formam contrariam" ("In any sort of generation through the induction of the form every contrary form is expelled, even the disposition to a contrary form"). Applied to baptism this means: the influx of grace expels all guilt. For Ockham, however, grace is objectively identical with love. And by sacramental grace one can understand God's merciful will, which, because of a promise (pactio) which he has given, coexists in the sacramental act and effects something in the soul (*Sent.* I, d. 17 q. 9).

Among the later Nominalists, who in large part adopt Ockham's doctrine of baptism, the best known are Pierre d'Ailly[39] (died 1420) and Gabriel Biel[40] (died 1495), the "last schoolman".

[39] Petrus de Alliaco (P. d'Ailly), *Super* I. III. et IV. *Sent.* (Argent. 1490).
[40] Gabriel Biel, *Super* IV. *lib. sent.* (Tubingae 1501).

Chapter Ten

THE BAPTISMAL THEOLOGY OF THE COUNCIL

OF TRENT AND IN THE MODERN PERIOD

BIBLIOGRAPHY: C. Ruch, "Le baptême d'après le Concile de Trente" in (*DThC* 2/1 (1905, new impression 1927) 296–328. H. Freericks, *Die Taufe im heutigen Protestantismus Deutschlands. E. dogmat. Studie (Münst. Beitr. z. Theol. 6; Mst. 1925). W. Tr. Hahn, *Das Mitsterben und Mitauf-erstehen des Christen mit Christus bei Paulus. Ein Beitrag zum Problem der Gleichzeitigkeit des Christen mit Christus* (Gü. 1937); cf. review by O. Casel in *ArchLW* 1 (1950) no. 291, p. 315–23. K. Barth, "Die kirchliche Lehre von der Taufe" (*Theol. Existenz heute,* NF 4; Mch. 1947). O. Casel, *Die Liturgie als Mysterienfeier (Ecclesia Orans 9)* (F.bB. 1922), esp. 46–106; *Mysteriengegenwart* in *JbLW* 8 (1928) 145–224, esp. 157–63, 203–5. G. Söhn-gen, "Die Kontroverse über die kultische Gegenwart des Christus-mysteriums" in *Catholica* 7 (1938) 114–49. Th. Filthaut, *Die Kontroverse über die Mysterienlehre* (Warendf. 1947) 81–5. — M. Barth, *Die Taufe – ein Sakrament? E. exeget. Beitrag z. Gespräch über die kirchl. Taufe* (Zollikon-Zü. 1951). W. Jetter, *Die Taufe beim jungen Luther. E. Untersuchg. über das Werden der reformatorischen Sakraments- u. Taufanschauung (Beitr. z. hist. Theol.* 18; Tü. 1954*). G. W. Bromiley, *Baptism and the Anglican Reformers* (Ld. 1953).

LUTHER wanted to maintain the sacramental nature of baptism under any and all circumstances. But his reformation standpoint created assumptions which fully uprooted the Catho-lic conception of what a sacrament is. According to Luther the sacraments serve only to forgive sins. They become efficacious not by being performed, but rather by being believed in. And this happens when the inner and enlightening word of God goes hand in hand with the external ministry of the word and the administration of the sacrament. The sacraments of the new covenant are efficacious for salvation only insofar as the word of the gospel is of saving power. They are merely a particular form of the word, and there is actually only one single sacrament, the word of God. Already in his early period the subordination of the sacrament to the word had become the cardinal thesis of Luther's sacramental teaching.[1] How this conception effected Luther's understanding of baptism is shown by the following sentences of his Small Catechism:[2] "Baptism is the water contained in God's commandment and joined with God's word." "It effects the forgiveness of sins." "Of course, water does not do this, but rather the word of God, which accompanies the verbal formulary, and faith, which trusts such a word of God, present in water. "Baptism signifies that the old Adam in us is to be drowned daily by contrition and repentance . . . and that daily a new man is to emerge and arise as well." Baptism effects a regeneration which is continually being renewed. Through baptism, however, original sin is not simply blotted out, nor is its after-effect, concupiscence, weakened. Indeed it is truer to say that the Christian in baptism hangs the devil round his neck, as Luther expressed it once, inasmuch as it is only when he becomes, in baptism, a man of grace, that he becomes fully aware for the first time of the sinfulness of his

[1] A. v. Harnack, *Lehrbuch der Dogmengeschichte,* vol. 3 (Tü. ⁵1932) 851, cf. 880; W. Jetter, *Tf. b. jungen Luther,* esp. 337–43, and 165 ff., 318 ff.
[2] Harnack 3, 852 note 1.

natural manner of existence and of the temptations which come from concupiscence. Sin remains in him who is baptized. But he is placed under different rule, the rule of the gospel and of grace. And because of this sin is not reckoned against him. Baptism, therefore, effects the forgiveness of sins merely as being a promise given on the strength of a pact made by God.

Luther did not follow up the revolutionary implication of his teachings. This is proved by his concern "to justify infant baptism as a means of grace in the strict sense of the term".[3] The Anabaptists and other fanatics were more consistent in this point when they threw over infant baptism. For if the basic Lutheran thesis, that grace and faith belong inseparably together, is really to remain valid, then infant baptism is no longer a sacrament, but nothing more than an ecclesiastical celebration.[4]

Whatever was to be found in the writings of Luther and other reformers in the way of destructive innovations in the doctrine of baptism was laid before the theologians at the Council of Trent, summarized in a few terse sentences.[5] These read: in the Roman Church there is no longer true baptism; the genuine baptism is "repentance"; baptism with water, being a mere external sign, is not necessary for justification; rather it is belief in the forgiveness of sins which is crucial; therefore

---

[3] *Op. cit.* 3, 881.

[4] *Op. cit.* 3, 882; Harnack appeals at this point to the passage in Luther's *Großer Katechismus* IV (496 ed. Müller): "Absente fide baptismus nudum et inefficax signum tantummodo permanet" ("Apart from faith baptism remains merely a bare and inefficacious sign").

[5] *Concilium Tridentinum. Diariorum, actorum, epistularum, tractatuum nova collectio*: ed. Societas Goerresiana, tom. 5 (ed. St. Ehses, FbB. 1911) no. 323, p. 836–8.

the baptism of John and that of Christ have the same value; infant baptism is to be omitted, or else children so baptized are later to be re-baptized – and the like.[6] The Council determined that the great majority of the theses laid before it contradicted the whole tradition, and must therefore be condemned anew. The only significant limitations were the declaration that baptism could actually in a certain sense be termed repentance,[7] and the wish expressed by a few theologians that the distinction between John's baptism and that of Christ should not be too strongly emphasized, because of earlier doctrinal opinions in this matter.[8] And finally the fathers of the Council established fourteen canons having to do with the sacrament of baptism.[9] They present an indirect defence of the old traditional doctrine of baptism, limited to those fronts against which the innovators had launched their attack. These canons preserve for Christian baptism a greater efficacy than that of the Johannine baptism (Can. 1); they defend the necessity of real, material water for baptism as against a merely metaphorical understanding of the sacrament (Can. 2); they forbid a reduction of the sacrament to the status of a mere sign of faith in baptismal grace, ascribe the validity of what occurs in baptism to the "opus operatum" of God, assigning to it in this way a certain independence from the personal faith of man; infant baptism is thereby justified and re-baptism outlawed (Can. 13). As long as there is in the administration of baptism an "intentio faciendi

---

[6] *Loc. cit.*; cf. 838 note 2, where a German text of Luther on infant baptism is given.

[7] *Op. cit.* 5, 866.

[8] *Op. cit.* 5, 867; on this whole question see *op. cit.* no. 342, p. 863–8.

[9] Sessio VII (3rd March, 1547): *op. cit.* 5, 995f., no. 395 (*Denz.* 857–70) about baptism; 5, 995 (*Denz.* 844–56) about the sacraments in general.

quod facit Ecclesia" the sacrament is certainly valid (Can. 4) and may not be repeated. The reason for this is the presence of the sacramental character, an indelible spiritual sign (Can. 9 *de sacr. in genere*). It can be seen from Can. 6 *de sacramentis in genere*, which places upon the efficacy of the sacraments the limiting condition "non ponentibus obicem", that there is no reference here to any mechanical or magical sanctification. Baptism is necessary for the attainment of salvation; its reception is in no way left to the discretion of the individual (Can. 5 *de baptismo*). Baptismal grace can be lost again through mortal sin (Can. 6). It is clear that these canons are nothing but a framework containing the patristic and scholastic doctrine of baptism.

There is in the following centuries nothing special to record with regard to the doctrine of baptism, save perhaps that the frontal position adopted in opposition to the reformers brought with it a certain narrowing of the field of vision to those portions of doctrine which had been attacked. Only in the modern period has there been an enrichment of baptismal theology. This has come about primarily through a more thorough study of what has been handed down with regard to baptism in biblical theology, in the writings of the Fathers, and in the liturgy. Fruitful as well has been the controversy with the comparative religions school and with liberal theology.

It is beyond doubt that liberal protestant theology has given the impulse to a new and more concrete attempt to answer the questions with regard to baptism which in recent centuries have been treated more within the framework of the doctrine of the sacraments in general. The comparative religions school brought to light the numerous forms in which Christianity was rooted in the common cultural ground of the ancient world.

225

People were, to be sure, all too easily inclined to statements
which no longer did justice to the uniqueness of Christianity,
and which even called into question the claim of Christian revelation to be the truth. It was claimed that primitive Christianity
had, under the influence of the religions of the Hellenistic time
and of the religious spirit of the period, ascribed to baptism a
"natural and magical efficacy", "meanwhile ignoring, or at
least with purely secondary emphasis upon, a psychological
mediation".[10] The general direction may be indicated by names
from the beginning of this century, such as H. Gunkel, H. J.
Holtzmann, O. Pfleiderer, W. Heitmüller and G. Anrich.[11] As
early as 1909 F. J. Dölger has asserted with regard to these
tendencies: "The parallels to be found in comparative religions
can do no damage to Christianity, especially if each parallel is
judged in the framework of its own religious system."[12]
Dölger is quite prepared to recognize the value of the contribution made by the researches undertaken in the field of comparative religions, provided that they are purged of their exaggera-
tions. He grants the truth of the claim made by W. Koch, who
said in 1906: "Today more than ever sacramental doctrine must
remain in contact with the study of comparative religions, and

[10] W. Koch, *Taufe im NT*, 15.
[11] Further details *op. cit.* note 1; cf. also the works of Dölger cited in note
15 below.
[12] F. J. Dölger, *Der Exorzismus im altchristlichen Taufritual* (Pb. 1909),
foreword, p. v f. In support of his argument Dölger refers to Origen's
answer to Celsus (*Contra Celsum* I, 21): "Good, Moses is supposed to
have found in the writings of others an older doctrine and to have passed
it on to the Hebrews. If this doctrine was . . . false, and therefore not wise
and worthy of honour, then he is culpable. But if he accepted wise and
true doctrines, as you say, and instructed his people in them, what did he
do for which he can be punished?"

must explain the frequently striking parallels between the sacramental rites of the various religions . . . ."[13] A few years later, in 1911, Dölger could write: "The conception of baptism as regeneration, as a mystic death or a mystic resurrection, holds at present the close attention of scholars in the field of comparative religions. I shall express my own view on this question in a study which I have almost completed under the title, 'The Ancient Mystery Rites and Christian Baptism'."[14] Dölger was not fated to publish his comprehensive work. But the works that have appeared from his pen are addressed in the main to this matter, which is today being taken up by many theologians.[15]

Still, Dölger was merely an exponent of the *common* line of development within Catholic theology. It was in general quite impossible simply to pass over the questions posed by Protestant theology in the form in which they were treated around the turn of the century. The question was no longer merely, "When did Jesus 'institute' Christian baptism?", but rather: "Did Jesus institute Christian baptism at all? Or did Christian baptism arise first in the earliest Christian communities? And if it were necessary to answer the latter question in the affirmative, how is it, then, that this sacramental baptism came

---

[13] *Op. cit.* p. viii. [14] F. J. Dölger, *Sphragis*, foreword, p. viiif.
[15] A small substitute is Dölger's review of a few works under the title, "Mysterienwesen und Urchristentum" in *ThRev* 15 (1916) 385–93, 433–8; also *Die Sonne der Gerechtigkeit und der Schwarze. Eine religionsgesch. Studie zum Taufgelöbnis* (Mst. 1918) and the extensive volumes of *AntChr.* The same point is taken up by H. Rahner, *Griechische Mythen in christlicher Deutung* (Zü. 1945), above all pp. 21–72 (E. T. *Greek Myths and Christian Mystery,* Ld. 1963); *Reallexikon für Antike und Christentum,* edited by Th. Klauser, vol. 1 (Stg. 1950).

into being?"[16] A. Loisy had attempted a solution of this problem within the Catholic camp.[17] It proved to be wrong and was rejected by the Church. According to Loisy it is the glorified Christ who speaks in the baptismal commission of Matt. 28:19. But the historian was incapable of saying anything on the subject of this glorified Christ. The historical Jesus could have inspired baptism, but he did not institute it. It was, rather, in the Christian community that the sacrament of baptism came into being. In the question of the relationship of baptism to the heathen mysteries Loisy had also gone much too far along the path of liberal theology.[18]

Catholic research has decisively rejected the view that the Hellenistic mysteries exercised any essential, causal influence on primitive Christian baptism.[19] The same scholar who had so energetically defended the independence of the Christian rites as against the heathen mysteries,[20] M.-J. Lagrange, also gained from comparative religions keener appreciation of the fact that baptism imparts a fellowship with the Lord's passion. He comments on Rom. 6:3: "Le baptême nous conduit au Christ pour lui être unis, et cette union commence par l'union

[16] W. Koch, *Taufe im NT,* 21.

[17] The view of A. Loisy which was condemned in 1907 in the Decree *"Lamentabili sane exitu"* (propos. 42ff.; *Denz.* 2042ff.), ought really to be more exhaustively refuted in the framework of his system as a whole. From his works one could cite perhaps: *L'Évangile et l'Église* (1902), *Autour d'un petit livre* (²1903); cf. here W. Koch, *Taufe im NT,* 21, 32f.

[18] Extensive bibliography in A. Oepke in *ThWbNT* s. v. βάπτω p. 527.

[19] See W. Koch, *Taufe im NT,* 38, and the bibliography given there; also perhaps, O. Casel (review of R. Reitzenstein, *Die Vorgeschichte der christlichen Taufe,* Lp.-Bln. 1929) in *JbLW* 9 (1930) no. 146, p. 206–19; K. Prümm, *Christl. Glaube u. altheidn. Welt,* 2, 273–321.

[20] M.-J. Lagrange, "Les mystères d'Eleusis et le christianisme" in *RevBibl* 16 (1919) 157–217; "Attis et le christianisme": *op. cit.* 491–40.

à sa mort. .... Le baptême était une image de la mort, parce qu'on était complètement plongé dans l'eau; quand on sortait de l'eau, on venait à une nouvelle existence. .... Les ancients protestants ne voyaient dans l'union qu'un symbole; de nombreux critiques reconnaissent aujord'hui dans les expressions de Paul une union, mystique sans doute, mais tres réelle avec le Christ."[21] ("Baptism leads us to Christ to be united to him, and this union begins in the union with his death.... Baptism was an image of death, because one was completely submerged in the water; when one left the water, one entered upon a new existence. .... The old Reformers saw in this union only a symbol; a number of critics today recognize in St. Paul's expression a union with Christ which is doubtless mystical, but which is very real.") He develops these thoughts in a special digression. He maintains that the reaction of Protestant theologians to Luther's mere symbolism shot over the mark at first by confusing magic and sacramentality. But after this distinction had been worked about afresh, especially on the Catholic side, this Protestant reaction rightly recalled the fact that St. Paul ascribes an "action réelle mystique" to baptism, which makes of the sinner a man freed from sin, who is bound in a mysterious way with the death and resurrection of Christ. It is to the credit of Odo Casel that he pointed out emphatically this retrospective relationship of baptism with Christ's saving work, and that he thus gave Catholic theology at the very least, as even his opponents admit, valuable new stimuli.[22]

[21] M.-J. Lagrange, *Saint Paul: Épître aux Romains* (Pa. 1915, reprinted 1931) 144; excursus 149–52.
[22] There are good reports of O. Casel's stimuli and the controversy which followed them in Th. Filthaut, *Die Kontroverse über die Mysterienlehre,*

These findings have found increasing recognition within Protestant theology.[23] Despite the advance of this more concrete conception, the old basic ideas of the Reformation are still so powerful that there is a readiness to draw the logical conclusions of these ideas for infant baptism, and to reject it as unbiblical.[24] M. Barth has brought this controversy to a head with his work, *Die Taufe – ein Sacrament?* (1951). He states at the outset – not without reason – that a controversy about infant baptism does not belong in a work of New Testament exegesis; for "the New Testament does not mention any baptism of immature children".[25] Shortly thereafter, however, he terms the Catholic Church's baptism of infants as "a falling away from apostolic Christianity". The equation of baptism

81–5, as well as in the works of R. Schnackenburg, *Heilsgeschehen,* and of V. Warnach, *Taufe u. Christusgeschehen* (see bibliography to chapter 1).

[23] A good witness to this fact is supplied by A. Oepke in *ThWbNT* 1 (1933) 527ff., even if the reserve with regard to the "Catholic sacrament" (*op. cit.* 541–3) has not yet disappeared completely. Definitely worthy of note is also the presentation of W. Tr. Hahn, *Das Mitsterben u. Mitauferstehen mit Christus bei Paulus.* Cf. the review of this work by O. Casel in *ArchLW* 1 (1950) no. 291.

[24] See the exhaustive arguments of H. Freericks, *Taufe im heutigen Protestantismus Deutschlands,* 84, 191, 228; and then K. Barth, *Kirchl. Lehre v. d. Taufe,* 29–40 (the work which gave the signal for the latest controversies). J. Schneider, *Die Taufe im Neuen Testament* (Stg. 1952) reports about the state of the controversy at present; cf. also E. Stauffer, *Theologie des NT* ([3]1947) 140f. Baptism is viewed either as a mere confirmatory sign, or as so bound up with a faith which must be personally confessed, that an immature man, and therefore an infant, cannot receive it. This is true even if one admits, as does J. Schneider for example, "that baptism is not a mere external visible sign for something which happens internally. In baptism something happens to the candidate which comes from God" (*op. cit.* 77). For witnesses for infant baptism from tradition see pp. 70, 88, 123 *seq.,* 147, (cf. however 146), 176, 183, 187, 193, 207, 212 *seq.*

[25] M. Barth, *Taufe,* 164.

with mystery was, according to him, the mother of infant baptism. This book, which admittedly offers a number of noteworthy contributions, is on the whole a shocking testimony to the results of an exegesis which is no longer willing to recognize any kind of tradition, not even that of the Reformers themselves.[26]

[26] *Op. cit.* p. 212: "A Church which is not tied to Scripture and which is not chained to its own tradition will dare at all times to re-examine its position and will not shrink back in the face of the results that such a re-examination may bring – even if this should lead to a decision which deviates theoretically and practically from Luther and Calvin." For more detailed critical controversy we refer to Ch. Masson in *RevThPh* 3, 3 (1953) 21–30; also to V. Warnach, "Taufe u. Christusgeschehen nach Röm. 6" in *ArchLW* 3, 2 (1954) 284–366; and finally to J. Hering in *RevHistPhRel* 33 (1953) 255–60.

Chapter Eleven

THE FULL RECOGNITION OF CONFIRMATION AS AN INDEPENDENT SACRAMENT IN ITS OWN RIGHT

BIBLIOGRAPHY: In addition to the works mentioned in chapters 1 and 2: G. Bareille - P. Bernard - C. Mangenot, "Confirmation" in *DThC* 3/1, 1026-93. K. Lübeck, "Die Firmung in der orthodoxen griechischen Kirche" in *Pastor B* 33 (1920/21) 111–18, 176–84, 219–26; same author, "Die Wieder-firmung in der griechisch-russischen Kirche" in *Kath* 95 = IV, 16/2 (1915) 198–214, 281–93. M. Jugie, *Theologia dogmatica Christianorum Orientalium ab Ecclesia dissidentium,* vol. 3 (Pa. 1930) 126–76; vol. 5 (1935) 289 ff., 685 ff. H. Weisweiler, "Das Sacrament der Firmung in den systematischen Werken der ersten Frühscholastik" in *Schol* 7 (1933) 481–523. J. A. M. Prein, "De Geschiedenis van de romeinse vormritus" in *TLtg* 39 (1955) 199–218.

OUR PREVIOUS investigations (see chapter 2 above) have yielded the certain fact that the Church was familiar as early as the age of the apostles with a second sacramental act subsequent to baptism and supplementing it. This is the laying on of hands, the effect of which finds expression in visible gifts of the Spirit. But it is just as certain that there is not a single Pauline text which points really compellingly to the laying on of hands as a part of the total rite of initiation. Even when he speaks of the various visible gifts of grace, which according to Acts are imparted to Christians only as a result of the laying on of hands, he traces them back to the Spirit which is active in baptism and

232

which incorporates us into the body of Christ, in order thus to show that these gifts of grace are bestowed for the good of the whole fellowship. Finally, we have interpreted the fact that St. Paul does not mention the laying on of hands in the general rite of initiation, and that he does not speak of the differing effect of the water-bath and the laying on of hands, as meaning that we must assume that the initiation rite of the primitive Church embraced both the water-bath and the laying on of hands. This total action was called quite simply "baptism", after its first and fundamental rite, which, as such, is both its most necessary as well as its most impressive element. This "baptism" imparts fellowship with Christ in "dying to sin" and in "rising again to a new life for God". It constitutes regeneration to a new life which is filled with the Spirit. But the individual stages of this total effect were not precisely distinguished from one another. Only later did it become necessary to distinguish consciously and exactly between the individual parts of the total action, and above all to define the difference in their effects. We might name, as definite witnesses to this process of development: St. Cyril of Jerusalem, who treats the imparting of the Spirit in a special catechism, following the baptismal catechisms, namely in his *Third Mystagogic Catechism* Περὶ Χρίσματος, and St. Ambrose, who distinguishes a "signaculum spirituale", through which the seven-fold Spirit is imparted, from baptism proper (and from the accompanying anointing which immediately follows it). This distinction he justifies with the words: "quia post fontem superest, ut perfectio fiat" ("for after the font perfection is still to be accomplished").[1]

---

[1] *De sacramentis* III, 2; see p. 5 above.

This state of affairs, however, certainly exists earlier. Evidence for this may be found in the tractate *De rebaptismate,* which makes a radical division between "baptisma aquae" and the "baptisma spiritus" (which is normally administered in the laying on of hands).[2] But in striving to refute Cyprian's view and to justify speculatively the validity of heretic baptism, the author of this tractate goes as far as to ascribe even the forgiveness of sins and the mediation of grace to Spirit-baptism; and he holds that in water-baptism only the invocation of the name of Jesus is given. He attempts thus to get around Cyprian's argument against the validity of heretic baptism – namely, that the Holy Spirit certainly could not be present amongst heretics. Of course, a special opinion of this kind, which grows out of a controversy, may not be generalized or given too much importance.[3] But even Cyprian holds that confirmation is the fulfilment of what happens in baptism; for the baptized "achieve the Holy Spirit through prayer and through the laying on of our hands

[2] *e.g. De rebaptismate* 10 (Hartel in *CSEL* 3 Appendix 82_{5-18}): "cum salus nostra in baptismate spiritus, quod plerumque cum baptismate aquae coniunctum est, sit constituta, siquidem per nos baptisma tradetur, integre . . . sine ulla ullius rei separatione tradatur . . . si vero ab alienis traditum fuerit, . . . tantummodo baptismate spiritali *i.e.* manus impositione episcopi et spiritus sancti subministratione subveniri debeat" ("since our salvation consists in the baptism of the Spirit, which is mostly joined with the baptism of water, so baptism should be performed completely, when it is imparted by us . . . without anything being left out . . . but when it is administered by others, . . . one should help the administration of the Spirit with spiritual baptism, *i.e.* through the imposition of the bishop's hand").
[3] G. W. H. Lampe has, in his book, *The Seal of the Spirit* (1951), criticized quite rightly G. Dix's interpretation of such passages and of others like them in the sense of an imparting of the Spirit which is fully separate from baptism. He also shows how in the third and fourth centuries the teaching that there was in baptism a pouring out of the Spirit receded somewhat.

234

and are fulfilled by the Lord's seal" (*Ep*. 73, 9). And Tertullian testifies that the candidate, after leaving the bath, is anointed like the priests of the Old Testament and like Christ himself. And then he speaks of a subsequent laying on of hands with a word of blessing which invokes the Holy Spirit (*De bapt*. 7–8). From this point the way back to Acts 8 and 19 is entirely natural and obvious.

These pieces of Patristic testimony do show definitely and clearly that confirmation is an independent act in the sense of the Church's later teaching. Nevertheless, even such evidence leaves this act so much within the framework of the entire action that it is often difficult to ascertain where the division lies, where one act begins and the other ends. It is, therefore, not surprising that, precisely for this interim period, the pressing question arises, where exactly we are to place the beginning of confirmation in the course of the rites which were customary in the third century (in Rome and Africa): the water-bath, anointing with chrism, laying on of hands, and the *consignatio* (or *signaculum*) without anointing. The so-called "post-baptismal anointing" can, of course, hardly be reckoned as forming a part of the sacrament of confirmation, but must be considered as belonging to baptism and as a symbol of the fundamental and initial imparting of the Spirit which occurs in baptism.[4] Confirmation is certainly "not in any exclusive way the sacrament of the imparting of the Spirit. Even baptism alone endows us with the Holy Spirit in a fundamental manner, so that the *chrismatio* (anointing with chrism), which is a symbol of the imparting of the Spirit,

---

[4] This opinion is maintained by P. Galtier in *RevHistE* 13 (1912) 467–76 and by H. Elfers (see chap. 2, footnote 19 above) as against B. Welte, *Postbapt. Salbung*.

does not stand in contradiction to the supernatural reality of baptism".[5] There is simply "in baptism a fundamental participation in Christ's priestly and kingly dignity, and a more intensive participation in confirmation".[6]

Once the post-baptismal anointing is thus eliminated, only the facts of the rite can inform us with regard to the symbol which is now peculiar to confirmation. In the East the anointing with myrrh occupied a central position already at an early date,[7] whereas the laying on of hands – at any rate as a rite different from the *consignatio* – gradually receded more into the background.[8] The situation is entirely different in the West. Here the laying on of hands constitutes, at first, the actual heart of confirmation. It gives "the full imparting of the Spirit, the completion and the conclusion of the rite of initiation", and was reserved to the bishop.[9] An anointing accompanying this act cannot be ascertained in the case of Ambrose, and even in Augustine's case it cannot be proved with certainty.[10] The letter of Pope Innocent I to bishop Decentius[11] is the first certain evidence in the West for such an anointing. Nevertheless, we can assume that this custom goes back to Pope Silvester, who could have taken it over from Hippolytus.[12]

---

[5] H. Elfers in *ThGl* 34 (1943) 341.   [6] *Op. cit.* 338.

[7] H. Elfers, Kirchenordnung Hippolyts, 147; "attested to for the Church of Alexandria as early as the time of Clement and Origen".

[8] *Op. cit.* 127–30; J. Coppens, *L'imposition des mains,* 295, note 3.

[9] H. Elfers, *op. cit.* 111, 153.   [10] *Op. cit.* 114–18.

[11] *PL* 20, 555 A; also in *Denz.* 98.

[12] *Liber Pontificalis:* "Constituit et chrisma ab episcopo confici. Et privilegium episcopis contulit, ut baptizatum consignent, propter haereticam suasionem" ("It determines that the chrism shall also be prepared by the bishop. And it confers upon bishops the privilege of signing the baptized, on account of the arguments of the heretics") (ed. L. Duchesne, vol. 1; Pa. 1886) 76;

Feeling our way back now from what has been established as certain, it appears that the essential core of confirmation both in the West and in the East consisted originally of a laying on of hands. Even in the Church of Alexandria a laying on of hands can, according to H. Elfers, certainly not have been lacking, although in this Church the connection between the laying on of hands and the anointing is attested at an earlier date than anywhere else.[13] Special emphasis is attached there to the anointing. That would lie quite along the line which leads back to the usage of the apostolic Church (according to Acts 8). Now we know quite well the significance attached to the "idea of anointing" by the Fathers, especially those of the second century.[14] But we know hardly anything about the concrete ritual form of the anointing, and we are quite unable to decide to which sacramental act such an anointing should, in a given case, be reckoned, despite a passage in the letter of Theophilus of Antioch to Autolycus (see chap. 3 above, footnote 119). We can agree with H. Elfers, when he says:[15] "The sacramental liturgy of anointing has come into being from three different sources which continually influenced each other. These are: the Old Testament ideas with regard to the anointing of kings and priests, the significance which was attached to oil in the whole ancient world, and ideas of a spiritualistic and symbolic kind. Only in the third century and later can one see more clearly how the liturgical rite of anointing has assumed concrete form from these three elements." In the Eastern Church the anointing (with myrrh)

---

quoted also by J. Coppens, *L'imposition,* 334, footnote 2. Cf. H. Elfers, *Kirchenordnung H.,* 113, 126.

[13] H. Elfers, *op. cit.* 147. [14] S. B. Welte, *Postbapt. Salbung,* 18–22.
[15] H. Elfers in *ThGl* 34 (1942) 336.

assumes a central position in the rite of confirmation already in
the third century, and gradually pushes the laying on of hands
completely into the background. In the West on the other hand,
and only in Rome, probably under the influence of Hippolytus
of Rome, who took his inspiration from Alexandria, a confirmation anointing appreared later on (in the fourth century
approximately) and at first only sporadically, alongside the
laying on of hands.[16]

Thus the symbol peculiar to confirmation took a different form
in East and West. But the teaching as to what was effected by this
rite of confirmation was not so different. According to Tertullian
the laying on of hands invites and invokes the Holy Spirit
(*De bapt.* 8). Ambrose called confirmation a "signaculum spiritale", in which Christ has given the pledge of the Spirit; and this
infusion of the Spirit takes place in response to the appeal of the
priest (*De myst.* 7, 42; *De sacr.* III, 2, 8). For the Eastern Church
in general, confirmation means "completion through the Spirit;
the chrism symbolizes ordination as the disciples of Christ;
the *sphragis* with myrrh imparts firmness and steadfastness".[17]
If a similar significance is attached in the West,[18] and especially
in Rome, to the chrismation which immediately follows baptism
(and which is, therefore, to be distinguished from the laying
on of hands), that does not compel us to hold that anointing and
the laying on of hands were in these places already combined
in a single rite. We shall be most likely to assess correctly the
facts of the situation if we see them as an expression of the fact

---

[16] H. Elfers, *Kirchenordnung H.,* 127–39; J. Coppens, *L'imposition,* 323–43.
[17] H. Elfers, *op. cit.* 128.
[18] B. Welte, *Postbapt. Salb.,* 41 refers to it.

that confirmation completes and strengthens something which has foundations that go right back to baptism.

More exact information about the gift of confirmation is afforded us by the *Third Mystagogic Catechism* of Cyril of Jerusalem. We have already discussed this (see above p. 143) in connection with Cyril's teaching about initiation as a whole. His interpretation of the anointing parallels that of the act of baptism in water. Through the anointing with myrrh the candidates become associates and partners of Christ, "who was anointed with the spiritual oil of joy, that is with the Holy Spirit" (*Cat. myst.* 3, 2). The myrrh is the antitype of the Holy Spirit, "Christ's gift of grace and the efficacy of the Holy Spirit through the presence of his divinity" (*op. cit.* 3, 3). The anointing of the soul with the invisible Holy Spirit corresponds to the visible anointing of the body (*op. cit.* 3, 3). Only through this anointing do the candidates become fully fit for the name, Christian (*loc. cit.* 3, 5). The Christian must from henceforth preserve unblemished this chrism, which is the source of all spiritual enlightenment (according to the biblical text placed at the head of this catechism: 1 John 2:20–8). The sacramental effects which Cyril lists here remain from this time on in Oriental theology always connected with the anointing with myrrh. This anointing is, quite simply, what we in the West call confirmation.[19]

In this connection we must, however, make one important limitation. In the *Acts of Thomas,* in the *Acts of John of Zebedee,* and in the Syrian *Didascalia* (third century) there is no anointing

---

[19] Thus *op. cit.* p. 46; extensive treatment by H. Elfers, *Kirchenordnung H.,* pp. 127–39; J. Coppens, *L'imposition,* pp. 325–33.

after baptism; nor is any to be found in the writings of Ephraim the Syrian. "In the Syrian rite this anointing is clearly prescribed for the first time in the *Apostolic Constitutions,* which come from Syria around the year 400."[20] But when W. de Vries[21] proceeds to dispute the existence of anything corresponding to our sacrament of confirmation in these Syrian (or Nestorian) circles, then that seems to us to go too far. If we consider impartially the *Mystagogic Catecheses* of Theodore of Mopsuestia, as well as Ephraim's texts and those of the Nestorian liturgies,[22] and especially if we apply the methods used in the comparative study of liturgies, we can be reasonably certain that even the Syrian Church had some further act after the baptism with water. This was, to be sure, not an anointing with myrrh or with other oil, but it was certainly a "marking", and perhaps even a laying on of hands,[23] which was connected with the imparting of the Spirit in such a manner that we can say that we have here what the other Churches call, and in exactly this position in the rite, confirmation.[24] It is certainly abundantly clear here that this act of

[20] W. de Vries, "Der Nestorianismus Theodors von Mopsuestia in seiner Sakramentenlehre" in *OrChrPer* 7 (1949) 143; cf. 132f., and E. J. Duncan, *Baptism in the Demonstrations of Aphraates the Persian Sage (Cath. Univ. of America, Stud. in Christ. Antiquities* no. 8, 1945).
[21] W. de Vries, "Sakramententheol. bei den Nestorianern" (*Or. Chr. Anal.* 133; Rm. 1947) 182–9.   [22] W. de Vries, *Sakramententheol.,* 182–9.
[23] Such a laying on of hands is certainly to be found in the texts quoted by W. d. Vries (*Sakramententheol.,* 188) – though it is true that they come from a later period, say from about 544.
[24] The opinion of M. Jugie (*Theol. dogm. Chr. Or.,* 5, 291) seems to us to be more pertinent than that of W. de Vries: "De sacramento confirmationis hic (in the works of Theodore of Mopsuestia) agi nemo infitias ibit" ("No one will deny that it is the sacrament of confirmation which is treated here"). He would like to suppose essentially the same for the present-day Nestorians: *op. cit.* 295.

confirmation remains completely a part of the total order of baptism, so that it is understandable that the Nestorians, for instance, hardly ever bothered their heads explicitly about the distinction between baptism and confirmation.[25] This state of affairs is by no means a deviation,[26] but rather an archaism in which the ancient Christian type is preserved to a later date, and according to which "baptism", considered as the entire process of initiation, imparts regeneration and the filling with the Spirit, without any exact distinction being made in detail. The only strange feature is that in the Syrian Church the symbol of anointing was placed prior to the actual water-baptism.[27]

No proper treatment of the anointing with myrrh has been handed down to us apart from that of Cyril of Jerusalem. This anointing is, of course, referred to, but always in the closest connection with baptism and as its crowning conclusion. Especially impressive treatments of this kind are to be found in the works of later systematic theologians, such as the pseudo-Dionysius and John of Damascus.

In contrast to this relatively clear situation in the East, there emerges in the West a process of duplication: there is an anointing immediately after baptism, then a rite for the imparting of the Spirit through the laying on of hands, and later a further anointing with chrism.[28]

It is true that the oldest witnesses in the West – leaving aside Hippolytus, for the time being – are familiar with only *one* post-baptismal anointing, which was in turn followed by the laying on of hands. The first that we hear of any anointing in connec-

---

[25] M. Jugie, *op. cit.* 5, 289.   [26] Cf., for instance, *op. cit.* 5, 294f.
[27] For this whole problem cf. also B. Welte, *Postbapt. Salbung,* 25, 39.
[28] See pp. 234f. above and B. Welte, *Postbapt. Salbung,* passim.

tion with confirmation is in a letter of Pope Innocent I to the bishop of Gubbio, written in the year 416; and the *Liber Pontificalis* has a report about the introduction of this custom by Pope Silvester.[29] The scholars have suspected that this custom was introduced in the light of the anointing prescribed by Hippolytus, under Oriental influences, as this point in the rite.[30] Gradually, however, this anointing gains in importance. The historical and liturgical connections are rather complicated, and the research has not yet reached any generally agreed conclusion here. So we shall simply have to content ourselves with saying that in all probability the laying on of hands in confirmation was already at an early date accompanied by an anointing. We find the two ceremonies connected in the writings of the Venerable Bede and Isidore of Seville.[31] People simply saw the laying on of hands as contained in the *consignatio,* as prescribed by the *Sacramentarium Gregorianum*. And it was therefore possible for people to accept the statement of Innocent III: "The laying on of hands is characterized by the anointing of the forehead with chrism, and is also called confirmation."[32]

Of course, in High Scholasticism the anointing with chrism was so strongly emphasized – probably for reasons connected with systematic theology – that in practice the laying on of hands was no longer discussed by the theologians. Thus we can understand the gradual development which took place from

[29] See notes 11 and 12 above.
[30] P. Galtier, "La Tradition Apostolique d'Hippolyte. Particularités et initiatives liturgiques" in *RechScRel* 13 (1923) 527, quoted with agreement by J. Coppens, *L'imposition,* 334, footnote 2.
[31] J. Coppens, *op. cit.* 311.
[32] Innocentius III, *Ep. ad Basilium archiep. Trinovitanum,* quoted by J. Coppens, *op. cit.* 312, footnote 2.

the Second Council of Lyons (1274) to the *Decretum pro Armenis* at the Council of Florence (1439). The former Council decreed: "The bishops administer confirmation by anointing those who have been re-born with chrism" (*Denz.* 465). But in Florence we read: "Confirmation is given in the Church in place of the laying on of hands." And confirmation is said to consist of the anointing with chrism accompanied by the (present) formula: "Signo te . . .".[33]

We find a theological interpretation of confirmation in the works of the scholastic theologians.[34] It is true that Peter Lombard, like his predecessors – as far as they mention confirmation at all – has only one very short chapter about confirmation (*Sent.* IV, d. 7). Its "forma", that is the essential sacramental form, consists of the words used by the bishop in signing the baptized on their foreheads with chrism. Only the bishop can administer the sacrament, in accordance with apostolic usage (with allusion to Acts 8). The "virtus sacramenti" is the imparting of the Holy Spirit "for vigorous action" (ad robur), whereas the Spirit is given in baptism "for the forgiveness of sins". Like baptism and ordination, confirmation may not be repeated. The patristic authorities cited in

---

[33] "Secundum sacramentum est confirmatio; cuius materia est chrisma confectum ex oleo . . . per episcopum benedicto. Forma autem est: Signo te signo crucis . . . hanc (unctionem) non nisi episcopus debet conferre . . . (Acts 8:14ff. follows in proof.). Loco autem illius manus impositionis datur in Ecclesia confirmatio" ("The second sacrament is confirmation; its matter is chrism made from oil . . . blessed by a bishop. The form is: I sign thee in the sign of the cross . . . this (unction) should not be administered by anyone but a bishop . . . Confirmation is given in the Church in place of the laying on of hands", *Denz.* 697).

[34] For the details see H. Weisweiler, *Sakr. d. Firmung in den systemat. Werken d. ersten Frühscholastik,* 481–523.

support of this statement are all to be found already in the Decretum Gratiani.[35] The first four canons are pseudo-Isidorian forgeries, but correspond completely to tradition[36]. Whether confirmation was a sacrament, or perhaps a sacramental belonging to baptism, was no problem for most of the commentators. They took it for granted, on the basis of tradition, that it was a sacrament. "The credit for raising in due form the question of the sacramentality of confirmation belongs probably to St. Thomas Aquinas."[37] But like his contemporaries he took the use of chrism already in the apostolic period so completely for granted that he hardly went back to the Acts of the Apostles at all, save to prove the bishop's prerogative of administering confirmation. People very often did not even interpret the laying on of hands in Acts 8 as a sacramental act.[38] Considerable uncertainty prevailed in the question as to when confirmation was instituted. An especially peculiar opinion is that of Alexander of Hales, who says that the apostles bestowed the Holy Spirit without any sacrament, and that the sacrament was instituted "Spiritus Sancti instinctu" only at the Council of Meaux (845).[39] Others taught that the sacrament was instituted by the apostles. St. Thomas Aquinas proceeds from the

---

[35] Gratiani *Decretum* P. III, d. 5 d. 1–10 (*PL* 187, 1855 C – 1858 C).

[36] See J. B. Umber, *Schriftlehre v. S. d. Firm.,* 2, footnote 2.

[37] *Op. cit.* 5.

[38] *Op. cit.* 7; but Acts 8 was interpreted as a genuine confirmation, and a later change was assumed nevertheless. This is the judgment even of St. Thomas Aquinas in his little work, *De articulis fidei et Ecclesiae sacramentis* (see note 41 below).

[39] Alexander Hal., *Summa theol.* in IV, q. 9 m. 1 quoted by J. B. Umberg, *Schriftlehre v. S. d. Firm.,* 8 f.; also in the scholion of Quaracchi's edition of Bonaventura, p. 165. Just how Alexander of Hales comes up with the Council of Meaux (Conc. Meldense) is hard to say. There is nothing of this

244

basic principle that the institution of a sacrament of the New Testament is the prerogative of Christ alone. Originally he sees the institution in the laying of Christ's hands upon the children (Matt. 19:15).[40] He later abandons such explanations and says (*Summa th.* III, q. 72 a. 1 ad 1) that Christ instituted this sacrament not directly but by promise (non exhibendo, sed promittendo), referring in support to John 16:7: for the fullness of the Spirit could not have been given before the Lord's resurrection and ascension.

St. Thomas sees the chrism alone as the matter absolutely essential for the sacrament. He does not mention the laying on of hands at all. He even says in his *Opusculum de articulis fidei et Ecclesiae sacramentis*[41] that confirmation has taken the place of the (apostolic) laying on of hands, a statement which, as we have seen, was later taken over literally in the *Decretum pro Armenis* (*Denz*. 697). Bonaventure likewise requires chrism as the necessary matter, but does also mention the laying on of hands in connection with the anointing: "The hand which is to confirm is strongly (potestative) imposed and the cross is imprinted on the forehead."[42] These statements reflect the Western tradition which already at an early date perceived the laying on of hands as contained in the anointing. Therefore

kind to be found amongst the many canons of this council. On the contrary canon 44 refers expressly to the relevant regulations of Innocent I; canon 46 requires merely the consecration of oil on Maundy Thursday (*Mansi* 14, 829 f.).

[40] Thomas Aqu. calls this an "opinio probabilior": *Sent.* IV, d. 7 q. 1 qc. 1 ad a.

[41] Thomas Aqu., *Opera omnia* t. 27 (ed. St. E. Fretté), opusc. 4 (Pa.: Vives, 1875) 171–82; the passage about confirmation (p. 179) is somewhat more comprehensive than the text of the *Decretum pro Armenis*.

[42] Bonaventura, *Breviloquium* p. 6 c. 8 (Quar.–Ed. 5, 272).

the present *Codex Iuris Canonici* sums up this development and again adopts more closely the diction of the ancient Church by saying: "Sacramentum confirmationis conferri debet per manus impositionem cum unctione chrismatis . . ." ("the sacrament of confirmation is to be conferred by the laying on of hands together with anointing with chrism . . .").[43]

The blessing or consecration of the chrism, which is testified to already at an early date, as for instance, by the *Euchologion* of Serapion,[44] and which we have met with in the works of Cyril of Jerusalem, as well as in those of the pseudo-Dionysius,[45] who emphasizes it strongly, is considered by the scholastic theologians, in accordance with the tradition, as essential for confirmation.[46] They unanimously emphasize the necessity of the word as well. The indicative formula provided in the present *Pontificale* appears for the first time in the tenth century in the Ordines Romani: "I sign thee with the sign of the cross and confirm thee with the chrism of salvation . . .".[47] For the East we have the formula, as early as the fourth or fifth century: "Seal of the gift of the Holy Spirit".[48] In the West

---

[43] *CIC* can. 780; cf. J. B. Umberg, *Schriftlehre v. S. d. Firm.*, 143–53.

[44] Εὐχὴ εἰς τὸ χρῖσμα ἐν ᾧ χρίονται οἱ βαπτισθέντες (F. X. Funk, *Didascalia et Constitutiones Apostolorum* 2 [1905] 186f.).

[45] See pp. 143 and 171 above; cf. also the connection made by Gregory of Nyssa, p. 151, footnote 48.

[46] Thomas Aqu., *Summa th.* III, q. 72 a. 3: "Sed contra: ad hoc sacramentum requiritur quod materia huius sacramenti prius per episcopum consecretur" ("but on the other hand this sacrament requires that the matter be consecrated beforehand by the bishop"); Bonaventura speaks in a quite similar sense, *Sent.* IV, d. 7 a. 1 q. 2 ad 1.

[47] D. Winzen, *Kommentar z. Deutsch. Thomas-Ausgabe* vol. 29, footnote 219.

[48] F. J. Dölger, *Sphragis*, 185: "in a letter of the Church of Constantinople to the Bishop Martyrius of Antioch"; cf. also M. Jugie, *Theol. dogm. Chr. or.*, 3, 138f.

deprecatory formulas were customary, as is indicated already by Tertullian (*De bapt.* 8).

The task of confirmation is "con-firmatio", the strengthening of the baptized Christian, that he may "like a front line fighter (pugil) confess the name of Christ boldly and publicly".[49] St. Thomas interprets the confirmation character similarly: "that a man may proclaim spiritual things by his bold confession" (*Sent.* IV, d. 7 q. 2 a. 1 sol.). In the *Summa theol.* (III, q. 72 a. 5) he speaks of receiving the "power to carry out what belongs to the spiritual struggle against the enemies of faith". Thus the grace of confirmation does not serve the forgiveness of sins, like the grace of baptism, but "the increase and defence of righteousness" (*loc. cit.* q. 72 a. 7 ad 1).

From the fact that confirmation cannot be repeated Scholasticism deduces, at least from the time of William of Auvergne and Hugh of St.-Cher, the existence of a character in confirmation, and Peter Lombard says this is "indubitanter".[50] It is true that we had to state (above p. 132f.) that, contrary to the assumption of a number of authors, the fact that baptism cannot be repeated was not established with complete certainty either for the Africa of Augustine's day or for the Rome of Pope Leo the Great. Pope Vigilius (died 555) was the first to give to the existing liturgical practice the interpretation which later came to be accepted in the West. According to this interpretation the laying on of hands which was given to the heretic upon his return to the Church is not identical with the laying on of hands for the imparting of the Spirit. Rather it is a mere rite of penance

---

[49] Bonaventura, *Breviloquium* p. 6 c. 8 (Aur.–Ed. 5, 273).
[50] Cf. F. Brommer, *L. v. sakram. Char.*, 64.

or reconciliation (see above, p. 133, note 77). Whereas it was in the entire Church undisputed that confirmation could not be repeated, at least when it had been validly administered within the Church,[51] considerable deviations in the application of this principle to apostates are to be found in the East. It can probably be taken as assured that there is not, prior to the ninth century, even in the Greek Church any solid evidence for an actual repetition of confirmation. A rite of reconciliation, which we may probably ascribe to St. Methodius, Patriarch of Constantinople (843–7), prescribes a bath upon completion of the period of penance, and then continues: "When he comes out of the bath, and is clothed with a linen towel, let him be anointed with myrrh like the baptized." A number of manuscripts add here as accompanying words the customary formula for confirmation: "Seal of the gift of the Holy Spirit."[52] But the context suggests that what we actually have here is merely a symbolic bath reminiscent of baptism, and thus also merely an action which recalls the bestowal of the Spirit in confirmation.[53] Only in this way can we understand the sharp rebuke administered to the Latins by a successor of Methodius, Photius, because they had reconfirmed a few Bulgarians who had already been confirmed in the Greek rite.[54] But it is also just as certain that Methodius' canon could be "through the terseness of its rubric . . . the cause and occasion for the subsequent Greek practice of reconfirmation, which endures to the present

---

[51] Cf. M. Jugie, *Theol. dogm. Chr. or.*, 3, 138 f.; also P. Galtier, *Imposition des mains* in *DThC* 7, 1397–1408.   [52] Thus M. Jugie, *op. cit.* 3, 145.
[53] This is the interpretation both of M. Jugie, *op. cit.* 3, 145–7, and K. Lübeck, *Wiederfirmung in der griech.-russ. Kirche*, 284 ff.
[54] Photius, *Epist.* lib. I, *ep.* 13, 6 f. (*PG* 102, 725 A–C).

day".[55] This unfortunate interpretation has come to the fore especially since the separation of the Churches.

The scholastic theologians, in their unanimous designation of the bishop as the minister of confirmation, are completely within the Western tradition. Even Hippolytus testified that the bishop, after the presbyters have carried out a previous anointing, lays on his hand and administers the anointing. And Jerome testifies to this episcopal prerogative, despite the peculiar way in which he evaluates it.[56] Innocent I states this right expressly and refuses to allow priests to administer confirmation, citing both ecclesiastical usage as well as the apostolic practice (Acts 8:14–17) in support of his argument.[57] But the theologians also found in the Church's tradition grounds for a possible exception, whereby, "when no bishop can be had, priests may also anoint the baptized on the forehead with chrism".[58] In the Orient, on the other hand, the priest was recognized as the minister of confirmation already at an early date, although the oldest witnesses say that it is the bishops who both baptize as well as anoint and lay on hands.[59] In fact,

---

[55] K. Lübeck, *Wiederfirmung,* 291; similarly, M. Jugie, *op. cit.* 3, 147.

[56] Hieronymus, *Dialogus ctr. Luciferianos* 9: "ad honorem potius sacerdotii quam ad legem necessitatis" ("more for the honour of the priesthood than for the law of necessity") (*PL* 23, 164 C): cf. here J. Coppens, *L'imposition,* 304.

[57] In the letter to Decentius of Gubbio (*PL* 20, 554 B; *Denz.* 98) quoted in footnote 11 above.

[58] Gregor. M., *Ep.* 26 *ad Januarium* (*PL* 77, 696 B), quoted from Thomas Aqu., *Summa th.* III, q. 72 a. 11 ad 1; cf. D. Winzen, *Kommentar z. Deutsch. Thomas-Ausgabe,* vol. 29, 473, footnote 231.

[59] As an example of the administration of the entire initiation rite by a bishop see Bishop Firmilian of Caesarea, *Ep.* 75, 7 (Hartel in *CSEL* 3, 814f.). The problem, of course, does not lie here, but rather in the fact that

however, it came to be customary for priests to administer confirmation as well, and this has been recognized by the Roman Church in the case of the East.[60] This is all the easier to understand in that the consecration of the myrrh, which is given great importance in the oriental confirmation rite, is reserved to the bishops.

The synthesis which the great Scholastics were able to create from these few elements in the tradition has remained in its essential parts authoritative for the entire subsequent period.

The sixteenth century reformers, in breaking with tradition, no longer perceived in confirmation a sacrament but merely "rites taken over from the Fathers", "without God's command and without a clear guarantee of grace" (*Apologia Confessionis Augustanae*), an "otiosa caeremonia" (Melanchthon).[61] The Council of Trient anathematized such views in the canons of Session VII.[62]. In response to the desire of the theologians, an article was drawn up against the attacks on the saving power of the chrism.[63]

In the period following the Council, people felt themselves in the face of the Reformers obliged above all to construct with greater care the proof from Scripture of the sacramentality of confirmation.[64] St. Robert Bellarmine played an important part

"presbyteri" may also administer confirmation. On the view of Orthodox theology cf. M. Jugie, *Theol. dogm. Chr. Or.*, 3, 166ff.

[60] See M. Jugie, *op. cit.* 3, 163f.

[61] *Concilium Tridentinum* vol. 5 (ed. Ehses) no. 323, p. 838; J. B. Umberg, *Schriftlehre v. S. d. Firm.*, 12f. quotes a longer text from M. Luther, *Von der Babylonischen Gefangenschaft*.

[62] *Conc. Trid.* vol. 5 (ed. Ehses) no. 395, p. 996; *Denz.* 871–3.

[63] *Op. cit.* no. 342, p. 868: artic. 2.

[64] As is shown quite well by J. B. Umberg, *Schriftlehre v. S. d. Firm.*, esp. 12, 32, and 59.

in this task. It is true that "not everything advanced by him is indisputable; . . . his appeal to John 14:16 in his principal argument is especially vulnerable". But he has "nevertheless the great credit of having advanced a scriptural proof aimed at the opponent, and of having demonstrated their objections in all directions to be untenable".[65] Even now it was still urgently necessary to demonstrate that a bestowal of the Spirit different from that in baptism was promised to all the faithful of all ages, that the Spirit which was bestowed in the primitive Church in the laying on of hands was not a mere charisma, and finally that the laying on of hands for the imparting of the Spirit can actually be traced back to Christ.[66]

That is, of course, merely the underpinning and defence of what has existed for a long time. However, two present-day facts can contribute to a proper and rich development of the theology of confirmation. In the first place, there is the newly attained recognition of confirmation's concluding and completing position in the foundation of the life of a "mature and fully grown Christian, who is placed through (confirmation) in the full strength and the full zenith of the spiritual life". And from the newly deepened understanding of the Passover and Pentecost which has come from the liturgical renewal, there is growing up a more profound view of this sacrament, which is related to baptism "as Pentecost to Easter. Confirmation is the sacrament of the messianic fullness of the Spirit. Therefore it elevates Christians to the highest ranks of

[65] *Op. cit.* 31f.
[66] *Op. cit.* 32. Umberg undertakes this task himself, presenting his material extensively on the basis of the "classic texts for confirmation", Acts 8:14ff.; 19:6, and also, though to a lesser degree, Heb. 6:2 (*op. cit.* 60–154).

the spiritual life, it ordains them to priests, to prophets and to genuine rulers in the kingdom of the Spirit. And because the Spirit of the Lord is destined to fill the whole world, confirmation makes Christians confessors and apostles of Christ's kingdom in the face of the world."[67]

But the second thing, which is of even greater importance for the speculative theology of confirmation, is the decree of Pope Pius XII, issued in the year 1946, giving all priests in case of necessity the right and the duty to administer the sacrament of confirmation.[68] The first thing to notice in this decision is that the Pope is in some measure able to "unbind" such a power in ordinary priests. And then we should take note of the fact itself, namely, that he relinquishes this power to be exercised by the ordinary priest, and thus brings the practice of the Western Church considerably nearer to that of the Eastern Church.

Right here we can see how the unfolding of the deposit of faith with regard to confirmation, which is laid down in Holy Scripture and transmitted to us in tradition, is still going on today in lively fashion. So that we, the distant descendants of that deposit of faith, may not lack the primitive strength of the Holy Spirit, who is the great gift of the Messianic age; but that he may be ours, to confess before the world, to the praise of the Father.

[67] D. Winzen, *Kommentar z. Dtsch. Thomas-Ausgb.*, vol. 29, 530.
[68] *S. Congr. de Disciplina Sacramentorum,* Decretum of 14th Sept. 1946 (*AAS* 38, 1946, 349–54).